'Kit and Caboodle'

To/ Tam

Best wishes fae the 'Wee toon'

Hamish.

'Kit and Caboodle'

A History of Football

in Campbeltown

Alex McKinven

'For we are, each of us,
a collection of memories
Our personalities are the
collective result of
everything that has happened to us, yeah
it is at the end of the day we look back
upon the days and years
through the looking glass of memory.
And when we are gone,
we become part of the memories
and personalities of others'

'Sons of Somerled'

Kennedy & Boyd

Kennedy & Boyd
an imprint of
Zeticula Ltd
The Roan,
Kilkerran,
KA19 8LS
Scotland.

http://www.kennedyandboyd.co.uk
admin@kennedyandboyd.co.uk

First published in 2013
Copyright © Alex McKinven 2013

Cover, including copyright photographs,
based on 'Kit and Caboodle' exhibition boards,
designed by Tartan Ink Ltd (http://www.tartanink.com/),
courtesy of Argyll and Bute Council: Culture and Library Service.

ISBN 978-1-84921-196-3

For my wife and family:
Fay,
Barry, Karen, David, Euan and Iona

Acknowledgements

First, I would like to thank local author and historian Angus Martin for his knowledgeable assessment, guidance and support of this work, and for constructing the index; in fact, 'thank you' is simply not enough cover my appreciation.

To Derek Corr, I extend my sincere thanks for finding time, at such short notice, to scrutinise and give advice on the content.

To Caroline Corr and Florence McEwan of Campbeltown Library, my appreciation of their patience and invaluable assistance during many visits to the local newspaper archives. I would also like to acknowledge the assistance of Murdo MacDonald, retired archivist of Argyll and Bute Council, whose supply of archival materials allowed me to make a start on this project.

I would also like to compliment Bob Clark and Robin Patel of Auchindrain Museum, Inveraray — this in respect of their professional expertise in setting up the supporting football exhibition at Campbeltown Museum — and Richard McBrearity, curator of the National Football Museum at Hampden Park, for exhibits loaned in connection with the display.

Many thanks to my two buddies, Iain Johnston— for assisting with IT queries — and Iain McMillan, for his unflinching support and patiently listening to all my worries and gripes along the way. My appreciation is also extended collectively to the many people who sent me letters, photographs and relevant information, a reservoir of knowledge that has helped make this book what it is.

Last, but certainly not least, my eternal gratitude to my wife and family whose encouragement and belief inspired me to complete a task that I thought was well beyond my capabilities. It was always my ambition to compile a history of local football, to record different times and the many characters that coloured the town's sporting scene. To everyone who helped me achieve this goal, please accept my thanks for your interest and exceptional kindness during the course of my efforts.

Contents

List of Illustrations

Introduction

On Saturday 27 May 2000, at Kintyre Park, Campbeltown Pupils AFC became Scottish Amateur Premier League Champions, the first club from Argyll to achieve success at this prestigious level. A long-awaited breakthrough, winning the league's top accolade, fulfilled the dreams of countless young players who, in their own time and generation, had worn the team's distinctive 'white jersey' with pride and dedication. Campbeltown Grammar School Former Pupils Association, to give the club its full title, was seeded from a scholastic background in 1919 and was nurtured to satisfy the sporting needs of ex-students. In its inaugural year, the Former Pupils team joined the ranks of the Campbeltown and District Junior Football League, a path followed faithfully until the outbreak of war ended the relationship in 1939.

After two decades in local junior football, the club's failure to reappear after the Second World War was a major disappointment. The years of absence had taken its toll on an aging squad: lack of numbers pushing a once-proud organisation towards its inevitable demise. Consigned to the historical scrapheap, the club's identity gradually faded from memory – that is, until reborn under unusual circumstances during the summer of 1961... Reformed to compete in the ranks of amateur football, the 'new' club established a formidable reputation as part of the Kintyre Amateur Football League – formerly the Artisans' League – a respected organisation which served the community's sporting needs for more than four decades (1952-98).

The game in Kintyre was fiercely competitive during the 1960s, a decade that signalled the end of the highly-successful Peninver Amateur Football Club, a club which had risen to prominence during the 1950s, a period in which the town enjoyed two separate grades of football. While junior football was being played at Kintyre Park to a standard widely accepted as the equivalent of non-league in England, amateur football could be seen on the wide expanse of

Kinloch Park, or, in the case of rural sides, the relevant village park.

The historic Campbeltown and District Junior Football Association came to an end on 14 October 1961, a troubled period in which the 'stars' of yesteryear finally called it a day. However, what arguably was the biggest catastrophe in the 'Wee Toon's' sporting history, in time would leave an unexpected legacy; the transfer of experienced talent into the lesser amateur ranks, improving the standard of play and heralding a renaissance of the game at 'grass roots' level.

As a result, amateur football thrived during the 1960s, a period of optimism in which the town was a hive of industry and sporting activity. Work in advance of the re-opening of RAF Machrihanish brought jobs aplenty, especially in civil engineering, with re-laying of the airport runway and construction of a fuel depot at Glenramskill. On the completion of work, the build up of service personnel brought a new source of competition blessed with first-class playing facilities and their own brand of skill to the playing fields of Kintyre. Unfortunately, the ever looming spectre of unemployment once more haunted the streets with the closure of Argyll Colliery in 1967, a sad loss, as the 'pit' was much more than a source of employment. The Miners' Welfare Association, the social arm of the industry, provided employees and their families with sport, entertainment and the arts, on occasion even catering for the needs of the wider community as well.

Although the game struggled during the early years of the 1970s, the shoots of recovery were already appearing by way of the wonderful Campbeltown Boys Football Association. In relation to work, the opening of Campbeltown Shipyard stemmed the haemorrhage of local labour, provided a base for new industrial skills, and, almost overnight, became a breeding ground for a new generation of sporting talent.

Nevertheless, a decline in standards persuaded Campbeltown Pupils to seek pastures new, a change of course in a new and challenging direction. So, while the hospitality of the Mid-Argyll Football Association was accepted from 1971 to 1973, a decision had already been taken to pursue a more ambitious path. Perseverance became an invaluable ally as the club sought membership of the Scottish Amateur Football League, an ambition finally realised in June 1977. It was a passport to competitive football, the beginning of a memorable period in the life of the club. Good news followed with the resurgence of the Kintyre Amateur Football League, and the game found a home in the unlikeliest of places. Teams were drawn from the fishing fleet, shipyard, creamery, and, as always, the local villages. The RAF played its part, as would a new and thoroughly well-organised Campbeltown Boys AFC.

All the while, a talented Campbeltown Pupils AFC swept through the Scottish Amateur Football League at breakneck speed, gathering success along the way. Championships were won, cups lifted, a national goal-scoring record broken, international caps and league representative honours secured – this as an outstanding team raced headlong towards the league's top division. The club also played its part in the formation of the Scottish Amateur Premier League, later adding the championships of the league's top two divisions to its collection of honours.

However, concentrating on a single era was never the purpose of this book. These pages are a simple attempt to highlight the game's historic past, a journey that will lead us through times of change, both social and sporting. It contains a wide spectrum of characters, some forgotten and others half-remembered; all with one thing in common – the part they played in the story that is Campbeltown Football. Some of their achievements exceeded my wildest expectations and, being local, it is a source of pride to bring these to your attention.

Owing to the dearth of material in the publications of yesteryear, writing this book proved difficult at first; however, problems were overcome by a wealth of information received from a wide variety of trustworthy sources, some, from far-flung places around the globe – much written down and lovingly conserved; the rest entrusted to memory and conveyed in the time-honoured manner by word of mouth. With this knowledge I was able to construct a snapshot of local football, surprisingly, a story that began before the genesis of the modern game.

The town's love affair with association football had blossomed earlier than first anticipated – a history pre-dating some of the 'giants' of the Scottish game. Although remote from mainstream football, the game flourished in Campbeltown despite its far-flung location. Local enthusiasts had first to overcome the barriers of strict Victorian society; nevertheless, once established, the game's patronage remained steadfast and loyal through to modern times – a journey in excess of one hundred and thirty years. These pages are a humble attempt to reflect on images of the past, a backward glance to reveal our obsession with football, a game that has been, is, and always will be a constant and loyal companion.

The Origins of the Game

The development of modern football began during the industrialised 19th century, a period when national associations were formed to regulate a sport that had gripped the imagination of the general public. The historical ball game had existed in its many forms since pre-Christian times, a modest pastime that evolved through the millennia to become the world's most popular team sport.

Taking its place alongside other athletic disciplines, the simple ball game proudly established a niche in the annals of the great classical civilisations, a pastime actively encouraged by the conquering hordes of history. Then considered a perfect outlet for the surplus energy of gathered troops, 'football' was adopted by the leading powers of antiquity, each in turn altering the rules to create a unique version all of their own. These early interpretations were a pale shadow of today's sophisticated spectacle, however, in the greater scheme of things the historical game mattered little. Ball sports were only an escape from the boredom of large military gatherings, a simple diversion from the harsh reality of life in ancient times. Normally found in association with the supremely fit warrior classes, the game became a routine of camp life during the extensive military campaigns of history.

Early records suggest that the Chinese were the first people to embrace a game resembling what we now call football. They called the sport 'Tsu Chu', which means 'kick with the foot the ball made of leather and stuffed'. The Ancient Greeks – famed as mathematicians and philosophers – also developed a fondness for a kick at the round object, a popular pastime called 'Episkyros' in the land that gave us the Olympic Games.

Another great civilisation of the ancient world adapted rules to suit its armed forces, the sport becoming a firm favourite of the mighty legions of Rome. The game evolved to offer a modern classic in the Lazio v Roma derby at the Stadia Olympico, an epic in its own right, but no match for the eternal city's main attraction of the gladiatorial era – the bloody fare 'served' within the confines of the majestic Coliseum!

Legend suggests that the Romans brought their favourite ball sport during the conquest of Britain, a version loosely based on the Greek interpretation, but renamed 'Harpastum' in the native tongue of the visiting 'team'. However, this show of continental flair did little to impress the indigenous Celts; threatened with imminent conquest, the home side preferred their own brand of sporting entertainment. Supported by a cast of thousands, not to mention the benefit of home advantage, the original 'Celtic team huddle' inspired all-out attack, a little bloodletting and the dispatch of their enemies to a celestial version of 'Paradise'.

The collection of trophies was just as popular in the past as it is nowadays; the ancient Britons being infamous for the decapitation of the fallen enemy. However, Rome's best were disciplined on the frontline of battle, a confidence gained from military superiority or maybe just the advice of a friendly centurion – a Latin version of 'keep the heid son'?

Moving swiftly on, there is little doubt that the legions of imperial Rome brought their own unique game to the shores of Britannia, a version recently touted as the template of modern football – at least in the opinion of one extremely opportunistic Italian newspaper. The ancient Latin game did encourage players to win the ball from an opponent; however, although a step in the right direction, in itself, it is hardly proof of Italy being the birthplace of modern football!

After its lengthy sojourn through ancient history, the once popular ball game suddenly disappears from view. Had it been forgotten or simply left unrecorded during a period called the Dark Ages? Its absence from this particular era remains a mystery; however, the game of football refused to go away. The ball game would reappear during early medieval times, a rowdy imposter popular with peasants and the ever-present ne'er-do-wells of the community. Normally held during religious feast days – a celebration of the saints – it was an aggressive communal sport that mirrored the wild nature of the age. These bloody confrontations were known as 'kicking games' or 'mob football' – basically the obscene brainchild of medieval hoodlums. Rules were few and the tactics simplicity itself – to kick and gouge a path into the other team's district! The use of a ball was little more than an excuse for the ensuing mayhem.

The occurrence of fatalities brought the game's aggressive nature to the attention of the authorities. More consistent with warfare than any known sporting pursuit, these wild confrontations even disrupted business on the streets of London. As a result, the city merchants petitioned King Edward II to halt the lawless practices. Consequently, on 13 April 1314, two months prior to the famous Battle of Bannockburn, a royal edict proclaimed: 'For as much as there is great noise in the city caused by hustling over large balls, we command and forbid on behalf of the King, on pain of imprisonment, such games to be used in the city in future.' The days of the medieval 'kick about' were numbered; the uncompromising nature of the game deemed only an excuse for rough and tumble. However, it appears there was a more relevant reason for the ban – in a warlike age, it interfered with a citizen's archery practice!

Football was still making a nuisance of itself one hundred years later, this time in Scotland. During the reign of James I, the people were forbidden from playing by an Act drawn up on 26 May 1424 – although the legislation fell into disuse, amazingly it was not repealed until 1906. The bill stated: 'It is statute and the King forbiddis that na man play at the Fut Ball under the payne of a fine of four pence.'

However, despite being unpopular in the eyes of the law, the game survived these inauspicious beginnings to gain respectability when the Football Association was formed on 26 October 1863. The inaugural meeting was held at the Freemason's Tavern, Great Queen Street, London, an august forum attended by the supporters of two vastly different sporting creeds. Academics tried in vain to bring uniformity to the game; however, the dribbling and carrying versions were at odds with each another. Unable to agree upon a common set of rules, both camps went their separate ways. Surprisingly, the cause of disagreement wasn't in the handling of the ball – the problem was the unsociable habit of hacking! Supporters of the carrying game wanted hacking – the unpleasant habit of kicking a person's shins – to remain part of the sport. The suggestion was rejected out of hand, and the followers of Webb Ellis left to invent a new version of the sport, the now popular game of Rugby Union.

The division of the two ideologies marked the birth of modern football, in the beginning a sport favoured by the middle classes. When the rich man's interest faded, the game was quickly adopted by the skilled working classes, especially in the inner cities during the latter years of the industrial revolution. The crowded workplace became the ideal place for the spread of football delirium, an employee's allegiance to his factory team the forerunner of greater things to come. Now an integral part of everyday life, the game's unrivalled popularity was responsible for a new phenomenon – the birth of the community club.

Football's meteoric rise to become the favourite pastime of the masses is unparalleled in the history of modern sport, a fact acknowledged in its affectionate but all-revealing name – 'the people's game'. The idea of forming a football governing body had surfaced around the same period in Scotland; however, a sparsely populated country had little chance of winning a race to the constitutional finishing line. There were only ten football clubs north of the border at the time of the world's first international match between Scotland and England in 1873. In comparison, England could muster close on one hundred clubs of varying standards. Nevertheless, the ingenuity of the Scots would lead to the game's most important development – the invention of possession play! North of the border a sporting revolution was in the making and a peculiarly 'tartan' version of football was poised to change the nature of the game forever.

Queens Park Football Club, founded in 1867, is universally accepted as creators of the modern game. The club's greatest achievement was the invention of the Scottish passing game, the template for organised football throughout the world. Another triumph of this wonderful amateur club was the building of Hampden Park, the spiritual home of Scottish football and the world's first super-stadium. Hampden Park has seen construction at three separate locations, the last on the Somerville Drive site in 1903. The ground broke all major attendance records and is rightly regarded as the most famous football stadium on earth. Still on the subject of records, it is interesting that English football league side Notts County has the distinction of being the world's oldest club. Founded in 1862, the 'Magpies' were responsible for the spread of the game to Italy. Notts County became the role model for a small organisation called Juventus, and the club known as the 'old lady' of Italian football is recognised by the black and white colours of the English club to this very day.

A shortage of competition in Scotland persuaded Queens Park to become members of the Football Association in 1870, a marriage of convenience that would have far-reaching consequences. The 'Spiders' were invited to compete in the first-ever FA Cup competition, and having entered at the semi-final stage travelled south for the match at Kennington Oval on 4 March 1872. The opposition that day were Wanderers FC, a 'giant' of the early game and a team steeped in the traditions of the old style dribbling philosophy. The game proved a severe test of physical strength for the Scots; however, the general play of the Glaswegians was infinitely more skilful than that of their English opponents. A match of contrasting styles ended in a no scoring draw; as it transpired, the worst possible result for the visitors. Queens Park was denied the opportunity of playing the replay at home and with a second trip to London financially impossible, they were forced to withdraw from the competition. The much-fancied Wanderers now had an unhindered path to the final, where a 1-0 victory over Royal Engineers saw them collect the first ever FA Cup. Did fate conspire to stop a Scots side achieving this lofty distinction? We will never know – but it's certainly an intriguing thought.

Queens Park's distinctive method of play was hailed as a revelation when first witnessed in England, a country still influenced by the old-fashioned dribbling game. An individualistic form of football, dribbling was developed to suit the courtyards and cloisters of universities and public schools, and, in truth, was almost a different sport to that practised in Scotland. Exposed to the admiration of the media for the first time, the Scots' innovative passing game was hailed a sensation. Teamwork was the name of the game, a template for other nations to follow and the way the game would be played throughout the world in years to come. While the rules of the game were the invention of English academics, it was the ingenuity of the men from Hampden who gave the game its method and flair, a spectacle admired today by billions of devotees across the globe!

The game had one more step to take, considered the national sport of both England and Scotland, it was natural these two countries should meet at representative level. Football had now become a focus of national identity, and a peaceful renewal of ancient cross-border rivalry created the world's first football international. Played at the West of Scotland Cricket Ground on St Andrew's Day, 30 November 1872, the match drew a crowd of 4,000 spectators – at the time, the largest gathering for a sporting event ever witnessed in Scotland. The match was also the first to charge for entry – another watershed in the development of the game. Unprecedented interest in football produced massive, paying attendances at new purpose-built stadiums, a step towards the capital needed for the introduction of professionalism in the latter years of the 19th century.

With Queens Park's hand 'firmly on the tiller', the Scottish Football Association was founded in 1873. The original members were Clydesdale, Dumbreck, Eastern, Granville, Rovers, Third Lanark, Vale of Leven and, of course, Queens Park Football Club. It also heralded the beginning of a new competition, the Scottish Cup, the world's oldest domestic football trophy. Queens Park's revolutionary approach to football would also create an era of dominance for Scotland's national side. The 'Dark Blues' remained undefeated for a period of fifteen years between 1874 and 1888, a fact which caused frustration for the FA who ordered a complete overhaul of the English game.

Another 'first' attributed to the Scots was the creation of 'professionalism', but the game's first wage-earners received their dues in a somewhat shady manner. At this juncture, football was organised by an amateur administration, and the payment of players was considered not only irregular, but also downright immoral. With vast revenue from burgeoning gates, the leading clubs of the period maintained their elite status by the reimbursement of out of pocket expenses – in effect a licence for illegal payments – another first attributed to Scottish players, although hardly one to be proud of. The passionately amateur Football Association was alarmed by the growing number of 'professional Scots' plying their trade with regional clubs south of the border, especially in the midlands and north of the country. Ironically, the offending clubs were dubbed 'Scots teams,' the likes of Blackburn Rovers and Preston North End owing their early success to the steady stream of 'Tartan mercenaries'. Bowing to the inevitable, the Football Association became the first administration to legalise professionalism in 1885 – modern football was now truly on its way

While Queens Park reached the FA Cup Final on two further occasions, in 1884 and 1885, both games ended in defeat to the first of the professional juggernauts, Blackburn Rovers. A number of amateur clubs tried to retain a presence within the professional structure, mainly the ones based in the south of England. One of the most famous amateur clubs of all time, Corinthians Casuals, was rich enough to launch a missionary trip to South America. This famous amateur organisation would survive into modern times, but the club eventually became a spent force in the lower reaches of the English game. Ironically, the world's most successful football nation still recognises the missionary work of this resolute amateur organisation – the name perpetuated in Brazil by Corinthians of Sao Paulo.

Like its counterpart south of the border, in the beginning, the Scottish Football Association presided over a host of regional systems, but in 1890 a national league was created – the Scottish Football League, an amalgam of the country's strongest clubs, the ones capable of embracing professionalism. The leading lights were Abercorn from Paisley, Cambuslang, Celtic, Cowlairs, Dumbarton, Hearts, St Mirren, Third Lanark, Vale of Leven and Rangers. Rangers and Dumbarton shared the first-ever league title in 1890/91, the latter winning the title outright the following season.

Declining overtures from the 'gang of ten', Queens Park steadfastly defended its long-held amateur principles. Convinced that professionalism was a lost cause, the opinion seemed justified when they, the oldest and most successful team in the country, won the Scottish Cup in 1890 and 1893. If further proof was required, two years later, non-league clubs St Bernard's from Edinburgh and Renton contested the Scottish Cup Final in 1895. However, 'the writing was on the wall' for those who ignored the march of time, and it was the beginning of the end for a commendable but idealistic view of football.

First casualties were the smaller, less well-off provincial clubs, the ones who were unable to compete for the services of the top players. As the standard of non-league football diminished, Queens Park had to reluctantly reassess its position. The Mount Florida club joined the Scottish Football League in 1900, although to this day it stubbornly clings to its amateur-only principles. Already committed to building a new Hampden Park, the move to a higher grade of football guaranteed the project's success and safeguarded the club's place at the forefront of Scottish football.

Professional football was here to stay, and the inequality that pervades our modern game had finally taken root. In future years the best supported clubs would simply get richer, a trend taken to its ultimate conclusion in UEFA's financially obscene Champions League.

The full potential of professional football was finally realised in the latter part of the 20th century, when the elite clubs of Europe became rich beyond belief. Multi-million pound transfers are now commonplace, made possible by profits from pay for view television, worldwide marketing, and, in some cases the attention of a billionaire 'sugar daddy.' Top professionals now earn vast amounts of money and in-contract players are transferred for millions of pounds on the market 'merry-go-round'. At the end of a contractual period, the player becomes his own master, no longer a commodity held to ransom. The thought of losing a player on a free transfer creates a stampede, a rush to sell early in an attempt to recoup part of the original investment. Fidelity is a thing of the past as money rules the game – a player's 'kiss of the badge' only a hollow gesture in an increasingly mercenary sport.

Life was less complicated in the past, a time when a player earned substantially less in his pay-packet. Normality was a few pounds for turning out on the Saturday, his earnings supplemented by a job on the side with the director's firm. Nevertheless, the early professional could expect to live reasonably comfortably, with earnings somewhat above that of the man in the street. Depending on circumstances, a reserve team player could also expect to fare reasonably well from the game. However, this was the exception rather than the rule. Commonly known as 'the stiffs,' reserves for less glamorous clubs were sometimes rewarded with a meal in lieu of cash, a situation which earned them the unenviable title, 'the Ham and Eggers'.

These days are long gone. Greater earnings mean more commitment to the club, and today's full-time professional hones his fitness, skill and tactical awareness to a much higher level than before. This in turn has produced the great sides of world football, household names like Real Madrid, Barcelona, AC Milan and Manchester United. Times have also changed from the days when an individual's rights were sacrificed on the altar of corporate control. Jan Bosman fought for his human rights and won, a momentous occasion to give players control of their own destiny. It should have been a new beginning, but once more it failed to address the cancer of the modern game – greed!

Like pop artists and film stars before them, modern footballers now boast professional negotiators in the form of agents. The boot is now firmly on the other foot and vast sums of money change hands to satisfy unrealistic demands. The casualty is the game itself, and the gap between the 'giants' and 'dwarfs' is now an almighty chasm. Smaller clubs live beyond their means to maintain a worthwhile challenge, embracing the spectre of closure as they chase impossible dreams. Winners have become predictable as wealth dominates the form book and for the time being, the game is lost in a maelstrom of self-destructive capitalism.

A Guiding Spirit and the Birth of the Blues

With the passing of time, it was inevitable that association football would eventually spread to the provinces. Set to a strict code of rules, the newly organised game replaced the boisterous folk version predominant in our society from time immemorial. During the early 1840s, some twenty-odd years before the founding of the Football Association in England, our local establishment brought forward legislation to curtail the nuisance of 'playing ball games on roads, bridges and quays'.[1] Its inclusion in the Argyllshire Road Act confirms the presence of the 'untamed' version of the game – at this juncture a pastime causing mayhem on the public highways. Incredible as it may seem, it appears that force of law was necessary to curtail the street urchin's 'kick at the bladder,' originally a harmless children's street game. Of course, there was a lot more to this than meets the eye...

The early nineteenth century saw the 'old game' hi-jacked by unruly youths as part of their adolescent posturing, its uncontrolled fury used to disrupt the peace of the general public – at least that is how it was perceived by those in authority. A maximum fine of 40/- (£2) was imposed as a deterrent – a vast sum of money for the period. However, the evolution of football and its march towards prominence was unstoppable and, even in its crudest form, the popularity of the game far outweighed the fear of legal action. Similar to working-class communities nationwide, the street 'kick-about' had cornered the imagination here in Campbeltown; however, it seems reasonable to ask why a game that had around for hundreds of years should suddenly prove so popular. The answer is fairly straightforward: previously considered no more than a children's pastime or civic amusement for public holidays, by the 1860s, football was busily turning into the world-class sport we know today. The historic 'folk game' was slowly being replaced by one adhering to a definitive set of rules, a pastime soon to be adopted by the masses and honed to perfection on the highways and byways.

Municipal facilities were unknown at this particular time, and organised team sports were the preserve of public schools and universities. Given the circumstances, it is hardly surprising football in its formative years was the plaything of the middle-classes. It was a similar story at the heart of the community where sport was the domain of the privileged few and games like cricket, bowls, golf and yachting were simply out of the working man's reach.

Private clubs made sure that the 'right' people gained admittance, but as middle-class interest waned, the man in the street was only too willing to fill the void. Football in one guise or another was historically familiar to the masses, a game with the distinct advantage of costing very little to play. The downside was the absence of proper recreational facilities, but the public solved this problem by taking to the streets ... unfortunately, without the blessing of those in authority. Free of traffic with the exception of the occasional horse-drawn vehicle, the Victorian highway was the perfect playground for football; however, these impromptu gatherings were generally unruly and soon became a nuisance to everyday life. The introduction and popularity of the 'new game' increased the problem, and people found themselves continually at odds with the law.

In today's tolerant society the solution would be simple – embrace the game and provide proper facilities, but there was no chance of this happening in an era dominated by social inequality. Football would have to prove its worth before being accepted by respectable society. The attitude of the establishment mellowed with the creation of the Football Association, but at the outset this renowned organisation had little in common with the working-classes. The FA powerbrokers set rules to a game born in the cloisters of Cambridge University, a dribbling version manufactured to suit the closeted environment in which it originated. The birth of Queens Park Football Club in 1867 – an offshoot of the YMCA movement – brought the game one step closer to the people. Glasgow's world-famous amateur football club rang the changes, not only in how the game was played, but also in the way it was organised and eventually perceived by Victorian society.

A commercially confident group of people, Queens Park provided a link between the professional business classes and the raw talent of the common working man. Ambitious to a fault, the club aspired to build the biggest stadium in the world and use an entertaining brand of football to fill it to the brim. Against the odds these ambitions were achieved; the club's innovative 'Scottish passing game' showed the world how the game should be played and in 1903 a 'new' Hampden Park – the club's third 'home' – became football's first 100,000 capacity stadium.

Football had developed slowly in the hands of the privileged few; however, supported by the masses, it now spread rapidly through the industrial heartlands of the nation. Next to inherit the game were the country's legions of skilled craftsmen – the artisans – a section of the workforce first to benefit from trade unions and reforms at work and it was at this point our own area entered the pages of football history.

Through all of this time, the game in one form or another had been fermenting on the streets of Campbeltown, but it was a major surprise to discover that the area's first organised football had taken place in the village of Southend. Part of the festive celebrations, the good people of the village were encouraged to play shinty and football on New Year's Day 1870.[2] From an historical viewpoint, the day would have been more significant had it been football in the modern sense of the word; however the occasion bore little resemblance to the recently-established game of association rules. People were encouraged to take part en-masse – to all intents, a free-for-all reminiscent of the folk games of old. By now, the formation of dedicated clubs had given the public a better understanding of rules football; however, at street level the game was still a trial of strength rather than a test of skill. This appears consistent with what was happening throughout the country, as around this period 20-a-side games were common in Glasgow at Queens Park Recreation Ground.

As football gradually took root it produced identifiable clubs and properly structured league systems, events brought to the public by a special breed of literalist – the world's first football correspondents. Cloaked in anonymity, the early sports writers adopted outlandish pseudonyms such as 'Horatio' and 'Bedouin,' for reasons known only to themselves, choosing oblivion rather than personal fame when writing about the game. These media pioneers brought us the names of future legends, players who emerged from simple beginnings during the closing decades of the 19th century. Around this time our own local newspapers – the *Campbeltown Courier* and *Argyllshire Herald* – described the town's introduction to the joys of association football. Snow fell on the day of the game; nevertheless, it couldn't deter 200 spectators' braving the elements on Thursday 2 January 1879 to watch the town's first-ever football match set to rules. It soon became apparent that the icy weather was not the only surprise on show that day.

Campbeltown at this point was approaching the peak of its economic powers, a vibrant community boasting the highest per capita earnings in Scotland. The town's population had reached its highest ever level, a figure boosted by itinerant travellers intent on securing a living. Many found employment in one or other of the town's traditional industries, where skilled work was plentiful, but actual prosperity remained in the hands of the few. The closing decades of the nineteenth century were industrial boom years, particularly for whisky in a buoyant market driven by record overseas sales to America and Australia. From the early 1800s, Campbeltown's status as a leading whisky producer attracted a select group of government employees – the officers of the Inland Revenue Department. By the late 19th century these gentlemen were a familiar presence around town, both from a business point of view and through a variety of social interactions. Nevertheless, given that they were part of a rather insular profession, it was surprising to find they were the source of the town's introduction to cricket and football.

They were not alone in their choice of leisure pursuits, as many arriving in search of work brought the latest sporting trends as part of their 'excess' baggage. Football, a game of the industrial workplace, would in a comparatively short space of time appear in south Kintyre. The game germinated in the fertile earth of the town's vibrant economy, embraced by a group of government employees who would unwittingly champion sport among the working classes. The development of local football was a ponderous affair, as the length of the working day left little or no time for recreation. The Saturday half-day holiday was still a thing of the future, although the introduction of the same would revolutionise the game by the end of the 19th century. Meanwhile, with the exception of long summer evenings, football could only take place on public holidays.

This certainly was the case when association rules football was seen for the first time in Campbeltown, a sport unveiled during the New Year holiday period. The game was advertised in elaborate terms as 'A Grand Football Match', in which the competing teams were Campbeltown Football Club versus a Scratch Eleven. [3] The

Campbeltown or Dalintober fishermen's team circa 1890.

description is decidedly 'over the top' by modern standards, but these were early days and the language being used simply confirms a sport in its organisational infancy. The newspaper also announced that the match would take place at 'the Showground on Thursday 2nd January 1879'. Admission was 6d and entry was by Castlehill. A touch of old-world etiquette then prevailed, as ladies were allowed to enter free of charge.

The match report describes a game played with 'considerable spirit and dash', an insight to the standard of football on offer. The report continued: 'Considering the short time the game of football has been practised by the present clubs, the play on the whole was fair', but 'they [the players] have a great deal yet to learn in the way of dribbling and close passing'.[4] These are telling remarks and suggest a group of beginners struggling with the intricacies of a new sport, but without question, the start of association football in the community. In what appeared a comparatively low-key introduction to the joys of football, the aptly named Campbeltown Football Club won the match by 3 goals to 1. There seemed little else of interest in the script, but after a second reading, a surprising revelation came to light.

Describing the best players on show, the writer mentions the fine play of D McArthur, R Wylie and N McEachran for Campbeltown, but things became really interesting when he turns his attention to the Scratch Eleven. The report continues with the statement, 'Kicking and tackling well for their side are Richardson and S. Wylie of the QPFC'. Was I seeing right? Anyone with a basic knowledge of football will recognise these distinctive initials – the players last mentioned were members of the famous Queens Park Football Club. Naturally, this posed a simple, but nevertheless relevant question, why would top class players pursue their sport in Campbeltown at this point in the game's history? After all, the town was hardly the centre of the soccer universe. So, what exactly was going on?

I must confess to being confused at first, but the 'penny finally dropped' when the same players reappeared a few months later, this time in a team representing the Inland Revenue Department. Of the original 'Scratch Team', no fewer than six players were listed to appear for the Revenue Officers against Campbeltown Football Club, known locally as 'the Blues'. This was the first of three occasions the clubs would meet during the early months of 1879, and the experimental side had now developed into a team representing the locally-based tax officers. From this connection, it is reasonable to assume that our two Queens Park gentlemen were in some way connected with HM Customs and Excise. The mystery of local football's distant past was beginning to yield its secrets.

However, what of the Showground – also known as Showfield – and the type of football on display during the early years? The ground was located on what is now modern-day Smith Drive, an open common used for agricultural shows, military camps and all sorts of community activities including sport. With regard to football, the Showfield was the hallowed ground in an era devoid of municipal sporting facilities, a refuge for the game during the formative years. Well-known or perhaps infamous for its sloping surface, the ground would accommodate football for the next 50 years, only to disappear under the sprawl of the town's first Council housing estate in the mid-1920s. The type of football played at the Showfield would seem strange to the modern gaze, as much of what we now take for granted had still to be invented.

Immediately noticeable was the absence of a crossbar, as a tape was strung between the uprights at this moment in the game's development. A conversion between posts counted as one point, the magical word 'goal' still missing from football terminology. In a short space of time, who would have guessed this small word would generate such excitement from Barrhead to Brazil? Goal nets and corner-flags were also things of the future, and with the exception of basic instruction tactics were non-existent. The original team formation consisted of a goalkeeper, two full-backs, two half-backs and no fewer than six forwards. Caution was never a consideration of early football philosophy – the aim of the game was attack and score. If in difficulty, a defender would simply dispatch the ball route-one to an eager, if overstaffed forward-line. Come to think of it – some things never change!

The early footballer's dress code was more like a fashion statement. Wearing a skullcap similar to his cricketing counterpart was considered 'the bee's knees'– the derivation of the international cap. The preferred headgear north of the border was the 'cowl', a hooded hat similar to that worn by fishermen and seafarers. Naked legs were simply out of the question, and the aforementioned appendages were discreetly concealed beneath 'knickerbockers' – loose breeches tucked into the socks at knee-level. The Victorian goalkeeper wore outfield gear similar to the rest of the team, a flat cap the only indication of his specialised position. Although provincial players were keen to appear as modern as possible, at local level they would have struggled with the fine arts of passing and team-play. The basic nature of local football can be traced in the columns of the press, the qualities admired being strength, speed and the ability to kick the ball long distances. Nevertheless, the young men were quick to learn as the game settled into its new-found home on the western seaboard.

Campbeltown's late-Victorian building boom was just around the corner, an opportunity made possible by the burgh's 19th century industrial success. Clearance of the old Georgian slums preceded an unprecedented period of reconstruction, a project to reshape the architectural character of the burgh (1890-1911). Reforms at work also helped the development of football, as the introduction of the Saturday half-day holiday gave employees more time to enjoy their favourite sport. First to benefit were craftsmen or artisans, their status in the workplace recognised well in advance of unskilled workers. Similar to elsewhere, the development of local football was now firmly in the hands of those with a little spare time, the skilled working-classes. In 1951, the origins of local football were commemorated by the formation of the 'Campbeltown Artisans League', a short-lived forerunner of the popular Kintyre Amateur Football League.

If gainfully employed, life was tolerable during the closing decades of the 19th century; however, poverty was still rife across the social divide. The absence of a proper welfare system left many to survive as best they could. The luckless legions included vagrants, the incapacitated or simply those without a proper trade or skill. The people who qualified for assistance were the responsibility of the Campbeltown Parochial Board, a well-intentioned, but grossly under-funded welfare initiative. Prime example of deprivation was the able-bodied unemployed, the unskilled masses who, although physically fit, were too numerous to have any chance of employment. The Scottish Poor Law had nothing for these people and their families, so many simply resigned themselves to the milk of human kindness. Notwithstanding, the community rallied to their aid by raising money at special charity events, and the town's fledgling football fraternity played its part to the full.

Curiosity was football's biggest asset, and with little understanding, many turned up in hope of witnessing the rough and tumble associated with the folk games of old. However, as they say nowadays – this was a whole new ball game! Association football had arrived, and, once properly organised, its officials were able to arrange special matches from which the admission money was gifted for charitable distribution. However, this gesture of public benevolence was a double-edged sword. At a time when all social activity was under the microscope of the Town Council, the game's commitment to charity created a favourable impression in the minds of the town's ruling elite. At this juncture, the progress of provincial football compared favourably with that of the main stage, as the game had developed little since the creation of the Scottish Football Association in 1873. Nevertheless, it was just 'the calm before the storm'. The introduction of weekly half-day holidays allowed the nation's skilled workforce the time to support their favourite team, and the masses turned football clubs into profitable businesses.

These events would come to fruition in the not too distant future, but at this juncture long hours of work confined the playing of football to fair days and public holidays. Easter week-end presented another opportunity for Campbeltown FC and the Inland Revenue to renew their recent acquaintance. A challenge match was arranged at the Agricultural Society Showground on Saturday 7 April 1879, the third meeting between the sides in as many months. The local newspaper reported that 'fine spring weather encouraged more than 200 spectators to climb Castlehill, for the first time bringing out the fairer sex in large numbers, which in itself ought to have encouraged the players to do their utmost, and we were glad to see they did'. [5] The description was light-hearted in nature, nevertheless, it left no one in doubt of the conduct expected at public gatherings in Victorian times. In comparison to previous encounters, it was favourably stated that 'the crowd at this match did not, as on former occasions, display such bad taste, which made it more enjoyable for players and onlookers.' The game ended with the teams level at 1-1, with Richardson and S Wylie recognised as towers of strength. It appears the experienced gentlemen from Queens Park made a real impact on the town's fledgling football scene, a presence that obviously influenced the early days of football in the burgh.

The beginnings of local football were heavily influenced by work and industry, a catalogue of secrets waiting to be revealed. Although the Inland Revenue's contribution to local football was indeed short-lived, its part in the founding of the same cannot be underestimated. The tax officers were here in numbers, as their presence in the burgh was extremely important to the nation's economy. Campbeltown had twenty-two working distilleries producing a combined output of 2 million proof gallons of whisky each and every year, a commodity that was liquid gold in the eyes of the Chancellor of the Exchequer. So vast was the quantity, it needed 'a team of tax officers' to control the financial interests of the state! Their presence can be found in Alfred Barnard's book *The Whisky Distilleries of the United Kingdom*, when on a visit to Hazelburn Distillery in 1887 he states: 'There are twenty-two people employed at the distillery and there are three Inland Revenue officers.' Given the town's unprecedented collection of distilleries, it is easy to gauge the size of this department – reputedly the largest in the country with over fifty serving officers.

Most if not all were incomers, as is clearly evident from their team list published in the columns of the local newspaper. It contained many names uncommon to Kintyre, an example of the settlement of people from various parts of the UK in the 19th century. From a sporting perspective, at a time when our near-neighbours were upholding their Gaelic traditions playing shinty, Campbeltown adopted the ways of the settler and wholeheartedly embraced 'the Beautiful Game'. Nevertheless, 'it takes two to Tango'. The birth of Campbeltown Football Club – 'the Blues' – the town's first club, is indicative of the beginning of association football in western Argyll. These people were not just a supporting act in the founding of the local game; along with the Inland Revenue they were the very origins of association football in 'the Wee Toon.'

Between 1880 and 1890, football witnessed an explosion of interest as reforms at work allowed a mass development of the game. Campbeltown joined the revolution in a period when craftsmen and skilled employees were the first of the working-classes to play football on a Saturday. At this point, a host of new clubs were formed; the Council constructed two pitches at Kinloch Green, and football would at last become what it had always threatened to be – 'the game of the people.' Campbeltown's contribution to the game nationwide could hardly be described as earth-shaking, but as the following pages will show, for a small town it has always 'punched well above its weight'. Considering its size, the town has produced quality sides in abundance, players who have turned professional, and some who have even worn the 'Dark Blue' of Scotland. These achievements are rightly commendable; but when we consider that the town's late Victorian prosperity allowed Campbeltown to embrace the game before many of our country's top professional clubs were even formed, that for me is truly amazing.

The teams from the two earliest games were as follows:

Campbeltown FC v Scratch X1 – 2 January 1879.

Campbeltown F.C:
R. McKay, R. Wylie, D. McArthur, N. McEachran, J. McInnes, Hamilton, W. Mustarde, N. Wylie, J. McLean, D.Vetters and Hamilton.

Scratch XI:
R. Weir, Cass, S. Wylie (QPFC), Richardson (QPFC) capt, Ashley, Livingstone, Scott, Hamilton, Waller, Bolger and Bolger.

Inland Revenue v Campbeltown FC – 7 April 1879.

Inland Revenue:
Ashley, Richardson (QPFC), S.Wylie (QPFC), Daly, Fitzgerald, Mulpeters, Cass, Robinson, Waller, Woulfe and Stewart.

Campbeltown F.C:
R. McKay, D. McArthur, R. Wylie, D. Vetters, McLeod, W. Mustarde, A. Hamilton, D. Hamilton, A. Smith, J. Chapman and R.Wylie.

Charitable Beginnings

The closing decades of the nineteenth century saw the Royal Burgh of Campbeltown reach its industrial peak. This success was made possible by a number of factors, not least the efforts of a select group of skilled workers commonly referred to as artisans. Despite the burgh's apparent wealth, a sizable percentage of the population was haunted by the spectre of poverty, people with no means of support who were simply living from hand to mouth. Their alternative was the ignominy of the 'Poor Hoose', a Dickensian institution with a local equivalent at the old Witchburn Hospital. In cases of extreme hardship, the authorities had the power of committal, a situation dreaded by every self-respecting citizen. Ironically, the building set aside to shelter the poor now houses the offices of Argyll & Bute Council Finance Department, a contradiction in terms if there ever was one.

Confinement of the poor in communal institutions was a convenient solution to a troublesome civic problem, an Establishment 'quick fix' to a glaring, social embarrassment. It certainly provided shelter as an alternative to life on the street, but it also stigmatised individuals in the eyes of their peers. Consequently, instead of conceding to a form of charitable incarceration, the majority were thankful to pursue the 'milk of human kindness'. All too familiar with the shortcomings of the Scottish Poor Law, the sympathetic folk of the 'Wee Toon' rallied round to help their less fortunate fellow citizens.

But what has this to do with football? Given the early game in Campbeltown was played by those who could comfortably support their families – 'everything,' is the simple answer! As always, the church was foremost in the fight against poverty, but the effort was also supported by a host of well-meaning community organisations. One such group was the fledgling, football fraternity, in the first throes of organisation and in need of a little popular support. In past times, the historical folk-game had been branded the domain of 'ragamuffins', but the sport's 'new order' was determined to change this negative image. While the efforts of the football fraternity were

Kintyre Football Club, 1898-99.
Back row, left to right: Turner, O'May, Pat McCrank, Mansfield, McNaughton and Robertson.
Middle row, left to right: Bob McCuaig, Brown, Joe Black, Danny McMillan and Sandy McMurchy.
Front reclining: P McMillan and W Mustarde.

undertaken in the spirit of kindness; nevertheless, their connection with charity helped to foster local prestige and, in the long term, improved the game's social standing.

In 1873, the creation of the Scottish Football Association popularised the game nationwide, and in many ways provincial football mirrored its senior counterpart. A benchmark had been set for those who had time and money, but grass roots football in general was still very much in its infancy. Football only became popular as a spectator sport between 1870 and 1880, and it was at that juncture some of today's best-supported senior clubs came into being. The game's most productive period followed, a decade of progress which culminated in the founding of the Scottish Football League in 1890. The level of interest was such that the game became known as 'the opium of the masses'. The 'new sport' grabbed the imagination of the general public and extended coverage in the popular press helped to fan the flames of enthusiasm. Here in Campbeltown it was a similar story. Following the national trend, a host of local clubs were formed during the 1880s, but the town was still devoid of proper playing facilities and the development of the game suffered. Not to be outdone, local enthusiasts went 'cap in hand' to the Kintyre Agricultural Society, and the Showground at Castleacres was eventually given over to the game. The arrangement suited both parties, as, apart from show days, military camps or the occasional athletics meeting, the park lay vacant for lengthy periods of the year. The only criticism was the field's infamous sloping surface, but local football was hardly in a position to pick and choose.

Having secured a proper venue, the football fraternity was free to organise a series of fixtures to help the unemployed of the burgh. In 1880, the town's earliest football clubs, Campbeltown and Kintyre, played a match at the Showfield to find funds for this very purpose[6,] which raised the princely sum of £1 sterling. At first sight this seems a rather piddling figure, but in reality it was equal to the weekly earnings of a skilled worker and therefore a fairly substantial amount. Football was relatively inexpensive to play, one of the reasons which made it the favourite pastime of the masses. If the vast numbers playing the game were remarkable, by comparison its development as a spectator sport was nothing short of spectacular. Across the nation, supporting a team was now every bit as important as playing and the volume of people attending matches increased dramatically with the arrival of the 'giants' of the game. This enthusiasm was replicated right here in Campbeltown, understandably on a scale representative of the community. The ropes of the Showfield were besieged each and every week by previously unheard of numbers, the game's popularity as a spectator sport increasing in line with the formation of a number of new sides.

Campbeltown FC, the founding club, was joined by Albion, Athletics, Rangers, St Kiaran, Kilbrannan and Kintyre, the latter still to the fore as a junior club until 1936/37. The next logical step appeared to be the introduction of a competitive structure, but the approval of the establishment was necessary before plans could be realised. Victorian Scotland was a class-ridden society, and the town councils of that period were dominated by representatives of the privileged minority – landed gentry, successful businessmen and members of the professional elite. The approval of social superiors was a necessity before any community venture could be taken forward. In Scotland's class-driven Victorian society, your worth as a person was secondary, in short, everyone needed to know their place. Patronage – the support of a person of substance – could pave the way to full acceptance, and progress for Campbeltown was found in an ardent football fan by the name of Huntley, a gentleman with the necessary credentials. He was the first of his class to openly acknowledge football by lending his name to a competition, if not the full-blown recognition the game desired, it certainly was at least a step in the right direction.

The first round of the 'Huntley Prize' brought together Campbeltown and Albion, a historic event in as much as it was the town's first competitive football match. The local press announced: 'There was great interest shown in the game, and, although the Albion captain played very well for his side, it was evident his men had very little practice.' The more experienced Campbeltown side ran out comfortable winners by 3-0, a match refereed by Mr C. McEachran, ably assisted by umpires A Horrocks and A Stewart. [7] The importance of the occasion wasn't lost on the town's football fraternity, as the support of a middle-class patron gave 'the new game' respectability – in effect, it acknowledged the need for organised sport among the working-classes.

Campbeltown's very own football revolution coincided with a massive undertaking on the part of the town council, the infill of the tidal mudflats at the head of the loch, 'the Mussel Ebb'. The area now known as Kinloch Park was initially earmarked as a botanical garden, the same to be designed by renowned architect Henry Clifford. The reclaimed ground was ploughed and seeded during spring of 1881; however, being almost at sea-level, it was blighted by drainage problems. Four years of remedial work was necessary before the town's first public park was ready for use in 1885, by which time, plans for an ornamental lay-out had been abandoned in favour of recreation. It was a popular decision welcomed by the general public – justification of how far society had progressed in such a short space of time.

In recognition of a massive increase in the popularity of association football, two parks were laid out on the 'Big Green', one at Lochend and the other on or near the site of what is now the War Memorial. Both parks were in regular use during the summer of 1885, but there were ominous signs with lack of drainage at high tide, and the onset of winter sent everyone scurrying back to the Showfield at Castleacres.

The Golden Jubilee of Queen Victoria in 1887 provided another landmark in the history of Campbeltown football. In honour of the occasion, the first Campbeltown & District Football Association was founded and the aptly named Charity Cup presented for competition. This special piece of silverware would in time become the 'Holy Grail' of local football, the Association's premier competition, a trophy played for annually until the demise of the 'juniors' in 1962. The Charity Cup found a special place in the hearts of all football-minded Campbeltonians and, in keeping with tradition, gate receipts were reserved in a 'Special Purposes Fund' to the very end. At this point, the cup and its sister trophies – Orr-Ewing, Sutherland and McCallum Cups – were passed into the safe-keeping of local solicitors Stewart, Balfour and Sutherland. Thanks to the efforts of the late Malcolm Lang and Willie McKerral – last trustees of the junior association – these prized possessions returned to 'active duty' under the auspices of Campbeltown Boys Football Association in the early 1970s.

It must have been a huge relief when the ambitions of the football fraternity finally came to fruition. Football was now firmly in the limelight with the inauguration of the town's first competitive structure in 1887 and it's hard to believe Glasgow Celtic was still an unknown quantity. The game had long since passed the 'acid test' of public opinion, but there were still some in society who were unconvinced as to football's long-term merit. The opportunity to change this opinion and showcase the benefits of a wonderful sport fell to Athletics and Kilbrannan, opponents in the very first Charity Cup Final.

A large crowd was present to witness a competitive first-half, a game in which Athletics drew first blood to lead 1-0 at the break. Although behind, Kilbrannan had performed well in the opening exchanges and their players were confident of retrieving the situation in the second-half. However, any thoughts of a dramatic come-back were quickly dispelled as the infamous Castleacres slope took its toll on their efforts. Using the terrain to full advantage, Athletics overwhelmed their opponents in a one-sided second-half, strolling downhill to an emphatic 6-1 victory. The cup-winners were roundly applauded by the spectators, 'Whose admiration for the neat dodging and accurate shooting of the winning team was unbounded'. [8]

The cup-winners made a slight adjustment to their name for the new season ahead and when play commenced, it did nothing to upset their recent outstanding form. Now termed Athletic F.C. in the singular, this talented eleven secured the Charity Cup no fewer than four times in the first six years of asking. Without doubt the best team of this particular era, the club also produced the town's first football personality, a star performer at fullback or halfback, Robert 'Lally' Cunningham.

Charity Cup Final, 30 May 1887.

Athletics F.C: C. Martin, R. Cunningham, D. Cameron, John Davidson, D. Campbell, John McCallum, P. Mitchell, N. Gilchrist, D. McLarty, D. Luke and C. Rice.

Kilbrannan F.C: D. McKinlay, J. Black, J. Meenan, J. Galbraith, D. Blair, D. McLean, P. Robertson, C. Spiers, D. Mathieson, D. McGeachy and T. McMillan.

Referee: W. Hamilton.
Umpires/Linesmen: M. H. Martin and J. McKinlay.

In any event, the purpose of the Charity Cup was to raise as much money as possible for the poor. As you would expect, business was usually conducted in a civilised manner, but the attraction of the cup final persuaded a few less conscientious fellows to stray from the straight and narrow – they decided to sneak in! Their actions were roundly condemned in the following week's newspaper and the perpetrators chastened with a few well-chosen words, albeit in a rather humorous manner. 'A sizable crowd was in attendance, and the amount raised for charitable distribution was £11 after deduction of expenses.' Unimpressed by the final arithmetic, the local reporter continued his criticism with a hint of caustic wit – 'the sum that should have been nearly doubled had all who witnessed the match paid as they should, but a very large number showed a decided, marked preference for other means of ingress than the gate, even though these means were less dignified and convenient and made calls upon their climbing powers.' Ah well, some things never change. The reporter certainly had a way with words and, although old-fashioned in style, his message came across loud and clear. In a final blast at the non-payers, he offered an opinion that the gate-shy perpetrators were 'less fastidious in their choice of exit,' – in other words, leave the park by a similar route – back over the wall from whence you came!

Flushed with success, Athletic F.C. decided to try their luck against stiffer opposition and in doing so, created another milestone in the history of local football – the first match against senior opposition. The game in question was played at the Showfield on Monday 3 January 1888, a match in which the local favourites defeated Queens Park Strollers by 4 goals to 2. With no suggestion of tiredness, the very next day our local heroes defeated St Mirren Reserves 1-0 at the same venue. [9]

The first of their kind, it is difficult to gauge public reaction to these ground-breaking events, but it certainly was a surprise to find senior opposition playing in Campbeltown this early in the development of local football. More to the point, to have them visit during the festive period was certainly most unusual. What exactly was going on? Amazingly, it looks as if the home club had organised a triangular holiday tournament. Whatever the reason, the track record of Athletic F.C. portrays a club not only well organised, but also extremely ambitious in its outlook.

The fact that senior clubs were willing to visit Campbeltown during the New Year period begs an obvious question – why bother if the games were only friendlies? Interestingly, it was all about money. We have to understand that football was still evolving and senior clubs across the country were playing in a variety of regional leagues prior to the founding of the Scottish Football League in 1890. The golden years of professional football were still in the future, a time when running costs could be easily covered by the revenue from enormous gates. During the interim period, in order to survive, senior teams had to hawk their wares to the highest bidder. But what was travel like in those far off days?

The most popular form of transport in Victorian times was the horse-drawn charabanc or 'brake,' a reliable, but laboriously slow method of travel. Horse-drawn vehicles were used in cities and towns, but were also convenient and available to link outlying areas to the nearest railway station or steam boat pier. Very much on the geographic periphery, it was essential for a seaport like Campbeltown to have its own shipping company, something that came to pass with the founding of the Campbeltown & Glasgow Steam Packet Company in 1823. During the latter years of the 19th century, the town had three renowned vessels serving its needs, the *Kinloch*, *Kintyre* and *Davaar*. There were twice-daily sailings to and from the Broomielaw in the heart of Glasgow, so it appears the town was anything but isolated in days of yore – in fact, we only became marginalised as a community with the demise of the Clyde Steam Packet Company in the early 1970s.

With efficient sea and rail links to the city, Athletic F.C. was well-placed to be the banner-carrier of local football. The club's organisational skills were far in advance of what seemed possible for the era, and this ambitious organisation became members of the Scottish Football Association in 1888/89, the same year Glasgow Celtic was formed in the east end of Glasgow. Campbeltown Athletic entered the Scottish Cup that season and has the distinction of being the community's one and only senior football team. Unfortunately, match results have so far proved elusive.

The holders of the Charity Cup repeated their success in 1889/90; a feat emulated in the following two years by newly formed Victoria FC. Suddenly there was a rival in the pack and it wasn't long before the 'top dogs' were at war. Football was now well-established in the burgh, nevertheless, being a competitive sport, it occasionally was its own worst enemy. Association officials feared the worst when the two main challengers clashed, a bad-tempered affair that soured local opinion. Negative press was the last thing the sport needed, but the area's top fixture was a magnet for the newspapers. Was behaviour in Victorian times any worse than it is today? Judge yourself from the following newspaper comments. 'The match was a unique one from the spectator's point of view and, the sooner this game falls into desuetude [disuse] the better, since the majority of the players cannot contain themselves on the field ... There was no falling off on the part of Victoria FC in their bawling, wrangling and use of bad language, and they were reinforced in their work by several of the Athletic F.C. players ... After a dispute with the referee, the Athletic F.C. captain ordered his men from the field.' It was the clash of the 'Titans,' a match full of the same indiscipline exhibited in many of today's top fixtures. Some things never change.

Nevertheless, apart from these moments of indiscipline, the game on the whole was relatively trouble-free. Mixed fortunes awaited the town's leading clubs; there was further success for Athletic F.C in the coming years, but a one-way ticket to oblivion for the short-lived Victoria FC. The mantle of power finally restored, Athletics' cup success continued with further wins in 1892/93 and 1893/94, a prelude to a prestigious meeting with the might of Greenock Morton. It was the first of many visits to Campbeltown by the Greenock club, a connection renewed on numerous occasions in years to come. The team from the 'Tail of the Bank' played the pre-First World War Academicals on two occasions and across many years, returned no fewer than five times to meet Campbeltown Pupils FC. Given the local club's previous record, it was no surprise when Athletic F.C. recorded another impressive win against top class opposition. Greenock Morton became the third senior club to be beaten in the space of five years, a record that speaks volumes for this fine old club.

For Athletic F.C, it was the last time they would 'cross swords' with senior opposition, a chapter of success never to be repeated by another local club. While I remember reading that Campbeltown only possessed an elementary knowledge of football in the early years, the facts tell a different story. This was a local club undefeated against three prominent senior teams, enjoyed membership of the SFA and was seen to compete in the oldest club tournament in the world – the Scottish Cup. There was nothing 'elementary' about this club. When all is said and done, Athletic F.C. made a major contribution to the development of football in the burgh, a proud sporting history that spans no fewer than 134 years and we are still counting. Arguably the most influential team in the history of the local game, the dawn of a new century saw its decline, despite time for one more Charity Cup success in 1908. Although the name of this famous football club would be utilised on a number of occasions in the future, the original Athletic F.C. disappeared from the record books shortly after its last cup final victory.

The closing years of the 19th century saw the pendulum of success swing towards teams who had chosen to identify with the prominent names of the Scottish game. In 1885, some twelve years after the founding of Glasgow Rangers, the burgh had its own version of the 'Light Blues'. Surprising as it may seem, in all this time, the town has never had an equivalent of Glasgow Celtic, but confusion must have reigned when the local Rangers' won the Charity Cup in 1899 and 1901 resplendent in hoops! At the time, there was nothing unusual about this, as the first colours of Glasgow Rangers were indeed light blue and white horizontal stripes. Around this period, football was stirring across the loch in Dalintober, a traditional fishing village now incorporated into the Burgh of Campbeltown. The new club's choice of name was made simpler by the outstanding form of Heart of Midlothian, at the time a team on the crest of the professional football wave. After deliberation, Dalintober gave life to one of the community's most famous junior clubs – its very own Hearts FC.

Campbeltown Hearts made an immediate impact on the local game, winning the coveted Charity Cup on 14 April 1900, the club's first season of competitive football. A remarkable story is associated with the team in the early years, an obscure piece of knowledge uncovered by local author and historian, Angus Martin. The information originates from Angus's uncle, Duncan Martin and is a perfect illustration of how football thrived in a tight-knit fishing community. The legend states that every out-field player on a particular match day had the surname McGeachy or Martin. The team consisted of Eddie 'Speed', Duncan 'Spud', Archie and Johnny – all brothers, then there was Duncan 'Muchan' and Alex 'Ferret' McGeachy. Making up the difference were Alexander 'Sandy', Archie 'Ringer', Neil 'Hairy' and Campbell 'Caimie' Martin. Last line of defence was Colin Mitchell.

A prominent member of the squad was Joe Black junior, part of a family who were master-bakers in the Dalintober area. They had moved to the head of the loch from their original town-based premises, the Geisha Tearoom in Back Street, now Numero Dix in present day Union Street. Business flourished at the new shop in Saddell Street, and an increase in trade prompted a search for larger premises. The solution was found after a short journey across the street to what became the family's long-standing address, a small single-story tenement next to West Coast Motors. The vacated shop in time became famous in its own right, remembered by older generations as 'Glundy's' fish and chip shop, latterly the Plaice for Taste. The bakery endured until the demise of another well-known personality, a third generation of the paternal name. Like his father and grandfather before, Joe Black was a Hearts supporter to the core

– both senior and junior varieties. An eloquent soft-spoken man, he often shared his thoughts with me on the state of the game, more so, when he discovered we both had an affinity with all things maroon.

This friendship brought me into contact with a woman with an amazing memory, Joe's sister, Mrs Chrissie McGregor. I was soon listening as she reflected on her childhood in the family home, describing her father and grandfather as first-class cricketers at Limecraigs, facts easily confirmed by the countless 'boundaries' attributed to the family duo in the local press. She also recalled her father's infatuation with traditional country sports; a crack-shot who liked nothing better than a day on the hill. Marksmanship, it seems, was an abundant quality in Campbeltown during the late Victorian era, a skill honed to perfection at the Volunteers Rifle Club. Shooting was the town's most popular pastime prior to the rise of football and as a result, local sharp-shooters were good enough to grace the national championships. When one of the local marksmen, Alexander Ferguson, won the annual Queen's Prize at Wimbledon, a coal-mine sunk at Drumlemble in 1881 was named after the venue in his honour.

Although Chrissie's father was a multi-talented sportsman, her lasting memory was of his dedication to the game of football, an enthusiasm shared by most of his neighbourhood pals. The introduction of the Saturday half-day holiday allowed them to play football on a regular basis for the first time. The people of Dalintober followed the team across the watery divide, a pilgrimage to the Showfield in support of 'the Reds.' Win, lose or draw the game dominated conversation at the Blacks' evening meal, much to the annoyance of Chrissie's mother. Reaching the end of her tether, she vented her frustration with a few well-chosen words. 'See youse men, a ye can think aboot is fur, feather and fitba!' Little did she realise that her inadvertent remark would soon become reality, for football would conquer the hearts and minds of the people, eclipsing other sports to become the game of the coming century and beyond.

The New Century

As Campbeltown stepped forward into the 20th century, it was as part of a nation embroiled in a major conflict against the Boers in South Africa. At the time, Great Britain had a sizeable professional army, a satisfactory situation as it eliminated the need for full scale conscription. Although the young men of Kintyre were spared the ordeal of enlistment, a small group of men inspired by patriotic fervour did register for active service. Three of the volunteers were wounded in action, with one of their number making the ultimate sacrifice – Lance Corporal William Gillespie was killed in action. His commemorative plaque, once displayed in Drumlemble Village Hall, can now be found in Campbeltown Heritage Centre.

Free from the demands of military service, our talented young footballers were able to participate with any one of a number of clubs active at the turn of the new century. The founders of the local game, Campbeltown Football Club – 'the Blues' – were still to the fore and, along with two survivors from the formative years, Kintyre F.C. and Athletic F.C, represented the origins of local football. Supporting the trail-blazers were Rangers and Hearts, clubs which chose to identify with their heroes when forming during the closing years of the 19th century. Newcomers on the scene were Drumlemble, Thistle and Heartfield, the former a team destined to have a long and successful passage in local football and one of the last to represent the area in the Scottish Cup prior to the collapse of the juniors in the early 1960s.

It was a one-season affair for Heartfield, and although Thistle had been around for a number of years, both became cannon-fodder for the more established sides and soon disappeared from the football scene. Nevertheless, a photograph of Thistle has survived which shows a group of very athletic gentlemen dressed in white shirts with a thistle emblazoned on the chest. They are also dressed in matching white knickerbockers. If this side was beaten regularly, it certainly wasn't for the want of fitness. Their perfectly honed bodies suggest a connection to athletics, but we will probably never know, however, a few names are available and could help with later identification. [10]

Thistle F.C. circa 1900: N. McPherson, P. McPherson, Angus McCallum, James Lamb, Archie Girvan, J. McKinven, Peter Rankin, Archie Rankin and Lachlan McCallum.

In 1900, Campbeltown was a confident, self-assured place in which to live, a town with the highest per capita earnings in the West of Scotland. The burgeoning success of the local economy had stemmed the tide of unemployment, the traditional sources of work now supplemented by new opportunities in ship-building and coal-mining. It was a prosperous time for the country as a whole, and Queen Victoria would pass into history as monarch of the richest nation on earth. The burgh would undergo major reconstruction between 1890 and 1911, the environment of the 'old town' swept away in an expression of the community's new-found affluence. Town centre slums were systematically razed to the ground and replaced by distinguished tenements designed by the brightest of minds. The hovels of the 'Wide Close' were demolished and a new thoroughfare created between Main Street and Back Street – Longrow South. Fashionable villas were built along the loch-side as Askomil and Kilkerran became retreats of the middle-classes and a second phase of the seafront promenade was completed between the quays at Hall Street.

Campbeltown's seafront boulevard now ran unbroken from the New Quay to Dalintober Pier, a popular walk across the wide expanse of the Esplanade. The two communities were now as one, leaving the old ferry service between the quays surplus to requirements. Notwithstanding, the joining of Dalintober to its larger neighbour failed to destroy the villagers' sense of insularity, as countless generations had been raised to consider themselves a breed apart. I was often confused, not to say a little amused, when asked, 'Ur ye a Dalintober man?' I failed, however, to understand what the question really implied. A little older and possibly wiser, it is now clear that it echoed a deep sense of belonging in the mind of the elderly inquisitor, the last vestige of a fiercely independent fishing community on the far side of the loch.

Attempts to conjure images of the town at the beginning of the 20th century proved difficult, that is until the chance discovery of an informative script published in 1966 by anonymous writer 'Sixty-Five Plus'.[11] In a short story entitled 'The Bells of Old Campbeltown,' the author portrays a vivid picture of the burgh in the early 1900s, a nostalgic account of what was then a vibrant community. It describes the familiar sounds that marked the passing of each and every day; a community guided by the peal of bells. The town crier, Mr Henry McLean – 'Harry' – brought everything to a standstill at Campbeltown Cross, then located in the middle of Main Street near the Town Hall. The attention of the public was drawn by the clanging of a hand-bell and his well-known cry, 'Notice!' He then conveyed the latest news to the congregation, a script covering everything from sales to water shortages. However, interest heightened when the list of local debtors was produced, a 'not-to-be-missed' opportunity for the ever-present gossipmongers in the crowd.

From the Old Quay Head came the sound of the 'Herring Bell', the prelude to David Robertson's familiar cry, 'Cam awa aal ye buyers!' It was a timely reminder that daily fish sales were about to get underway. You can almost smell the working pier as the fish were gutted, salted and barrelled for the Continent and far-off Russia. The early morning silence was broken by the sound of the embarkation bell, a last call for passengers travelling to the upper reaches of the Clyde on the local mail steamer. Close on its heels was the 'Trench Bell,' a wake-up call for the workforce as foreman John McCorkindale signalled the start of a new working day at Campbeltown Shipyard. A symphony of sound called the people to worship on Sunday – no escape for the wicked as the church bells demanded immediate attendance. Revelry and reckless behaviour were curtailed by the peal of the 'Curfew Bell', a duty performed by the burgh surveyor, Mr Fullerton, every night at ten o' clock from the Town Hall. It was a warning that legitimate business had ceased and the streets should be cleared of stragglers. It is difficult to believe something as simple could have worked; but it surely must have had some effect, as the practice was maintained until the First World War.

A relation of mine had a part to play in the street scenes of this particular era, as Charlie McLean was gainfully employed as the town's lamplighter. A well-known figure as he made his twice-daily rounds of the lamp standards of the Campbeltown Corporation Gas Company – a forerunner of Scottish Gas – his job was to illuminate the streets at dusk, and return the following morning to extinguish the 'leeries' with the start of a new day. These observations give a fleeting glimpse of times gone by and allow us to understand what life was like at the 'dawn' of the 20th century.

In truth, sport was still a comparatively new experience for the working-classes, as organised recreation was only possible after the introduction of the half-day holiday during the closing decades of the 19th century. Prior to this, sport was the preserve of the well-to-do, with golf, cricket, bowls, lawn tennis and yachting simply out of the working man's reach. Physical team-sports, particularly one as aggressive as football, were tolerated rather than embraced in an age governed by strict moral standards. First to benefit from shorter working hours were the artisans – skilled working classes – the very people who were instrumental in founding local football. Across the social divide, Campbeltown Cricket Club was rich enough to engage the services of a resident professional and have its pitch at Limecraigs re-laid in 1892. However, although wealth and recreation were inextricably linked during the 19th century, class division in sport was gradually disappearing. A time was coming when people would be judged on ability alone, and sport would become the vehicle of the masses.

By 1900, the existence of football could be numbered in decades and the amount of people enjoying the game had increased dramatically. By now, winter football was commonplace, although the game was still dominated by craftsmen and the self-employed, the ones with free time at the weekend. When football was first introduced in 1878/79, the average working week was 56-and-a-half-hours, so it was hardly surprising that most matches took place on public holidays. However, reforms at work and a change in social attitudes led to the founding of a local football association and the introduction of football on a Saturday.

The development of unions for general workers was much slower than for tradesmen, a situation that caused inequality in the workplace. Nevertheless, depending on the time of year, some games were scheduled for late afternoon to allow the unskilled to take part. This is of course a generalised view, as many employers had their own rules and regulations, and the half-day holiday only became law at the end of the First World War.

The acknowledgement of football by Charles Lindsay Orr-Ewing, Honourable Member of Parliament for the Ayr Burghs, was in a social sense a major breakthrough for the local game. Campbeltown was part of this gentleman's wider constituency, and the sitting MP donated a handsome silver cup to the local football association in

Hearts Football Club, 1900-1901.
Back row, left to right: Dan Black, J Rae, James McKay, Dan Watson, Campbell Martin and Trainer, Donald Brown. Middle row, left to right: Alex Bell, Duncan McCallum, Neil Martin, Alex Morrison, Duncan McGeachy, Archie McGeachy and Mathew Stewart. Front row, left to right: Johnnie McGeachy, Joe Black and Jim Scott. Foreground: The Orr-Ewing Cup and Charity Cup.

1900. It was the endorsement the game had prayed for, although a short announcement in the local press is all there is to commemorate the occasion: 'The trophy is presently on view in the shop window of Mr R. McCuaig in the Main Street'.[12] Local businessman Bob McCuaig was a committee member of Kintyre FC.

At this point – 1900/01 – there were four contenders for the medals: Rangers, Hearts, Campbeltown and the newly formed Drumlemble F.C. Competition was fierce between these sides, but Campbeltown F.C. emerged as league champions and Hearts secured the Charity Cup. All that was left was the brand-new Orr-Ewing Cup, a competition run in league format to maximise its potential. The winners of the earlier competitions, Hearts and Campbeltown, were 'neck and neck' going to the last game. They would face each other at the Showfield on 1 April 1901.

A single point was all that separated the sides, and Campbeltown entered the fray knowing a draw was good enough to secure the MP's coveted trophy. This made 'the Blues' hot favourites to lift the cup, an opinion shared enthusiastically by a member of the local press. The first half proved an exciting affair with the scores level at 2-2; nevertheless, our latter day reporter was determined to nail his colours to the mast and his match report contained more than a hint of favouritism. He described Campbeltown as 'persistently storming their opponent's goal' and 'pressing hard for the opening goal'. Later he described a Hearts defender as 'wilfully touching the ball to deny Campbeltown a third goal'.[13] No account of the second-half action is available, although all was revealed in the last few lines of the report. A tribute to understatement, it concedes that 'the reds' were the superior team in the second half, and netted the ball five times, but one was disallowed, and thus the game ended in favour of Hearts by 6 goals to 2. A one-sided second-half with goals galore had been completely ignored!

The excellent play of Alex Morrison and the McGeachy brothers helped to capture the very first Orr-Ewing Cup for Hearts. 'Camie' Martin also played 'a first-class game' for the winners at left-back. A postscript to the game states 'that defeat will perhaps teach Campbeltown a lesson in future not to count their chickens before they are hatched'. Victory was then grudgingly conceded, and 'the cup was carried off to Dalintober to lie beside the Charity Cup – for the meantime!' A salutary lesson learned – when it comes to football, you can never trust those Dalintober men!

Orr-Ewing Cup Final, Saturday 30 March 1901.

Campbeltown: A. Mathieson; D. O' May and P. McPherson; L. McCallum, J. Davidson, and W. Sharp; P. McArthur, R. Robertson, J Izzet, C. Campbell and W. Mustarde.

Hearts: J. McKay; D. McCallum and C. Martin; N. Martin, A. Morrison and D. McGeachy; J. Scott, J. McGeachy, J. Black, D. Black and A McGeachy.

Referee: T. Taylor (Rangers).

The winning eleven is captured for posterity in a photograph taken near the Limecraigs Cricket Club, now a modern housing estate, also pictured are committee members J.Rae, Dan Watson, Alex Bell, Mathew Stewart and a man who easily stands out in a crowd, club trainer Donald Brown. This gentleman was responsible for the fitness of the team, a man of military bearing with a fine set of regimental 'handlebar' whiskers (see photograph). Known to the players as 'Trainer Brown' – he obviously was a man who commanded respect. Duncan Brown, his grandson, owned a toy and souvenir shop in Longrow, a business still operational in Main Street and run by Donald's great-granddaughter Marjory. Football runs deep in the veins of the family, and it was little surprise to learn that Donald and Archie McCallum – Peninver Football Club, 1950/60s – were also grandsons of the early football pioneer. The football connection continues to this day through great-grandson Peter McCallum, past player, manager and mentor of the now defunct Campbeltown Boys Football Club and currently an SFA qualified referee. The founders of local football, Campbeltown Football Club, eventually dominated the sporting scene they started way back in 1878. It was a long time coming, but the famous 'Blues' finally gained their reward by winning the Charity Cup every year between 1902 and 1905.

In 1905, one of the most famous names to grace local football appeared for the very first time. Arguably the finest team of the 'junior era', Campbeltown United opened its account by winning the Orr-Ewing Cup at the first attempt. The club survived a protest from Drumlemble over the eligibility of one of its players, but the objection was deemed frivolous and the result stood.

Campbeltown United's original team was: C McMichael, D Gilchrist, D McCallum, W McLellan, M Prosser, N McCallum, K Taylor, G McFarlane, J Quinn, A McPherson and A McCallum.

Campbeltown also had an active youth league around this period, and, although termed a junior league, it was an under-age system and not to be confused with the later professionally-registered grade. Teams involved were Kilbrannan, Academicals, Rangers, Kintyre and Victoria, the last-mentioned an associate of the adult organisation dissolved fourteen years earlier in 1892. St Kiaran, a new club representing the Good Templars Lodge in lower Millknowe, set the pace in the Charity Cup of 1906. Once more masters of the late run, Hearts came from behind to carry the cup on a familiar journey across the loch to Dalintober. Last word comes from our intrepid *Courier* correspondent. Covering a match between Campbeltown and St Kiaran, he writes: 'Campbeltown kept pegging away at the top goal and finished masters of the situation'.[14] The final score: Campbeltown 0 St Kiaran 3. Without doubt the eternal optimist!

So we come to a period in which the 'Wee Toon' first made an impression on the senior game. Robert Pursell of Campbeltown Rangers signed for Queens Park in 1909, before moving on to Liverpool and an FA Cup Final appearance against Burnley. He was followed a few years later by James Brown, who joined Glasgow Rangers from Campbeltown United and later played with Kilmarnock. Robert Pursell's brother, Peter, signed for Queens Park and was capped at full international level against Wales in 1914. He later had a glittering career with Glasgow Rangers. Neil McBain played for Ayr United, Manchester United, Everton and Liverpool, a career which carried him to three full international caps for Scotland.

The early years of the 20th century were the golden times, a period of national prosperity which heralded the invention of the turbine driven steam ship and the beginning of mass tourism. The presence of the *King Edward* and *Queen Alexandra* on the Clyde gave rise to a new form of traveller, the 'day tripper'. It was now possible to leave the confines of Scotland's largest city, spend time on Kintyre's Atlantic coast and be home in time for supper. The Campbeltown and Machrihanish Light Railway moved quickly to grab its share of the market, upgrading its coal-carrying railway to accommodate passengers in 1906 – 'the Wee Train'.

Campbeltown Rangers, 1909-1910.

Back row, left to right: D Brown (Trainer), J McLean, W McLellan, A McLean, J Brown, T Blue, R McCuaig and J McNeill. Middle row, left to right: J Kerr, J McPherson, A McCallum, A Thomson, J Rankin, R Buchanan and J McClay. Front row, left to right: P Pursell, W Pursell, C Scobie, K Taylor and W Mustarde.

Tourism wasn't a new experience for Campbeltown, as the town had a healthy holiday market as far back as 1867. The Campbeltown & Glasgow Steam Packet Company – founded in 1826 – built a number of ships to service the expanding tourist market, the *Gael, Kintyre, Kinloch* and *Davaar*. Early visitors were middle-class travellers, but the steamers also brought football teams to Campbeltown from as early as 1888. However, there was a massive expansion in tourism during the early years of the 20th century, for the first time the working-class of Glasgow and beyond headed 'doon the watter.' By 1906, visitors of all social classes were able to use the 'Wee Train' to reach the sands at Machrihanish. Six years on, it was utilised by football supporters going to the game. They disembarked in their hundreds at Plantation Halt to watch their favourites at Moy Park, a venue long since vanished in the mists of time.

Famous Sons

In the days preceding the outbreak of the First World War, the standard of football in Campbeltown was as good as at any time in its history. During this particular period the community was blessed with young men of prodigious talent, many of whom progressed to the professional ranks, with a few even climbing the heady heights of the international stage. At this time, the town's main sporting venue was the Showground at Castleacres, but in January 1912 a new ground was opened on the outskirts of town to accommodate the ever-increasing popularity of the game.

Midway between 'Mile End' and the village of Stewarton stood Moy Park, yesteryear's answer to what is now a very modern concept – the building of sporting Stadia on green field locations. Well in advance of its time, this 'little gem' was well-served by various modes of public transport. However, its convenient location on the edge of residential Witchburn kept it within walking distance of the town centre. The ground was situated on the left-hand side of the Moy Farm Road, approximately 100 yards from its junction with the main road west to Machrihanish. Spectators could reach the ground by wagonette, horse-drawn bus or bicycle; however, with its own stop on the local railway system, the 'Wee Train' was the favourite mode of transport.

In May 1877, Campbeltown's world-famous narrow gauge railway started life carrying coal from Kilkivan workings to the New Quay. However, as already mentioned, an expansion of tourism during the early part of the twentieth century prompted the addition of carriages in August 1906. The improvement in the living standards among the urban working classes gave Scotland's coastal towns a new commercial opportunity. The train's new passenger service satisfied the demands of an ever-increasing holiday market, a situation made possible by higher wages and the beginning of unpaid annual leave for employees. With market potential, the railway line was extended to the village of Machrihanish, a destination soon to be the haven of Edwardian visitors because of its wide expanse of beach and superb championship golf course.

The 'Wee Train' was an extremely popular mode of transport, never more so than at the opening of the Moy Stadium in January 1912. Working non-stop from its terminus in Hall Street, the locomotive *Argyll* pulled the train's distinctive carriages by way of Limecraigs Cutting to the heights of Tomaig hill. From here passengers could view the lush Laggan plain as it spread westwards towards the sea, this before a slow descent brought the train to the tree-lined Plantation Halt. Renamed 'Stadium Halt' by local football supporters, 'on match day it was transformed by spectators disembarking from football specials run by the Campbeltown & Machrihanish Light Railway'. [15] Football was by now a source of entertainment for all social classes, the game's widespread appeal instrumental in a gift of land to Campbeltown and District Football Association. The new stadium was built on ground donated by a local farmer, and, with the help of public subscription, the firm of R. Weir & Son completed its construction for the princely sum of £400. The opening ceremony was conducted by Provost James C. McMurchy in front of 2,000 spectators on New Year's Day 1912, a gathering graced by a meeting of the area's finest athletes. Football enthusiasts had to wait one more day for the stadium's first match, an Orr-Ewing cup-tie between Kintyre FC and Campbeltown United. The game finished in a 0-0 draw, so the honour of scoring the first goal at Moy Park was 'still up for grabs'.

An interview conducted by local author/historian Angus Martin was successful in capturing a valuable insight into this very period. In 1974, his subject was a gentleman called John McWhirter, a former member of Glenside Juniors and an eyewitness to early sporting events at the stadium. John's vivid account is a unique record of football in the days prior to the Great War, the only known oral history of Moy Park in its heyday. His colourful description captures the essence of the period, in particular the importance of this long-forgotten venue to the people of that time. Only too willing to share his recollections, he began: 'Travelled by the "Wee Train" to play fitba at the Moy.' 'The park had a stand an all.' 'Tuppence ta'en ye oot there and she'd be packed on a Setterday efternoon for the fitba.' Clearly excited by the memory, he continued: 'Away wi the wee train for the match.' 'Queens Park, Kilmarnock and Hamilton all played there – a great field!'

As well as expressing an appreciation for what was the town's first custom-built sports facility, these precious memories convey the level of support the game enjoyed in the days prior to the First World War. Constructed primarily for the use of the Campbeltown & District Football Association, the ground's facilities included a grandstand, grass running track, spectators' enclosure, changing accommodation, and by far the best playing surface in Kintyre. No trace of the stadium remains, but the train's westward route from Plantation to Machrihanish can still be identified by remnants of the track's enclosure fencing.

The Moy district was an extremely busy place on match day and, despite its rural location, the needs of many were satisfied by one of the area's historic country inns, the 'Hungry Hoose'. Situated on the Stewarton side of the level crossing, this establishment was so called because of the thrifty nature of its landlord. The time-honoured tradition of serving an oatmeal bannock with a customer's dram of whisky was often ignored, a desertion of duty immortalised in the building's appropriate by-name. Vitally important in days of the horse-drawn carriage, the aptly named 'Hungry Hoose' was one of many inns dotting the landscape of rural Kintyre. The rise of the motor car in the early part of the twentieth century heralded the demise of these historic premises, sadly rendered obsolete by the pace of modern transport.

The new stadium at Moy was a first-rate facility, a ground fit to complement the undoubted skills of a particularly fruitful period in local football. This fact was demonstrated when the cream of an extremely talented crop competed for the laurels in 1912/13. A titanic struggle had developed for the league championship, the capture of which would also give the winners the 'bragging rights' in local hostelries. Such was the quality of local football in the days preceding the Great War, it was deemed 'junior' in standard. At this level players could receive payment for their services, although, I suspect, few did at the time. Paid or not, there was a general acceptance that football in Campbeltown was good enough to be considered semi-professional in standard – junior grade in Scotland being the equivalent of non-league in England.

Academicals, arguably the most prominent local club of the pre-Great War era, were at the time leading the league table by a single point from their great rivals Campbeltown United. Other teams involved were Hearts, Kintyre, Rangers and Glenside, with a seventh, Campbeltown FC, listed for cup competitions only. After a feisty start to the campaign, the championship was reduced to a two-horse race, the destination of the trophy still undecided as the final match of the series approached. The Academicals club contained some the most famous names ever to play in local football, a team with ex-professional presence and a galaxy of 'stars' who would play at a higher level in the not-too-distant future. Nevertheless, these were exceptional times in local football, a period of strength in depth when games of highly-competitive nature were commonplace. Campbeltown United trailed their more-fancied opponents for most of the league campaign, but dogged determination brought them within touching distance at the 'eleventh hour.' One more win would confirm the underdogs as champions, something that was extremely unlikely a few weeks earlier. The opportunity was too good to refuse, and on 23 January, 1913, an emphatic 5-1 victory over Campbeltown Rangers confirmed United as league champions.

Given the quality of their nearest rivals this success was particularly sweet for the players. In the final reckoning it was the team's forwards who received most of the plaudits, a bunch of pals extremely knowledgeable of the route to goal. As we have come to expect in the peculiar ways of the 'Wee Toon', they are best remembered by their nicknames, 'Wattie', 'Dooda', 'Bockie', 'Panks' and 'Greenyins', respectively, Walter Brown, J. Lambie, Dan McNaughton, W. McDonald and Malcolm McCallum, the latter best remembered as the putting green attendant at Quarry Green during the 1950s and early 1960s.

To celebrate victory, a jubilant squad gathered at the Kinloch Bar in Main Street, an establishment with longstanding ties to Campbeltown United. Strains of their club anthem filled the air as the team savoured success, words of a popular music hall song by Charles K. Harris conveniently altered to suit their needs. Had 'After the Ball' ever sounded so sweet or been sung more passionately? Fragments of the club song have survived, words lovingly remembered by the family of United's free-scoring centre-forward Dan McNaughton. Plentiful they are not, but the remnants are enough to convey images of the past, a fleeting glimpse of events that coloured the local football scene all those years ago.

'After the Ball.'

After the ball was centred
After the whistle blew

Campbeltown United, 1912.
Team only, back row, left to right: Alex McCallum, D Cook and H McCallum. Middle row, left to right: D Thomson, H Sinclair and J Rankin. Front row, left to right: Walter Brown, J Lambie, Dan McNaughton, W McDonald and Malcolm McCallum. Back row left in flat cap: James Brown, Glasgow Rangers.

48

'Bockie' passed tae 'Wattie'
And down the wing he flew.

'Wattie' passed tae 'Greenyins'
'Greenyins' he shot for the goal
Out dived the keeper
But in went the ball.

Campbeltown United 1913. Line-up in 2-3-5 formation:

Donald Cook, A. McCallum and H. McCallum, D. Thomson, Hugh Sinclair, and J. Rankin, Walter Brown, J. Lambie, Dan McNaughton, W. McDonald and Malcolm McCallum.

Remarkably, a framed photograph of this very team was found in the cellar of the Kinloch Bar (MacGochan's) on the corner of Main Street and Longrow South in the early 1980s. It had lain there undiscovered until the premises were taken over by a new owner, Mr Hugh Little, who promptly gifted the same to his newly sponsored football team, the Pupils. For a number of years it was displayed in the pavilion at Kintyre Park, but during a period of refurbishment, it was first transferred to Campbeltown Museum and subsequently to the Heritage Centre for safekeeping – where it can be found to this day.

'Sensation' was the name of the game when Academicals withdrew from the Campbeltown & District Football Association in February 1913. The local administration refused to affiliate to the Scottish Junior FA, a controversial move which left the fully registered Academicals with no option but to secede from membership. The national association tried to intercede by asking the CDFA to reconsider its position, but a compromise could not be reached. Eyes firmly focused on entry to the Scottish Junior Cup, Campbeltown's top club refused to take part in what was now an illegal competition. The stand-off was described in the local newspaper as a 'unique crisis' in local football.[16]

Local clubs were exempt from mainstream competition, but the isolation was hardly noticeable as things continued very much as usual at Moy Park. On the other hand, it really was a serious matter for the Academicals, a club innocently deprived of competition and left to find other ways of maintaining an interest in the game. Surprising as it may seem, instead of heralding the downfall of local football the hiatus would benefit the sporting community on a number of levels. At this juncture Academicals made a remarkable decision, in an act of self-preservation it turned to senior football for its salvation. Returning to its old stamping ground at the Showfield, Academicals invested in the most ambitious programme ever undertaken by a Campbeltown team – a programme of fixtures against the elite of the Scottish game.

It was a courageous undertaking, as the nearest source of opposition was a hundred-plus miles away. The cost of such a venture was prohibitive, and the pessimists gleefully predicted the demise of this famous local club. Thankfully, the complete opposite was the case, and a brilliantly organised Academicals became the only team in the history of Campbeltown football to engage senior opposition on a regular basis. It was great news from a spectator's point of view, but it also opened up a hitherto untapped source of talent to the gaze of the professional scout. The result was an exodus of players to the senior ranks, some to achieve moderate success, with a select few becoming household names and future 'stars' on the international football stage.

Back in familiar surroundings, Academicals enlisted the services of Glasgow Rangers, Greenock Morton, Hamilton Academicals, Motherwell and Queens Park. From the junior ranks came Petershill, Shettleston and Greenock, all to meet the local favourites at their famous Castlehill fortress. Daunting times lay ahead and immediate action was taken to strengthen the squad. Kintyre FC yielded a strong quartet in Neil McBain, Robert McGeachy, Archie Armour and Hector 'Beck' McMillan. The new signings joined the likes of Peter Pursell, John Durnin, Rev B. B. Blackwood and Rev M. B. Houston – ex-Greenock Morton – to form arguably the most formidable team ever assembled in the history of Campbeltown football.

With preparations complete, the club readied itself for the first match of an extremely challenging programme, an encounter with Glasgow Rangers on Saturday March 22 1913. The Ibrox management agreed to send its 'A' eleven, a team fresh from winning the Scottish Reserve Cup and hot favourites to add the Scottish Reserve League Championship to an ever-growing list of achievements. [17] Included in the squad were free-scoring forwards J. Parker and A. Brown, both included in the first team against Hearts at Tynecastle the previous week-end. Parker's reputation was such that an unnamed English League club had reputedly offered £1,000 for his services – a phenomenal amount of money for the period.

The organisers breathed a sigh of relief when a healthy crowd of 1200 mustered for the occasion, more than enough to support the lofty ambitions of an extraordinary project. You could describe what followed as unexpected, but that would be a gross understatement! The home side's performance had many rubbing their eyes in disbelief, and when the final whistle blew the Ibrox superstars were beaten by 1-0. The only goal of the game came in the fifteenth minute from the incomparable Peter Pursell, a low strike deceiving Rangers' goalkeeper Farrington at his near-post. Home goalkeeper Archie 'Mog' McCallum, a flamboyant character who turned out in all-white, made a number of important saves in the second half and a combination of industry and resolute defending saw Academicals record an unlikely but nevertheless sensational victory.

If the club's new venture depended on public support to survive, a win against the mighty Rangers was the right way of achieving it. The Accies' giant-killing performance grabbed the imagination of the national press, but it also provided a warning to future opponents that a visit to Kintyre was not without its pitfalls. Glasgow Rangers had cause to remember one young man from Campbeltown, a quality player who tormented the club's defence at the town's Showfield. Peter Pursell, a versatile performer, grabbed the headlines later in the year when he joined Queens Park and became an instant hit at Hampden Park. His rise to fame was little short of meteoric, and within months he was touted as a possible SFL player of the year. Peter won the sports writers' version of this accolade in his first season of senior football and, as if this wasn't enough, within six months of leaving junior football he earned a full international cap against Wales at Parkhead in February 1914. Peter's dream of stardom had finally arrived when his outstanding form drew the attention of Glasgow Rangers, and a short trip across the city was the start of a long and successful career at Ibrox Stadium.

Although overshadowed by recent events at the Showfield, football at Moy Park continued to have its fair share of attention in the local press. However, human nature being what it is there were times when controversy would rule the day. A case in point was an Orr-Ewing cup-tie between United and Hearts in March 1913, a day local football would rather forget. A large crowd witnessed a volatile match, an extremely rough encounter in which proceedings threatened to get out of hand. Goals from 'Dooda' Lambie and 'Wattie' Brown had Campbeltown United in command in the early stages, but the game started to swing in favour of the Dalintober

Campbeltown Academicals, 1913. Back row, left to right: D Quin, J McGougan, A Armour, A McCallum, W McEachran and J Finnie. Front row, left to right: R McGeachy, J Durnin, P Pursell, N McBain and D Johnstone.

men when Sweeney McGeachy reduced the leeway. Temperatures were set to rise. There was no love lost between the sides and, with football forgotten, 'several unpleasant incidents occurred'. Passions were running high and there were a number of 'incidents which caused the competency of the referee to be impeached'. [18] The award of a controversial penalty kick to United was the last straw. Enough was enough and the entire Hearts team walked off in disgust. Diplomacy now exhausted, the referee decided the penalty-kick should be taken with or without the opposition. As the Hearts team retreated to the dressing room, left-back H. McCallum had the easiest of tasks of converting into an empty net.

Matters were less contentious at the Showfield; the Accies' prestigious victory over Glasgow Rangers 'A' had given the team celebrity status in the national press, the standard of football in the 'Wee Toon' had taken everyone by surprise. Fully aware of what awaited, Greenock Morton travelled to Kintyre with a full-strength league side, a team containing no fewer than four Scottish internationalists – Bradford, Stark, May and Craig. Morton's celebrated goalkeeper Bradford had just won the equivalent of today's player of the year award, beating illustrious names like Tommy Walker of Hearts and Jimmy Quinn of Celtic to the title 'King of Football'. [19] Roared on by a crowd of 1500, Academicals' new-found reputation seemed justified when the local team stormed into the lead on the half-hour mark. A perfect cross from Robert 'Bobba' McGeachy found the head of Bruce Blackwood, whose firm parting header sailed into the top corner of the net. A rousing game reached the mid-way point with the home side's lead still intact, and a second major upset was not beyond the realms of fantasy. The 'Accies' started the second half on the front foot, but Morton's 'star' goalkeeper Bradford displayed his undoubted class with a string of outstanding saves. Deputising at centre half for the injured M. B. Houston (ex-Morton), young Andrew Armour's day was about to go downhill. The home defender's attempt at a headed clearance found the back of his own net, a lifeline for Morton at a crucial stage in the match. Luck was about to go right out the window, with fifteen minutes of the match remaining, a cross from Morton winger Thomson rebounded off the legs of team mate Brown, and a surprised McCallum in the home goal could only parry the ball into his own net.

Although beaten by 2 goals to 1, there was no despondency in the Accies camp; after all, it was a tremendous performance considering the presence of four Scottish internationalists. In an after-match interview, player of the year Bradford complimented the ability of the home side. He described Blackwood's scoring header as 'a fine thing' adding, 'I stood a poor chance of saving it'. He elaborated by saying: 'If I had two whole legs I would have had done better ... I received a 'dunt' (knock) in the previous week's match against Dundee'. [20]

No one could accuse the local favourites of slacking, as next on the agenda was a game against Hamilton Academicals, Scottish Cup finalists just two seasons earlier in 1910/11. As a compliment to the home side, the visitors once more travelled with a full-strength league side, which was, in the opinion of many, the best team to visit Campbeltown during this unique period for football in Kintyre. While a spirited performance by the home eleven kept the game goal-less at half-time, the superior fitness of the seniors became evident in the closing stages of the match. Hamilton made the breakthrough in the 80th minute of an enthralling game, adding two more, as the home side tired, to win 3-0. The result of the match was never in doubt, but a gallant effort from the home side ensured that defeat was only conceded in the closing stages.

It was the turn of Motherwell to visit the following week, the 'Steel Men' on the crest of a wave after securing a second league victory of the season over Glasgow Celtic. The Lanarkshire side selected nine first team members in their starting line-up, but Academicals were up to the task and finished the day with a creditable 0-0 draw. The game did have a rather unusual ending however, as the match ball burst with minutes remaining. Surprise quickly changed to embarrassment when the home side realised it was the only one available. Although retiring a few minutes early, both camps were suitably entertained at the post-match reception which reputedly came off without a hitch. The games against Hamilton and Motherwell were played in mid-week, a fact that speaks volumes for the commitment of the senior teams. It also highlights the standard of pre-First World War transport, as the Campbeltown and Glasgow Steam Packet Company offered a year-round service to and from the Broomielaw in the heart of Glasgow. Travelling by sea made for a relaxed journey in civilised surroundings, a better alternative to the long road trip regularly experienced by today's sporting gladiators.

Circumstances took a turn for the better when the local association joined the SJFA in April 1913. Now in full membership, the CDJFA was rewarded with permission to entertain senior opposition in the shape of Kilmarnock and Airdrie. Subsequent events at the Showfield had presumably brought everyone to their senses and, spoiled for choice, the obvious winner was the town's football-minded public. Atrocious weather greeted Kilmarnock to Campbeltown for the first of these fixtures, but a sizable crowd watched as fine play helped to brighten an otherwise bleak day. A hotly disputed second-half penalty-kick was all that separated the teams, the award duly converted by Templeton to give the Ayrshire seniors a narrow 1-0 victory.

Airdrie provided the opposition the following Tuesday, but any similarity to the previous weekend's spectacle was merely coincidental. Sitting joint third in the Scottish 1st Division along with Heart of Midlothian, the visitors were considered to have the best forward line in the country. The Lanarkshire men lived up to their reputation by demolishing the local select by 7 goals to 1. The visitors' line-up included the league's top goal scorer J. Reid, ably abetted by former English League 'cap', R. Thomson. Peace officially restored, the national association approved the visit of Petershill Juniors to Moy Park in May 1913.

Campbeltown Select v. Kilmarnock: A. McCallum (Hearts), R. Armour (Hearts), H. McCallum (United), D. Thomson (United), J. Taylor (Hearts), J. Rankin (United), W. Brown (United), S. McGeachy (Hearts), D. McNaughton (United), D. McEachran (Glenside) and E. McGeachy (Hearts).

Campbeltown Select v. Airdrie: J. McKinlay (Glenside), R. Armour (Hearts), W. Mustarde (Campbeltown), T. Cameron (Campbeltown), J. Brodie (Campbeltown), D. Thomson (United), W. Brown (United), W. McDonald (United), D. McNaughton (United), S. McGeachy (Hearts) and E. McGeachy (Hearts).

There was no shortage of talent in Campbeltown during the period immediately preceding the First World War, and to suggest these were the best days of local football is a fairly accurate assessment. At this juncture, the town was capable of producing players to match the best in the game; and this hitherto untapped reservoir of talent became the focus of the senior scouting system. Into this rich pool of sporting talent stepped a young man of undoubted ability, a gentleman who arrived in the community to pursue an ecclesiastical vocation. In time, the Reverend Bruce B. Blackwood would become a football legend in his new-found home. His reputation as a player preceded his arrival as the newly appointed minister of the Lochend

United Free Church was a proven Scottish Junior internationalist. He soon became a target for a club at the top of its game, his inclusion in the Accies squad adding further quality to a team destined to leave its mark on the town's sporting history.

At this particular point, fact and fiction become slightly blurred, nevertheless, an unusual tale from the past is certainly worth retelling. It has become part of Campbeltown's football folklore, a story of the streets to survive the passage of time. I have no way of confirming whether it is true or not, but it certainly deserves the benefit of the doubt. Reputedly, a large crowd had gathered at the Showfield to watch Academicals play an unnamed visiting eleven, often quoted as Greenock Morton. During the course of an evenly-contested game, the home side were awarded a somewhat dubious penalty – a soft one in football terminology! The gallery hushed in anticipation as Bruce Blackwood stepped forward to take the kick. Placing the leather on the spot, he intentionally interrupted his run-up to casually lob the football into the astonished crowd. Asked later to explain his actions, he insisted that he could not take advantage of what clearly was an unjust decision. Did it actually happen? In this case you will have to decide for yourself, but if true, it is a splendid example of a moral dilemma solved by actions rather than words.

In preparation for their assault on the Renfrewshire Cup, Academicals hosted Shettleston Juniors and won by 3 goals to 1. The inclusion of an Argyll club in this particular competition was at odds with geography, but, the success of their 'senior adventure' could well have paved the way. In any case, Academicals did themselves proud by making it to the cup final, a match against Neilston Victoria at Love Street, Paisley. The game ended in a 1-1 draw, a result which prompted outlandish travel arrangements for the following week-end's replay at Beresford Park, former home of Ayr United. Faced with an arduous journey by road, a better solution was found when the owner of a fishing boat offered to ferry the team across the Firth of Clyde. Ninety minutes from glory, disappointment followed when Neilston Victoria edged the replay by 2 goals to 1. Major players were missing from the Academicals line-up, the most notable being Peter Pursell, who had recently signed for Queens Park. Also missing was the club's excellent left-winger D. Johnstone and the highly influential B. B. Blackwood. It would be the last game for a number of players departing to the senior ranks, with Neil McBain leaving for Ayr United, Andrew Armour to St Johnstone and John Durnin to Plymouth Argyle.

Campbeltown Academicals v. Neilston Victoria, 1914: Archie McCallum; Dominic Quin and Willie McEachran; J. Taylor, John Durnan and Andrew Armour; Robert McGeachy, Hector McMillan, Sweeney McGeachy, Neil McBain and Eddie 'Speed' McGeachy.

The unprecedented success of this extremely ambitious club would eventually contribute to its demise, its abundant talent plundered by the senior scouting system. As players departed to the higher firmament of the game, the thinning of the ranks had an adverse effect on the health of the club. The team for the Renfrewshire Cup final also contained a number of changes, with stand-ins J. Taylor, Sweeney McGeachy and Eddie McGeachy all recruited from Hearts. Academicals would never again aspire to the heights achieved in the years prior to the Great War, and, sadly, the club disappeared altogether on completion of season 1934/35.

Campbeltown Academicals, 1912/13: Archie McCallum, Dominic Quin, Peter Pursell, John Durnin, Andrew Armour, Rev M. B. Houston, Willie McEachran, Jimmy Finnie, Robert McGeachy, Neil McBain, Hector McMillan, D. Johnston, Rev Bruce B. Blackwood, Johnny McGougan and Monroe.

The years immediately preceding the First World War were without question the most prolific period in local football, a time when Campbeltown was capable of sending a regular supply of players to the professional ranks. The quality of the local game also benefited from people who settled in the community in the years prior to military confrontation, as was evident with the arrival of two high profile players, the Reverend M. B. Houston, ex-Morton, and Reverend Bruce B. Blackwood, former international player at amateur and junior levels. Here are a few of our famous sons who made it senior in the first quarter of the twentieth century. Will we see their likes again?

'The Great' Neil McBain – Ayr United, Manchester United, Everton, Liverpool and Scotland.

Neil McBain was born in Campbeltown on 15 November 1895, where he emerged during his teenage years to become a member of one of the oldest and most respected football organisations in the town, Kintyre Football Club. He joined the ambitious Academicals Football Club in 1913, and no one was surprised when he progressed to become the closest article to a complete player as one could find. His reputation was such that he soon became the target of senior scouts, a man regarded in his own community as 'an outstanding forward'. [21] A record-breaking career in football followed, and he starred for the likes of Manchester United, Everton and Liverpool. Neil's outstanding ability was rewarded with international recognition, and he was selected to play for his country on three separate occasions, only the second player from the 'Wee Toon' to be capped at full international level. Arguably the most prominent player that Campbeltown ever produced, Neil McBain progressed to become a 'giant' of the game in the years following the end of the First World War.

During his early years in football, he accidentally found his true position at centre-half, a surprising choice considering his distinct lack of height. Standing no more than 5 ft. 8 inches tall, he was described as strong-built, mobile, extremely skilful and a superb header of the ball – not your stereotype British central defender! However, a centre-half in the 1920s was more of a free spirit, a player who had a roving commission virtue of the old offside law – three players required goal-side instead of the present two. When in possession, a team could keep the minimum number of players behind the ball. This allowed the centre-half to push forward into an attacking role – more of a playmaker than a stopper. The rule was ready-made for a player of Neil's talent, and he loved nothing better than to move forward and make defence-splitting passes. His stylish play made him a favourite of the terraces and he was recognised as one of the great players of his time and generation.

After playing in the Renfrewshire Cup Final with Campbeltown Academicals, in 1913 at the tender age of eighteen he joined Ayr United. Military service then put his football career on hold, although while stationed on the south coast he played as a guest with Southampton and Portsmouth. At the end of the war he returned to Ayr United, where he matured into a seasoned professional playing in the SFL 1st Division. Now considered the finished article, he moved to Manchester United for a fee of £4,600 in November 1921. After little more than a year at Old Trafford, he was transferred to high-flying Everton for a fee of £4,200 in January 1923. A superstar of his day, the amount of cash changing hands for his services was unprecedented for the period.

International recognition was just around the corner and he was selected to play for his country on three occasions. In a period rich in talent, he was capped against England at Villa Park on 8 April 1922, where a goal by Andy Wilson of Rangers was enough to claim success over the 'Auld Enemy'. This was followed by an appearance against Northern Ireland, when another Andy Wilson strike secured victory as the Scots lifted the British International Championship for the second year in succession on 3 March 1923. His third and final cap was against Wales at Ninian Park, Cardiff, on 16 February 1924, but on this occasion the home side claimed victory by 2-0. The standard of player available to Scotland in the 1920s was simply immense, as Neil shared company with the wonderful Alan Morton of Glasgow Rangers – 'the Wee Blue Devil' – and Queens Park's goalkeeping legend, the unflappable Jack Harkness. These 'giants' of Scottish football appeared in the fabulous 'Wembley Wizards' of 1928, a team which also included the equally amazing Hughie Gallagher and Alex James. The public were astounded when 'Old Firm' favourites Jimmy McGrory of Celtic and Bob McPhail and David Meiklejohn of Rangers were left out of the Wembley line-up, but these omissions were quickly forgotten when Scotland won convincingly by 5 goals to 1.

St Johnstone paid Everton £1,000 for Neil's services in 1926, the beginning of a two-year stint at Muirton Park. Further moves included spells at Liverpool then Watford, both sides benefiting from his experience in the latter years of his playing career. Retirement didn't keep Neil McBain away from his beloved sport, for in 1931 he changed direction and launched into a new career in management. Adopting a schedule that would leave most in a state of nervous exhaustion, he managed Watford (1931-36), Ayr United (1936-37), Luton Town (1938-39), New Brighton (1946-48) and Leyton Orient (1948-49). This should have been sufficient for one lifetime, but he then returned to Ayr United (1955-56), Watford (1956-59) and finally back to Ayr United (1962-63). He also managed to scout for Mansfield Town, Everton and Chelsea – in his spare time, of course!

During his time as manager of New Brighton he encountered a dilemma when both his regular goalkeepers succumbed to injury on match day. Left without cover between 'the sticks', he made the most unlikely decision of his long and illustrious career – he decided to turn out himself! Not only had he never played in goal before, there was also the small issue of his age. At 51 years and 120 days, against Hartlepool United on March 15 1947, Neil McBain became the oldest player to appear in a Football League match. Needless to say, the record still stands today.

Unbelievably, his lengthy managerial career included a trip to Argentina to coach the famous Estudiantes de la Plata (1949-51), this before returning home to take charge of his first senior club, the love of his football life, Ayr United. His return to Scotland prompted the *Daily Record*'s chief sports correspondent, 'Waverley', to write a piece entitled 'This Man McBain', an article copied by his hometown paper, the *Campbeltown Courier*, on 5 May 1955. It included a pledge by Neil to lead the Ayrshire club back to the first division. He flatly refused to disband the club's reserve team, placing his belief in a squad rotation system nurtured during many years of coaching both at home and abroad. Although he parted company with Ayr United for a second spell at Watford, his heart was always in Scotland with his former club.

Ironically, Ayr United regained first division status in 1958, and Neil returned for a last stint as manager in 1962. It was the final chapter of a truly amazing football story. At the age of 67, with a career spanning all of 49 years, he finally retired from the game. He had scaled the heights both as a player and manager, and richly deserves the accolade 'The Great Neil McBain'.

Robert Pursell – Queens Park, Liverpool and Port Vale.

Robert 'Bob' Pursell made the transition from the local game to the heady heights of senior football when he signed for Queens Park from Campbeltown Rangers in 1909. Along with fellow Campbeltonian, James Brown, he had earlier been on trial at Ayr United, and both men were invited back after impressing the manager. The initial trial match against Annbank Juniors was a personal triumph for Bob, as he scored a hat-trick playing at centre-forward in a game which Ayr United won by 4 goals to 1. As interest was now being shown by a number of senior clubs, both men were persuaded to keep their options open, a sound piece of advice as future developments would prove.

Queens Park was next on the scene when inviting Bob to take part in a mid-week friendly against near-neighbours Third Lanark. His outstanding performance in the 1-1 draw at Cathkin Park convinced the Mount Florida hierarchy to make a move for his signature, and remarkably he made his full league debut a few days later against Heart of Midlothian at Hampden Park. As if quicksilver promotion wasn't daunting enough, the task of replacing the injured Scottish internationalist Harold Paul made things more difficult. However, all such worries quickly disappeared as his debut became something of a fairy-tale experience. Bob's powerful display of front running was embellished by a magnificent individualist goal. With Hearts leading by the only goal of the match, in the words of a leading newspaper 'Bob Pursell saved the day when he scored with a low, fast shot that left Muir on his back fairly beaten'. [22] Another major newspaper was suitably impressed. 'Equally prominent at inside-right was a tall young fellow from Campbeltown named Pursell ... This youth is developed on the best football lines and infuses dash and pluck to the line ... He was the means of saving the game in the second-half, and throughout gave Hearts no end of trouble'.[23] Robert Pursell's senior career was off to a flyer!

Liverpool/Everton Select v International Select circa 1911.
Robert Pursell, back row, second from right.

Back home in Campbeltown, there was incredible excitement as the news filtered through. They even composed poetry to commemorate the occasion.

O' fitba folks an' did you hear
the news that's going round,
That Campbeltown is for players now
to be a hunting ground.

Nae mair tae Showfield Park we'll go
tae see our favourites run,
But we must hie to famous parks,
where higher laurels are won.

Then, here's success to Pursell who
reliable is and true;
He's shown them up at Hampden what
old Campbeltown can do.

And why should we our players grudge
when enthusiasm it is low,
But rather when some warrior's asked
encourage them to go.

Anon.

After spending two years at Hampden Park, Bob once more hit the headlines when he signed for Liverpool, albeit in a somewhat controversial manner. The Anfield hierarchy made the mistake of not including Queens Park in the signing talks, a serious breach of inter-league rules. Found guilty of illegal practices, 'the Reds' were fined £200 and the chairman suspended. The formalities of transfer having been finally settled, the Merseyside club was allowed to keep its prize acquisition, much to the disappointment of the other bidders waiting in the wings with cash at the ready.

Bob eventually moved south to concentrate on the business of playing football, a case of second nature to an extremely talented individual. In 1914, he was one of seven Scots in a Liverpool side which defeated Aston Villa in the semi-final of the FA Cup. This win set up a clash with Burnley at Crystal Palace, a match made famous as the first FA Cup Final attended by a reigning monarch. King George V was joined by 72,000 spectators to watch a tense struggle between two evenly-balanced sides, the only goal of the match scored by England international Bert Freeman of Burnley. Cup success had eluded Bob Pursell, but the disappointment of losing was tempered by the knowledge of his being the only Campbeltonian ever to play in an FA Cup Final. Bob made 113 appearances for Liverpool before moving to Port Vale, a club he considered the best of his sporting career. Although just another player at the time, in partnership with his brother Peter, Pursell would attain legendary status in 'the Staffordshire Potteries'.

Peter Pursell – Queens Park, Glasgow Rangers, Port Vale and Scotland.

By 1913, another member of the Pursell family had started to make his way in the game. This time it was the turn of 'wee' brother Peter to grab the football headlines. The heroics of Peter Pursell in the colours of Campbeltown Academicals didn't go unnoticed by the professional fraternity, his rich vein of form attracting a number of well-known clubs to the negotiating table. Like his brother before him, Peter decided to place his future in the hands of Queens Park. However, never in his wildest dreams could he have predicted the unprecedented chain of events that followed his arrival at Hampden Park.

Peter was nothing if not versatile, so when the team's regular centre-half was sidelined through injury, he easily moved from fullback to cover the vacant position. He was completely unfazed by playing out of position, so relaxed, indeed, that his subsequent performances at the heart of the Queens' defence made national headlines. Playing at centre-half for the first time in his life, his form proved so consistent he was quoted as a potential SFL player of the year. He then received the staggering news that he had been selected to play for Scotland against Wales in a Home International Championship match at Parkhead on 28 February 1914. That day, 19-year-old Peter Pursell became the youngest centre-half ever to represent Scotland – a record broken only recently by 18-year-old Danny Wilson against the Faeroe Islands – and the first Campbeltonian to play at full international level for his country. It is difficult to imagine how a young man in his first season of senior football could comprehend such an honour, a rise of meteoric proportions from junior to full international in fewer than six months. In terms of time-scale alone, it was a feat of progression unparalleled in the Scottish game.

Peter's progress had been closely monitored by the 'big guns', and it was no surprise when Glasgow Rangers became interested in signing him. It was an offer he could hardly refuse and he moved

Peter Pursell wears his international cap, 1914

from the comparative tranquillity of Mount Florida to entertain the heaving galleries of Ibrox Stadium. Now a full-time professional with one of the biggest clubs in the country, his career in 'light blue' spanned all of five years and 154 first team appearances (1915-20). In his time at Ibrox he occupied no fewer than seven different positions, his renowned versatility being tested to the full. Peter's honours included winning the Scottish 1st Division Championship, Glasgow Cup, Charity Cup and Belgian Cup, the latter a cross-border Anglo-Scottish tournament organised to assist troops on their return from the Western Front.

His Rangers career finally at an end, Peter was transferred to English 2nd Division outfit Port Vale for a fee of £2,500. At 'the Potteries' he was reunited with Ibrox team-mate Willie Aitken and, slightly later, with his brother, Bob. That season – 1920/21 – the Pursell brothers formed a full back partnership in front of Welsh International goalkeeper John Peers, a formidable rearguard according to the press. The defensive trio attained legendary status at the club, and they were remembered in a local press feature on past players as an 'impregnable partnership'. 'It was the three 'Ps' that Vale relied on'.[24]

The Pursell brothers' partnership was dissolved when Bob broke his leg in 1922, an injury which unfortunately brought his career to a premature end. Peter carried on and was honoured to serve as captain for three of the five years he spent at the club. He played in one more international trial match for Anglos against Home Scots, but failed to add to his solitary Scottish cap. He then moved to Wigan Borough in the English 3rd Division, where he acted as player/coach before moving to Holland and a new contract with Dordrecht FC – in more recent times, the club from which Mark De Vries moved to Heart of Midlothian. Peter's 'swan song' as a player was at non-league Congleton Town, although he did return to Springfield Park for a second spell with Wigan Borough – this time as coach, before retiring.

I was fortunate to make contact with Peter's son, who was himself a professional footballer in the late 1940s. Named after his uncle Bob, he kept family tradition alive by also playing for Port Vale at fullback, a rare occurrence of father and son having played for the same professional club and in the very same position. Sadly, he passed away before our paths could cross, but memories of my research were brought into focus during a holiday I spent in London in 2008. Scouring music festival trade stalls on the banks of the

Port Vale 1948. Robert Pursell junior, third from left back row.

Thames near Southwick, I stumbled across an old photograph of Port Vale dated 1947/48. Sure enough, there in the line-up was the very same Bob Pursell Junior – needless to say it was purchased immediately!

Bob and Peter Pursell were every bit as inseparable off the field as on it. Away from the focus of the terraces, after retirement they became partners in a small tobacconist shop in Tontine Street, Hanley. Known affectionately as the 'Hanley Highlanders', they ran the shop for all of 43 years, happy to live their lives in an area they had come to love. Celebrities to the end, in countless interviews with the local press they never forgot their roots – always remembering their days in the 'Wee Toon' with Rangers, United and Academicals. The place where it all began.

James 'Jamie' Brown – Glasgow Rangers and Kilmarnock

James Brown was another local player who caught the eye of senior scouts in the days prior to the First World War. A defensive stalwart with Campbeltown United, he was spotted playing for local rivals Academicals in a Scottish Junior Cup tie at Port Glasgow during 1911. In the crowd was a representative of one of the biggest clubs in Scottish football, Glasgow Rangers and, after an impressive performance, he was invited to appear on trial for the Ibrox reserves against Dundee the following weekend. Jamie excelled playing at left-back, and was rewarded with a place in the second team against Partick Thistle the following weekend, a match that just happened to be the Scottish Reserve Cup Final.

He quickly adjusted to the rigours of senior football and became a consistent performer for the rest of the season. He helped Rangers secure the Scottish Reserve Cup and a runners-up spot in the Reserve League Championship. He was also promoted to the first team for games against Hibs and Clyde, a valuable learning experience as the senior squad swept to the 1911/12 league championship. However, a familiar story began to emerge at Ibrox as youth was overlooked for the big money signings. Jamie was forced to reconsider his options when John Robertson was signed from Southampton. Faced with experienced competition for a starting place in the first team, he opted to accept an offer from Kilmarnock. The Ayrshire club was suitably impressed when he played for Rangers at Rugby Park, and the guarantee of first team football clinched the deal.

His acquisition proved extremely popular, especially with the club's faithful support. A glowing testimonial confirmed this when sports writer 'Horatio' declared: 'One of the best captures made during the close season is the securing of James Brown from Campbeltown.' [25] Once an untapped source, football in the 'Wee Toon' was set to come under the microscope as never before. At the end of his senior career, James Brown returned to Campbeltown to open a fish and chip shop in Cross Street, premises situated on the Union Street side of the present day dental surgery.

John Durnin, Plymouth Argyle and Swansea

Following in his friend's footsteps, John Durnin was another outstanding player promoted to the professional ranks in the wake of the Academicals' pulsating run to the Renfrewshire Cup Final. He joined English League side Plymouth Argyle in 1914, making 24 first team appearances in his only season with the south coast side. His career was put on hold when war disrupted the league programme, but the end of hostilities saw him move to Swansea Town – now City – a club which only turned professional in 1912. Prior to the war, Swansea had been promoted to Division 2 of the Southern League, a division which was integrated into the national league set-up as the English 3rd Division in 1918.

The Welsh club struggled to make ends meet in post-war professional football, but, as team captain, John Durnin is remembered for his unswerving loyalty and dedication during extremely difficult times.

Having survived the lean years, Swansea went from strength to strength by reaching the FA Cup semi-finals in 1925, a period in which the club was also promoted to the English 2nd Division as champions. At the end of his time in senior football John returned to Campbeltown to pursue life as a fisherman. His love affair with the game continued in the colours of Campbeltown Grammar School Former Pupils – 'the Pupils' – claiming his place alongside a number of outstanding individuals who represented the club during a highly successful period between 1926 and 1928.

Sporting interests, however, were tempered by the gloom of a faltering economy. As a concession to the temperance movement, Chancellor of the Exchequer David Lloyd George increased the tax on wines and spirits, a move that dealt a hammer blow to the whisky industry. The influential temperance lobby had infiltrated the political arena and, in an effort to control the level of alcohol consumption, the duty on spirits was doubled during the course of the following decade. It was devastating news for a town with twenty-plus distilleries. 'Is Campbeltown done?' raged a letter to the editor, the contributor's sentiments an echo of community frustration. All of this has a familiar feel to it, as after a lapse of almost a century we are still singing from the very same hymn sheet.

On a much brighter note, the Picture House, one of the earliest custom-built cinemas in Scotland, opened its doors for the first time on Monday 27 May 1913. Unfortunately, the world was poised to plunge headlong into war, and any thought of progress was a complete irrelevance. The approaching conflict would cripple society and claim the lives of a host of young men, ordinary citizens who in more carefree days found simple satisfaction on the playing-fields of the 'Wee Toon'.

One such person was Alex McCallum, right back of Campbeltown United FC and winner of a league championship medal in 1913. Along with many of his friends, Alex enlisted in the 8th Battalion of the Argyll & Sutherland and was sent to the Western Front. He was promoted to Sergeant and found himself in charge of a group of six bomb-throwers. At 1 a.m. on 14th June 1915, after four days in the fire trenches, the 8th Battalion was stood-down and began a 4-6 mile march back to the billets near the village of Locan. No sooner had they arrived, the tired men were ordered to return to the firing-line to help the Seaforth and Sutherland Terriers. It was a prelude to one of the horrors of the First World War – a full frontal assault on enemy lines.

The charge at Festubert on 15th June 1915 was preceded by the bombardment of the enemy lines by the British Artillery, and when the guns ceased an eerie silence descended before the order came. Over the top went No 10 Platoon, each line maintaining 10-yard intervals into the withering fire of German machine guns. We can only imagine the terror felt by the men involved in this action, as old soldiers are not renowned for relating their war experiences. Sergeant Alex McCallum was never seen again. He had been in France for six weeks only. Private T. K. Ritchie, one of Alex's men, had this to say of his leader. 'He was a gallant lad and a splendid soldier under fire; what more can one want to say of his sons in a time like this?'

Everything pales into insignificance when compared to the carnage of war – a sobering thought as one reflects on a man's sporting achievements. Thanks to relatives, Alex's league winner's medal was exhibited in the 'Kit and Caboodle' Football Exhibition in Campbeltown Museum during 2012.

Old Masters – New Pupils

The Great War lasted marginally in excess of four years, a small space in time when one considers its enormity in loss of life and human suffering. Campbeltown War Memorial bears testament to those who paid the ultimate price, in terms of numbers alone a major sacrifice for a town of its size. Given the legions of missing friends, it is impossible to imagine how a return to normality could have been achieved, nevertheless, a programme of social regeneration was put in place and, as you would expect, the community played its part to the full.

Removed from the rigours of warfare, the interest of young men once more returned to the challenges of sport, particularly football, a game of excellence in the years prior to the conflagration. The task of rebuilding a competitive structure was first on the agenda, and to that end Campbeltown & District Junior Football Association was reconvened in the autumn of 1917. Prior to the war there had been seven clubs of junior standard active in the town, so hopes were high of organising a similar structure when the troops returned. Four pre-war clubs responded to the initial rallying call, Glenside, Campbeltown, Kintyre and Hearts, and, before commencement of competition, they were joined by a team from the town's historic past, a club that had taken part in the first Charity Cup final in 1887, Kilbrannan FC. So, after a lengthy absence, the boots were back on, and the healthy rivalry groomed over three decades of competition was restored to the playing fields of the town.

Surprisingly, the top pre-war sides were noticeable by their absence, with Campbeltown United and Academicals both being unable to answer the association roll-call. The tragedy of war was all too evident as well-known clubs struggled with a shortage of manpower. In this climate, no single team would dominate, the baton of success passing with predictable regularity from one club to another. Post-war pride disappeared as the faithful fought to save their favourite team from extinction. As one club folded, another would take its place, realism finally dawning when the league's capability was reduced to four teams only. Football would have to wait a number of years for youth to swell its ranks, and, although the game's popularity was restored, the standard set in the years prior to the First World War was never fully recovered.

In 1919, a new organisation by the name of Campbeltown Grammar School Former Pupils Association tossed its hat into the ring. Formed to cater for the sporting needs of ex-students, its lengthy title was considered cumbersome and impractical, so in the interests of simplicity it was abbreviated to CGSFP. Supporters were less than happy with the decision, and, although a list of letters was good enough for officialdom, the rank and file decided to use their own affectionate by-name, the now familiar Pupils Football Club. That year the original team was photographed in the vicinity of the old Campbeltown Cricket Club at Limecraigs, a favourite haunt of football since the demise of the aforementioned club in 1905. Pictured in the line-up are two members of the local clergy, the Rev Bruce B. Blackwood of the Lochend United Free Church and the Rev C. V. A. MacEachern, at the time recently appointed minister of Castlehill Church. Mr Blackwood's ministry at Lochend Church was an epic of biblical proportions, a journey through five decades before his retirement in the late 1950s. The church he loved was demolished in 1985 to make way for a supermarket car park, in the opinion of many an act of sacrilege.

Cricket at Limecraigs had been in abeyance for over a decade, the empty clubhouse now utilised by football groups as a backdrop for photographs. Built in the latter years of the 19th century, the wooden building added a touch of Victorian class to row on row of extremely sombre faces. A common trait of early photographic groups, the image of happiness was often rejected in favour of a sterner persona. The vacant pavilion at Limecraigs served the purpose extremely well, but it seems ironic it was the popularity of football that caused the demise of local cricket in the first instance. If nothing else, football is a survivor, as even the depredations of war failed to halt its onward march. The remnants of the post-war game gave birth to the Pupils Football Club, a team managed by a man of steely determination, Mr A. D. McLeod. Although he set the pattern for future generations, I'm sure he would be astounded to know his club was still around in the second decade of the 21st century.

Campbeltown Grammar School Former Pupils, 1919-1920.
Back row, left to right: C Brown, J McMillan, J McMillan, R Stewart, L McKechnie, T McCallum, M Henderson, H Mustarde and A McLeod. Middle row, left to right: G Quigley, C Henderson, Rev CVA McEachern, Rev BB Blackwood, J Boyce and T McPherson. Front row, left to right: J McDonald, H Smith and L Mustarde

Members of the original CGSFP are as follows:

R. Stewart, Lewis McKechnie, T. McCallum, C. Quigley, C. Henderson, Rev MacEachern, Rev Blackwood, J. Boyce, Tommy McPherson, John McDonald, Hugh Smith and Lachie Mustarde.

The club's first match was a 'friendly' at the Showfield against pace-setters Kintyre FC, an organisation whose history dates back to the early years of the 1880s. Success evaded the Former Pupils in the first year of competition, but a winning mentality was developed and the team went from strength to strength. Campbeltown & District Junior Association was reduced to four sides in the early 1920s, Drumlemble, Glenside, Campbeltown and Former Pupils. Five pre-war football clubs had simply vanished: United, Academicals, Rangers, Hearts, and, after a short appearance, Kintyre as well. The survival and future of the local game was in the hands of youth, and the Campbeltown Churches and Sabbath Schools Football League would rise to the challenge. All the well-known clubs were re-established in due course, but it would take a generation before a full recovery was complete.

The breakthrough was just around the corner for the Former Pupils, but the exploits of the founding group were unknown when members of my family resurrected the club some 40 years later in 1959. Recovery of the club's history was down to a meeting with Archie McDiarmid, a member of the original team in its heyday. This was not a chance encounter, as Archie had been studying the sports pages of his local newspaper the *Greenock Telegraph* and, in his own words, was astonished to find his old club listed to play Port Glasgow Hibs. Not sure of what to expect, he travelled to 'the Port' to establish the facts for himself. To say he was delighted is an understatement as, on arrival, he found his old club stripped and ready for action, still sporting the traditional club colours of yesteryear. Questions came thick and fast, this before our journey in Scottish League football continued with a comfortable win against the host club – to the obvious delight of our newfound friend.

From that day on, Archie's attendance at away matches was something of a regular occurrence and our travelling support doubled in the coming weeks when his good friend, Malcolm Galbraith – an ex-Campbeltonian living in Giffnock – joined the happy throng. Both were ever-present that season and the public parks of the Central Belt echoed with the enthusiastic sound of

Campbeltown GSFP, 1926-28.
Back row, left to right. Team only: Malcolm Wilkinson, Walter Brown, Dougie Bannatyne, Alex Baird, John Durnin, A Sharp and Archie Mustarde. Front row, left to right: I McKinnon, McGeachy, Archie McDiarmid, A McQueen and Lachie Mustarde. Inset: Johnny Moscardini and Robert McGeachy.

our 'away support'. They became valuable members of the team, almost lucky mascots, as the club strode to the SAFL 7th Division Championship in 1978. Attending every away match without fail, the touchline echoed with the conversation of two animated fans – naturally reminiscing about the 'good old days.' Their enthusiasm for the club was infectious – a deep interest responsible for restoring the 'lost knowledge' of earlier times. Archie McDiarmid's wonderful story 'Pupils of Yesteryear,' a newspaper article supported by a photograph of the all-conquering squad of 1927-28 was – in his own words – the direct result of rediscovering 'his team'. It was a meeting that 'gave us back our history.'[27]

It is not surprising that manager Mr A. D. McLeod was considered the cornerstone of the club as he was responsible for building a team known as 'the best ever to play in Campbeltown'. It was a bold statement considering what had gone before, nevertheless, the original team was extremely successful in the decade following the end of the First World War. The breakthrough came in 1920/21, a season in which the Former Pupils won their first trophy, the Orr-Ewing Cup. A clean sweep of the trophies followed in 1921/22 and '22/23: League Championship, Charity Cup and Orr-Ewing Cup. I am fortunate to have three of these medals in my possession, the same gifted to the club by Moira McGeachy, niece of the team's original centre-forward, Hugh Smith.

While the men blazed a trail at football, not be outdone the ladies challenged the students of the Grammar School to a game of hockey. As both sides shared an affinity with the local secondary school, from a reporter's point of view the match was a nightmare to cover. However, the problem was solved by referring to one group as 'the Students', and the more mature team as 'the Pupils'.[28] It was the first time this particular terminology had been used to describe a Former Pupils group, and proved so popular it survives in the same form to the present day.

Around this time, Drumlemble FC – founded in 1900 – lost its 'star' goalkeeper Dan McPhail to the senior game. After short spells with Falkirk and Third Lanark, he moved south to join English 1st Division side Portsmouth in January 1923. Dan made his first team debut on 28 April 1923 and became the senior club's first-choice goalkeeper in 1925. A regular with 'Pompey' for the next four seasons, he made 128 first team appearances before his final match against Leeds United on 29 March 1929. Dan came within a hair's breadth of being the second Campbeltonian to appear in an FA Cup

Final, only denied by a broken wrist that ended his career at the south coast club. After recovering from what proved a complicated injury, he joined his last senior side, Lincoln City, in August 1931. Dan became club record-holder for most appearances by a goalkeeper in the Football League, keeping 97 clean sheets in 309 outings. His total number of games, including cup-ties, amounted to 344, with 104 completed without loss of a goal. On retirement, he settled in Lincoln to open a bookmaker's shop. One of the many outstanding Campbeltown footballers of the post-First World War era, Dan McPhail died in October 1987.

The Pupils celebrated their successful campaign of 1921/22 with a match against Scottish Cup holders Morton at the Showfield, a hard fought 3-1 victory for the Greenock club. The outing was so successful the Cappielow side returned the following year for more of the same. Games against St Mirren and Queens Park followed in 1923, history repeating itself as the teams that influenced the early years continued their association with the town. Meanwhile, that year Sir William Sutherland MP donated an attractive silver trophy to the football association and Glenside FC emerged winners in the first two years of competition. The Dalaruan club took its name from the area's famous Glenside Distillery and its roots can be traced to the Sabbath School that once stood at the top of Mill Street – now modern housing at the end of Glentorran Terrace. Founded in 1908, 'the Glen', resplendent in their familiar black and gold stripes, were a well-supported and much-loved football team, an organisation still held in high esteem by those who remember the halcyon days of local junior football. However, the club ceased to exist in the mid-1950s, although the name re-emerged as an amateur organisation in the early 1960s and as a youth team between 1971 and 1994. The later reinventions had no association – other than sentiment – with the original organisation.

The post-First World War period was a difficult time for the British people. Far from David Lloyd George's 'homes for heroes to live in', the country was plagued by overcrowded tenements. The economic collapse created rampant unemployment and widespread poverty, the subsequent unrest prompting trade unions to demand shorter working hours – a maximum 40 hour week. The plan was to steer demobilised troops into gainful employment, but it foundered immediately as industry was intent on retaining its experienced workforce. Strikes were commonplace as ruthless employers reduced wages at a time when post-war prices remained high. Soup kitchens reappeared in Campbeltown during the coal strike of 1921, and once again as the country descended into full-blown economic depression in 1929. The demise of the town's traditional industries compounded the distress of a community now virtually on its knees.

Hard times followed, with short-term solutions provided by government-funded work schemes – community initiatives to help troops into work on their return from the trenches. Four examples of job creation were started in Campbeltown, but only the Kilkerran embankment project and new football ground at Limecraigs were successful in providing long-term employment. In order to provide accommodation for key employees, the town's first Council housing scheme was built at Castle Park in 1923. The nearby Showfield was also earmarked for housing – Smith Drive – and the subsequent loss of recreation space redressed by the creation of Kintyre Park.

Against this background of economic uncertainty, the game of football at least provided a few hours of escapism. The Pupils gained most of the plaudits in 1926/27, winning the Orr-Ewing Cup, Sutherland Cup and a competition simply referred to as 'the Badges'. However, the cake was shared when Glenside claimed the Charity Cup, and a name from the past, Campbeltown Rangers, became league champions. It was time of mixed emotions with the final days of the famous Showfield now in sight.

Football at Moy Park also appears to have ceased, as the ground is noticeable only by its absence from the post-war sports pages. An area of prime arable land, it probably reverted to its original purpose in a time of economic need; however, without proper knowledge this is only conjecture. A state of the art facility in 1912, the ground not only disappears from view, it seems to have been wiped from local consciousness as if never having existed at all. As football made its short journey from the Showfield to a new beginning at Kintyre Park in 1930, Moy Park would simply be forgotten.

By the mid-1920s there appears to have been a conflict of interest in Campbeltown football. A number of groups become involved in Mid-Argyll football, playing in a competition called the Ainsworth Cup. All had different names from those competing in the CDJFA, some using the identity of prominent teams from the past. Without information it is difficult to understand what was going on, but the obvious attraction was competition against teams from other parts of Argyll. The Ainsworth Cup was won by Rothesay St Blane's in 1921/22 and the following season, 1922/23, by Lochgilphead Thistle. Thereafter, the competition was dominated by Campbeltown sides until the end of the decade:

1921-22: Rothesay St Blane's.
1922-23: Lochgilphead Thistle.
1923-24: Campbeltown Strollers.
1924-25: Campbeltown Academicals.
1925-26: Argyll & Sutherland Highlanders.
1926-27: Argyll Colliery.
1927-28: Campbeltown United.
1928-29: Campbeltown Academicals.
1929-30: Campbeltown United.

Whether these sides were of the hybrid variety or not is difficult to say, but as this was the only competition in which they took part, it certainly is a curious anomaly. An incongruous name on the winner's list is Argyll & Sutherland Highlanders, a team representing the Campbeltown Territorial Detachment of the regiment. Back at base, a very special Pupils team was reaching the height of its power, sweeping all before it in season 1927/28. It was during this extremely successful period that an intriguing tale began to unfold. The club signed a free-scoring centre-forward, a player from a far-flung shore who captured the imagination of an adoring public. A genial man in possession of a well-kept secret, he arrived in Campbeltown to help run his uncle's cafe in Hall Street. That person's name was Giovanni 'Johnny' Moscardini.

Former Pupils squad 1926-28: Malcolm Wilkinson, Walter 'Wattie' Brown, Dougie Bannatyne, Alex Baird, John Durnin, A. Sharp, Archie 'Purba' Mustarde, Ian McKinnon, Tommy McGeachy, Archie McDiarmid, Angus McQueen, Lachie Mustarde, Robert 'Bobba' McGeachy and Johnny Moscardini.

The Italian Connection

As life in their homeland was extremely difficult in the mid-19th century, many Italians decided to migrate to far-flung places across the globe. Tired of scratching a meagre living from their native soil, they settled in more affluent countries in hope of providing a better standard of living for their families. Without exception, it was a migration that left its mark culturally wherever they settled. Around 1850, the new arrivals established a community in London, where they earned a living by the manufacture and sale of religious figurines. In an attempt to create a wider market for their products, the aptly named 'figurinai' travelled extensively throughout the country, a few crossing the border to settle in Scotland.

Numbers were small at first, but by the start of the First World War the Italian immigrant population had swollen to 4,500 and a clearly identifiable ethnic community had been established. Instinctive entrepreneurs, the Italians quickly identified opportunities within the catering industry, disposing of their traditional skills to reinvent themselves as café and chip shop proprietors. They also embraced a policy of dispersal, spreading far and wide to maximise commercial opportunity at a time when the host country's industrial confidence was at its greatest.

Great Britain at the time was reaping the benefits of more than a century as the world's industrial powerhouse, with a buoyant economy which brought reform and change by the end of the Victorian era. Social conditions improved as mass-manufacturing provided guaranteed employment and for the first time there was disposable income in the pockets of the working-class. It was no real distribution of wealth, but the improvement in living standards was good news for the catering business. The man in the street could now afford the luxury of a hot carry-out meal – the beginning of the 'fast food' industry. A novelty at first, for good or bad the chip shop would revolutionise the eating habits of the nation. Society also succumbed to the delights of the ice-cream parlour as a touch of the 'continental' invaded the high street.

A venue that catered for the whole family, as opposed to the male orientated public house, the Italian café was an example of a society in change. The emigrant population posed little or no threat to traditional business, as the goods on offer were a reflection of the proprietors' own cultural background. Towns and villages throughout the land acquired their very own Italian family, or if large enough the extended family as well. Cafes with grand-sounding names like Mayfair, Royal and Locarno opened in Campbeltown, a trend replicated the length and breadth of the land. New phrases and words entered the vocabulary: fish supper, poke 'a' chips, ice-cream slider and 'pokey hat' – the latter derived from the call of early street ice-cream sellers *'Gelati, ecco un pocco!'*

Surprising as it may seem, the Italians who settled in this country originated from just two regions of their homeland, Lucca in Tuscany and Frosinone in Lazio south of Rome. Nestling among the sun-drenched olive groves of the Garfagnana region, the idyllic hilltop town of Barga was most prolific in the export of its people to Scotland. Almost two thirds of Scots of Italian descent can trace their roots to this particular town or surrounding area, known locally as *'Bargo esteri.'*

In 1911, the Grumoli family from the village of Renaio near Barga settled in Campbeltown. First to arrive was Leonella ('Leo'), his wife Maria and their daughter Emma. They were followed by Leo's brother Umberto ('Berti') and wife Claudina. Maria's maiden name was Moscardini and it is from this thread of the family that we derive one of the most fascinating tales in the history of Campbeltown football. The Moscardini family settled in Falkirk during the latter part of the 19th century, and it was here that Maria's nephew Johnny was born. A talented footballer, Johnny was destined for stardom on the international stage, an unlikely candidate to later grace the humble surroundings of the game in remote Kintyre. Quiet and unassuming, after a number of years working in Campbeltown he left behind not only a clear memory of his individual sporting ability, but also the suggestion of a concealed illustrious past. However, given his down to earth manner, it seemed less than credible that he had actually worn the azure blue of Italy, a secret so guarded that even his good friend and team-mate Archie McDiarmid failed to mention it in his reminiscences.

Years passed and the memory of Johnny's time among us slowly faded, his exploits forgotten except for the occasional dated reference to 'the outstanding Italian from the bottom café'. My father often spoke of him in this way, however as 'Barney' considered anyone of his own generation infinitely better at football than any modern counterpart, I'm ashamed to admit his opinion was taken with a 'pinch of salt'. Nevertheless, from an early age I was well aware of local football's Italian connection; but nothing could have prepared me for the amazing revelations yet to come.

My knowledge of Johnny Moscardini was greatly enhanced during a visit to Glasgow for the Scotland v. Italy World Cup Qualifier in 1993, a journey made with my good friend Duncan L. McMillan. As custom demands, we enjoyed a few refreshments while reading the pre-match comments in the daily newspapers, a precursor to the main event later in the evening at Ibrox Stadium. The newspapers were full of quirky stories highlighting the special relationship that existed between two of the world's most passionate football nations, but one report in particular dominated the pre-match script. It was an amazing tale of the only Scot to be 'capped' by Italy and while most newspapers concentrated on the Italian restaurant and café connection, the *Scotsman* carried the unusual story of a Falkirk-born man who had played for Italy during the 1920s. It is fair to say that the name Moscardini jumped off the page!

Footballers born abroad of Italian decent and later capped by the mother nation are called the *Oriundi*. The majority are of South American extraction, notably Juan Alberto Schiafinno, who originally played for the land of his birth, Uruguay, between 1946 and 1954. He then transferred his affections to Italy, the birthplace of his father. In more recent times, the Argentine Mauro Camoranesi of Juventus played 55 times for the *Azzuri*. All very interesting, but a Scotsman from Falkirk during the 1920s? Although the article in question claimed he had never played for a Scottish club, we were immediately taken by similarities to our own gentleman of Royal Café fame. Family information soon confirmed Johnny's illustrious credentials and the gaps in our limited knowledge were at last filled.

The Moscardini family settled in Scotland during the latter years of the 19th century, part of an influx of Italian citizens who moved here purely for economic reasons. Their roots lay in the Valle de la Corsonna, an idyllic location in the hills above Barga in Tuscany. A hard-working sturdy mountain race, they were resolute people who freely embraced the arduous challenges of life in a foreign country, all to create a better standard of living for their families. Johnny Moscardini was born in the historic town of Falkirk in 1897 and developed his love of football playing on the streets with

Johnny Moscardini – on the ball in dark shirt – in action for Genoa against Uruguay, 1923.

school friends. However, there was little opportunity to participate in organised sport as most of his spare time was spent helping his father run the family business. Although an accomplished player, for this reason alone his latent talent would go unrecognised in Scotland.

With the First World War raging throughout Europe, at the age of 18 and with dual nationality, Johnny fulfilled his patriotic duty and enlisted in the Italian army. In 1915, he joined the *Alpini*, an elite corps of mountain troops stationed on the country's northern border. He was wounded in action against the Austro/Hungarians at the Battle of Caporetto, a blast of shrapnel destroying his elbow, a perpetual reminder of his days on the front line. After a period of recuperation at Palermo in Sicily, he retraced his family roots to settle in the hilltop town of Barga. Post-war years in Tuscany were spent playing football with the local team; however, unknown to him at the time, his every move was being monitored by a senior scout. Trials followed with Union Sportiva Lucchese – 'the Rossonero' – the area's senior team from the city of Lucca, birthplace of famous Italian composer Puccini. Impressed by his all-action style, he was immediately signed to play for the 'red and blacks' in the Italian Championship/Tuscan Section. An old-fashioned British style centre-forward, he terrorised defences with his direct running, but he was also very skilful and could pick a pass with the best. An immediate hit with fans, he was adored by the terraces who called him 'Mosca' or 'Gioni' out of respect for his British upbringing. Johnny soon became the club's top scorer and in time drew the attention of an elite band of administrators – the international selection committee.

The following season he was the league's top scorer and international recognition was assured. Johnny was capped for Italy against Switzerland in a 1-1 draw at the Servette Stadium in Geneva on 6 November 1921. The name Moscardini made national headlines when he scored Italy's only goal on his international debut. A band welcomed him on his return from international duty. He was capped eight times while playing for Lucca, three times against Austria, twice against both Czechoslovakia and Switzerland and once against Belgium. International goals kept coming, his debut strike against Switzerland followed by two more goals against Austria, and one each in the games against Czechoslovakia and Belgium.

Johnny's football odyssey continued with an invitation to join Italy's top club Genoa on a tour of South America in 1923. A prelude to the adventure was a game against Senegal in Dakar, a little light relief before the long Atlantic crossing. Games followed against the national sides of Argentina and Uruguay, before the tour continued at Santos and Rio in Brazil, unique sporting experiences in those far-off days. A few years later, Uruguay was controversially selected to host the FIFA World Cup in 1930, a decision severely criticised this side of the Atlantic. Most of the leading European nations snubbed the invitation, as the majority simply couldn't afford the trip. The insular-minded home nations took matters a stage further and refused to join FIFA in the first place. Of the top European nations, only France, Yugoslavia and Belgium made the trip. Surprisingly, the United States of America and Yugoslavia reached the semi-finals, although both were heavily defeated by their South American opponents. The final between Uruguay and Argentina proved a spicy affair, the hosts eventually winning the first Jules Rimet Trophy by 4 goals to 2.

In the following year Johnny became the target of a host of top Italian sides but in an effort to stay close to his roots, he signed for Sporting Club Pisa in 1924 – Italian Championship/Northern League. Much later, Pisa developed another Scottish connection in the form of Paul Elliot, a fine player who played at centre-half for the Tuscan club before moving to Glasgow Celtic. The northern Italian league was the country's top division, with elite clubs such as Juventus, AC Milan and Genoa, to name but a few. At this time, these renowned clubs were still considerably short of the world class names they are today, but formidable opposition nevertheless. Johnny remained unfazed by all around him and his prolific strike rate continued with 18 goals for Pisa in the 1924/25 season.

Johnny Moscardini played his last game for Italy against France in Turin on 22 March 1925. He scored twice as the 'Azzuri' won by 7-0, taking his international goals tally to seven in nine appearances – prolific in any language! The Italian press described its team as no more than novices at this time, and, although holding their own against continental opposition, it was freely accepted that British teams were *i maestri* – the masters. While British football would dominate the international scene for some time to come, failure to acknowledge progress and adopt modern coaching methods would be its undoing.

The life-style of Italian players in the 1920s was anything but lavish; in fact, many simply played for expenses and the honour of representing a top club. Even in Britain, at the time considered the masters of world football, wages were hardly inspirational. This in part may explain Johnny's sudden departure from the Italian game to return to Scotland. His family had been subsidising his time abroad, and, now newly married, it was time to earn his way in the world. He was content to give up his career in football and sever the unseen bond that first attracted him to Italy – it was time to repay his family. Italian café owners worked long hours to make their businesses successful and Johnny realised it was his turn to share the responsibility. His uncle, Leo Grumoli, had worked tirelessly to build trade at the Royal Café in Campbeltown, and after 15 years at the tiller he was due a well-earned break. Johnny Moscardini was asked to step into the breach. The headline-maker of Italian football surrendered his fame to become interim manager of a small seafront café on the west coast of Scotland.

Accompanied by his wife Tecla, Johnny arrived in Campbeltown to take over his duties and moved into the family flat at 49 Main Street. It was their base for the next two years, and happy times followed with the birth of their son Anthony, 'Tony'. Twenty-eight years old and still at the height of his athletic prowess, Johnny was delighted to be given the opportunity to play football with Campbeltown Grammar School Former Pupils – 'the Pupils' – so, contrary to popular misconception, he did play for a Scottish club. Astonishing as it seems, the centre-forward of Italy donned 'the white jersey' of the local favourites for two seasons in the Campbeltown & District Junior League – 1926/27 and 1927/28. You simply couldn't make it up! He joined a team of unquestionable quality, adding his own considerable talent by leading the line at centre-forward. The 'man from the bottom café' was an instant hit with the fans and caused quite a stir with his outstanding football skills. Fast, with a powerful shot, a deadly dribbler and extremely shrewd, these were a few assets attributed to this talented individual. For two years he set the heather alight, terrorising defences at the Showfield, a period in which his team dominated local football.

Family commitments honoured, Johnny travelled to Prestwick to open his own business, the Lake Café. He spent the rest of his life in the relative obscurity of the small Ayrshire town, a complete contrast to days entertaining thousands of adoring Italian football fans. Every summer he returned to Barga and took the children for football practice, in turn being feted as the local hero he surely was. Umberto Sereni, editor of the local newspaper *Giornale de Barga*, remembered being captivated when Johnny coached the

Johnny Moscardini in Italian national colours – circa 1924.

young players. 'We looked at him with eyes full of marvel.' 'Then, even better, we stayed to listen to him when, in a clear flowing voice, he recalled memories of games against Milan, Genoa, Pisa and Juventus.'

In response to a proposal by the local newspaper, the Municipal Council of Barga decided to name the local sports stadium in his honour. At 82 years of age, Johnny travelled to Italy for the naming ceremony in 1979. At this point he was rediscovered by Italy's overtly passionate football media, the country's top sports writer, Gianni Brera, comparing his skills to the wonder boy of Italian football, Paulo Rossi. At the same time, a report by Sergio Casci for BBC Television's Reporting Scotland highlighted the extraordinary tale of the Scotsman who played for Italy. The Scottish press were slow to recognise Johnny's 'Wee Toon' connection, but with information gleaned from the *Kintyre Magazine* and the Scottish Amateur Football League Centenary Brochure, the story was at last made complete. As Scotland prepared for a World Cup Qualifier against Italy at Hampden Park on September 2005, the story of Johnny's football odyssey appeared in the *Scottish Daily Mail* and for the first time his two-year spell in Campbeltown was recognised.

With the full story now in the public domain, I wondered if anyone could possibly remember Johnny Moscardini during his playing days in Campbeltown. If such a person existed, he would have to be of an advanced age, so expectations were extremely low. However, the unexpected happened as I visited George McMillan's in Main Street to pick up my daily newspaper. John McDougall clearly remembered the strong-running Italian, and his enthusiastic account said it all. 'Aye, Johnny Moscardini, he plehed well for the Pupils, he was a lovely pleher.' 'He never got involved in anything rough, he dinna need tae, he wiz that good.' After all those years, here was an eye-witness account of Johnny Moscardini in a Pupils jersey!

Many of Johnny's relations still live in the Campbeltown area, and some are very well-known, like Maria Grumoli and retired art teacher Ronald Togneri. There still is a Barga connection in the present-day Pupils squad, with Sean, Paul and Gary Grumoli the great-grandsons of Umberto Grumoli. Along with their father Paul, all four made a nostalgic journey to Tuscany in 2010. The following year, I had the privilege of joining Paul and his brothers, Michael, Ronnie and Nicky, at the Johnny Moscardini Stadium to watch AS Barga play San Piero a Sieve. Cheered on by five Campbeltonians, Barga won the game by 2 goals to 0.

Johnny Moscardini spent the remainder of his life in Prestwick, where he was a valued member of the local community and an Ayr United supporter to boot. His latter years were spent on the bowling green, a member of the club he helped to found. He was a man who spoke Italian with a Scottish accent and someone who continued to embrace his heritage by returning to his Tuscan roots as often as possible. In 1979, on a special day to honour his football achievements, he was joined by his old friend and international team-mate Fluvio Bernardini, a chance for both men to remember old football battles won and lost. Four years later in 1983, Johnny Moscardini died at Prestwick aged 88. The passing of both these gentlemen inspired Umberto Sereni to pen these poignant words of farewell. 'Now these friends of that time will find themselves in a grass field which is always green and, having reacquired the appearance of youth, will return to chasing the ball which cannot be caught.'

It only remains to be said that the path of life, once trodden, can never be retraced, but the memory of Johnny's exceptional journey will endure for many years to come – in the small Tuscan town of Barga, possibly forever.

The Curran' Buns

Campbeltown has always had its fair share of street corner philosophers, an undying breed of men still to this day holding court at the well-known places of public debate. Given the benefit of an appreciative audience, for generations these renowned orators have entertained at 'Cook's Corner' or any one of a number of popular meeting places around the town. While listening to a well-spun yarn is certainly entertaining, the really good ones are nearly always the product of vivid imagination. This being so, during the early 1960s my attention was drawn to a group of gentlemen in animated discussion, the topic of their conversation a long defunct and obviously much admired football team. Given the level of admiration and genuine feeling of affection on display, in this case there was little doubt the story was authentic.

The debate took place at the town's most popular meeting place, the Weigh-House – 'Wee-Uss' – at the Old Quay Head. The purpose of this long demolished building was to weigh cargo before it was shipped from the quay, but it was also the favourite haunt of local characters and the birthplace of many a tall tale. It was here I first encountered the story of a group of neighbourhood pals, a bunch of lovable rogues who refused to take life seriously. Like most boys of their age, the focus of their attention was food and football, in the case of the former, not always available during a time of mass unemployment and chronic poverty in the 1920s.

Sunday schools were extremely popular during this period, not only for the gift of spiritual guidance, but also for the breakfast of tea and bread offered to children at the end of Bible classes. In times of rank poverty, the Church had a major role to play in people's lives, both spiritually and socially. This was particularly true in its relationship with children, a bond established through the provision of organised sport and leisure activities. Originally dismissive of the game of football, it soon recognised the benefits of the sport as a healthy outlet for the abundant energy of Christian youth. In the years between 1920 and 1930, the Sabbath schools, Christian youth clubs, Boys Brigade and Girl Guides were the mainstays of sport and leisure in the community. These well-meaning organisations advanced the physical wellbeing of youth, but they also created a better society by improving the discipline and morals of future citizens.

During the years of economic depression the young people of Campbeltown rushed to join church groups, this at a time when organised sport and recreation were offered in exchange for regular attendance at prayer meetings and Bible classes. Formed in 1926, the Campbeltown Churches and Sabbath Schools Football League was the first of its kind in the community, and, as the name suggests, its membership was closed to secular organisations. Remarkable as it may seem, in less than half-a-century a game once frowned upon had become the cornerstone for building a better society.

As you can imagine, our young friends were completely oblivious to these commendable ideals, to them the next game of football was all that mattered. At this point it is difficult to separate historical fact from local legend, but reliable sources assure me the boys' Christian affiliation was to the Salvation Army. At this point a problem occurs, as this worthy institution has never at any time been involved with football. My research had drawn a blank. In the long run it mattered little, the very fact that the boys were still revered thirty-plus years down the line was more important. While there is nowhere quite like Campbeltown for the use of nick-names, this peculiar preoccupation had been taken a step further to include a favourite football team. Comical it may seem, but there was a good reason for calling these lads 'the Curran' Buns'.

The Curran' Buns played their football on 'the wee park' at the Showfield, a ground adjacent to the present-day Creamery in Witchburn Road. Some years ago, my work brought me in contact with a gentleman called Duncan McLachlan, and many a conversation we had at his home in Smith Drive. Like me, he had a deep interest in football and was also a supporter of the now defunct Campbeltown Hearts. He was blessed with a bright and comical personality, and often referred to his house as standing on the site of the 'wee park.' In fact, he assured me that he dreamt of football every night as his bed rested exactly where the penalty spot used to be. I had no idea the Showfield had more than one park, but it should have been obvious since the main ground was often referred to as the Laundry Park, a reference to the laundry which once operated at Castleacres.

Free of responsibility and in the prime of youth, the boys of the Curran' Buns were completely unaware of the legends they were destined to become. In the long run, the team's extraordinary name only served to mask its true identity, as not a mention can be found in the columns of the local press. This proves that they were unique in being unattached – rebels without a cause – possibly the very thing that endeared them to the public in the first place. As the years passed, the legend grew stronger in the minds of an older generation, almost to the point of cult status. This said, 'Why would anyone in their right mind call a football team after a bakery product?' In time the truth would out and, given the difficulties of the period, the name was not only relevant but also extremely well-crafted.

The 1920s were infamous for mass unemployment, which led to hunger marches, soup kitchens and widespread social deprivation. Government-sponsored work schemes brought some relief to a society ruined by industrial collapse. One such project was the creation of our own Kintyre Park, completed at a cost of £15,015, of which only £134 was spent on materials – mainly corrugated iron – a truly astonishing feat. The Salvation Army mobilised a soup kitchen and children's breakfast club at the Burnside Citadel and if our young footballers had an association with this resourceful organisation, it is easy to understand why. All of the boys lived in the vicinity of the 'Wee Dyke', a name synonymous with present-day Burnside Street. A favourite meeting place when the weather was fine, 'the Dyke' was a feature of past times when the Witch Burn ran untrammelled to the sea.

Behind every success story there is always a driving force. In this case the guiding light was a gentleman called James McMurchy, a well-known merchant of his day and it was no surprise to discover he was a master baker by trade. Mr McMurchy produced his wares from his bakery in Burnside Street, now the ship chandlery business of Charlie Campbell. He also had a shop and tea-room in Union Street, and appears to have been a Christian gentleman with an interest in the well-being of a certain young football team. My mother spoke highly of the wonderful currant bread handed out free of charge to the children on the street and also his kindness in giving similar goods to help stock the soup kitchen at the Salvation Army. Although a long time ago, I'm certain this is where the name originated. The boys frequented the neighbourhood, and obviously gained the aforementioned benefits, all of which left them at the mercy of an agile mind. So it seems was born the Curran' Buns.

Even in those bleak times, Campbeltown was still a holiday destination for the lucky few. Through the years, the annual Glasgow trades' holidays brought thousands of visitors to the 'Wee Toon' and for one family in particular it was home from home. The Caskies had a holiday home in Millknowe Terrace, an ideal opportunity for brothers Alex and Jimmy to let off steam playing football with their friends. Later in life, Jimmy Caskie found fame in the colours of Glasgow Rangers, but at this time he had other battlefields to conquer. Both brothers were members of the famous Curran' Buns, contributing to a legend still being extolled all these years later at the 'Wee Uss'.

Jimmy Caskie remained unaffected by the fame he found in later years at Ibrox Stadium. He maintained his close affinity with the 'Wee Toon' and, in due course, presented a trophy to boys' football. His memory was kept alive through the Caskie Cup, a popular competition in the Campbeltown Juvenile Football League between 1948 and 1954, the Miners Welfare Boys League from 1957 to 1964 and more recently the highly successful Campbeltown & District Boys Football Association, 1970-1994.

The uniquely named Curran' Buns are remembered for their acts of football mesmerism on the 'wee park doon by the burn'. Here, Archie Gillies ('Boorax'), Archie Smith ('Smeesh'), John McLellan ('Shimmie'), Willie Scally, 'Curly' McLellan, George Simpson, 'Monkey' McSporran, 'Neilly' Hart, Duncan McLachlan, 'Stonewall' Gillies, Neil McLellan ('Kipples'), Alex Caskie and the soon to be famous Jimmy Caskie, gained access to the halls of local football legend.

The Skilful Thirties

As part of the worldwide economic crisis, Scotland descended into a state of acute depression in the period between the two world wars. Rampant recession wrought havoc within the country's financial institutions and the industrial collapse to follow left millions unemployed. Despite this period of unprecedented gloom, our enthusiasm for the game of football remained intact, in fact, the game appeared to flourish in the face of adversity. During the lean years of the 'thirties', Campbeltown boasted no fewer than six junior clubs, with the long-established Glenside, Hearts, United, Pupils, Kintyre and Academicals still to the fore. However, although these pillars of the local game offered a brief respite from the harsh realities of daily life, even with a host of willing participants, the organised game was in a state of flux. The local junior football association ceased to exist in 1931, with all competition left in abeyance until the league reformed under the presidency of Archie McMillan in June 1934. The problem appears to have been a shortage of officials, but the clubs remained active by taking part in 'friendlies'. In order to retain its competitive status, Campbeltown United joined SJFA, a wise decision, as it secured a place in the Scottish Junior Cup for club and community.

By now the old jousting grounds of Moy and Castleacres were but a memory, the haunts of past legends superseded by a new ground at West Park on Limecraigs Estate. The completion of Kintyre Park was the only bright spot on an otherwise gloomy horizon. Overseeing the project was Burgh Surveyor Neil Ferguson – 1917 to 1937 – a man fresh from steering the long-overdue Kilkerran Promenade to its completion. He was the ideal candidate for such an important task, not only owing to his expertise in civil engineering, but also as a man who had sport close to his heart. Neil Ferguson in his heyday was the area's top athlete, someone with a sporting pedigree second to none. Almost unbeatable in local track and field, among his many accolades was success in six separate disciplines at the Kintyre Athletics Championships in a single day – a work exile in Australia for many years, before returning home he crowned a glittering career by winning the half-mile race at the Australian Amateur Athletics Championships. [29]

The construction of Kintyre Park tested his competitive streak to the limit, a project which required exceptional skills in social awareness and man-management. The objective was to spread assistance as far as possible, so the job was strictly labour-orientated to achieve this purpose. A rota system was set up to distribute a minimum of two days' work for each employee in any given week, a fair distribution of the assistance, but a nightmare as far as job efficiency was concerned. Work commenced in 1926, was three years in completion and a further year added to allow for seeding and settlement of the playing surface. Considering the disadvantages of an ever-changing workforce, the finished article was nothing short of incredible.

An air of anticipation gripped the town as the opening day approached, but the citizens of one of the most passionate football communities in the country were in for a major surprise. Unbelievably, the inaugural event was a shinty match between Inveraray and Oban! Can you imàgine the supporters' comments? During the austere days of the 1930s, people had little else but football as a source of entertainment, a situation which makes the Town Council's decision even less understandable. However, the beginning of the park's long association with football was only delayed, and 24 hours later the legend was finally set in motion. Their favourite sport downgraded to a bit-part in the opening celebrations, the paying public voted with their feet and saved the entrance money for the 'main event' on Sunday. Football mad, they turned out in their thousands to watch Campbeltown United defeat Greenock by 2 goals to 1. Keeping it in the family, the first goal at the new ground was scored by the home side's M. Watson.

Being part of today's consumer-mad society, it is impossible for us to appreciate the level of deprivation that existed in the period between the two world wars – the earlier years described as the 'Great Depression'. The collapse of the global economy created ever-lengthening dole queues and, surprising as it may seem, events in far-off America would influence the health of our local industry. The decision of the US government to ban the production and sale of alcohol was a disaster for Campbeltown – a nail in the coffin of the town's whisky industry. Prohibition was a huge victory for the temperance movement on that far side of the Atlantic, and although alcohol remained legal in the United Kingdom, the industry was crippled by unrealistic taxation driven through Parliament by the abstinence lobby. The result was the mass closure of distilleries in the self-styled 'whisky capital of the world', a life-changing event for a community already reeling from the demise of Campbeltown Shipyard in 1922 and the closure of Argyll Colliery in 1927. The town's economy was on the 'rocky road to ruin'.

Prohibition gave rise to organised crime in 1920s America, the era of Al Capone and other infamous gangland leaders. Although a visit to the cinema is hardly the best way to discover history, a well made movie can sometimes draw back the veil of time. A favourite of mine is the Billy Wilder comedy 'Some Like it Hot', starring Marilyn Monroe, Jack Lemmon and Tony Curtis. Largely tongue-in-cheek, the film's depiction of the Mafia mobs, racketeering, bootlegging and the infamous 'speak-easy' drinking dens, is generally considered a fairly accurate representation of post-First World War America. In Scotland, the misery of unemployment was made worse by overcrowding in the home, a period in which large family groups were consigned to living in room and kitchen accommodation – the infamous single-end. The people of Campbeltown suffered these conditions until the Council constructed housing on land vacated by the distilleries at Parliament Place and Broad Street in 1936. Most unfortunately, further housing initiatives at Princes Street and John Street were interrupted by the outbreak of war in 1939.

Some people were less affected by the bleak economic climate. Cushioned by years of accumulated wealth, the town's successful middle-classes were able to weather the storm relatively unscathed. Evidence for this can found in the pages of the *Campbeltown Courier*, its columns crammed with adverts for servants of all descriptions. During the 1930s, domestic service was the main source of employment for women and young girls, scant reward for an army of 14-year-olds graduating from what was then regarded as 'the finest education system in the world'. For men, best opportunities were on farms where most of the work was labour-orientated, or the fishing, an industry now a pale shadow of its past.

Lack of employment during the years of economic depression created poverty and malnourishment, the prevailing legend of 'the good old days' no more than a social myth. Nevertheless, people would prevail in times of need by sharing what little they had and a caring society emerged from the friendly environs of the neighbourly tenement close. Conditions in rural Scotland were distinctly better than the highly-populated Central-Belt, and in times of need a rabbit from the hill or a 'rasher' of fish at the quay sustained the family when the cupboard was bare.

While entertainment was bottom of the list for people with large families, during the inter-war years a night at 'the pictures' was the main source of amusement. Dancing was also extremely popular and attracted enormous crowds to the Victoria, Town and Templars Halls, the latter affectionately known as 'the Bowery'. In trying times, both were a cheap source of entertainment. Football hypnotised the masses during the 1930s, an era of world-record attendances at both club and international level. It was also a time in which the local 'juniors' attracted bumper crowds to Kintyre Park.

Supporting a neighbourhood or district team was a trait peculiar to Campbeltown, a situation born of geographic necessity. Remote from mainstream football, to achieve a competitive structure, it was necessary to have a fair distribution of talent. In order to achieve this, local sides were required to represent districts, places of work or voluntary groupings. Campbeltown became the only town in Scotland to have its own junior standard league: Hearts representing the district of Dalintober, Glenside serving Dalaruan, and Campbeltown United the town centre. Then there was the ex-students' club, Campbeltown Grammar School Former Pupils Association – the Pupils – and Kintyre FC – the town's oldest surviving club – representing the unemployed of the burgh. Add Academicals and Lochgilphead to the equation, and it was the basis for a very tasty little league indeed.

The popularity of the game was never greater than in the decades between the wars, an unbridled enthusiasm displayed each and every week at Kintyre Park. There was no love lost between the teams and their respective supporters – with every game as passionate as an 'Old Firm' encounter. The opening of the new park brought an end to the Showfield at Castleacres, but the traditional route to the match was unchanged due to the close proximity of the two locations. On Saturday afternoon, the streets would be jam-packed with supporters making their way to and from the game, a brief escape from reality accompanied by a generous measure of skilful entertainment – be assured, 'fitba' in the 1930s was a partisan affair!

Around this time, a strange-sounding word found its way into the local sporting vocabulary, 'caboodle', old English in origin, but now more familiar as an Americanism of the 'silver screen' variety. This unusual word integrated into the local vernacular with comparative ease and, although sounding like a tribal war-cry or a secret initiation rite, the true meaning was a lot less sinister. 'Caboodle' – defined as a collection or group of items – was a makeshift clubhouse, a simple but highly revered meeting place for players and officials. It also doubled as the strategic nerve centre, where plans to conquer the local football world were hatched. The humble 'caboodle' was an indispensable feature of the local game in the days prior to the Second World War – a legendary meeting place for 'the lads'. While for the most part football orientated, as gambling was illegal at the time, it was the perfect venue for the odd game of cards!

My first recollection of hearing the word was in my father's reminiscences of his playing days with Campbeltown Hearts, a club he absolutely adored. He stood six foot three inches in his stocking soles, but on finding a job as a long-distance lorry driver, Big Barney's days between 'the sticks' were numbered. Goalkeeping dreams in tatters, he sustained his allegiance by visiting the 'caboodle' on days off work, 'just for the blether, of course', a story he steadfastly stuck to. It was probably just coincidence that his card skills were absolutely second to none. Quick with an answer when questioned about the quality of football in the 1930s, his thoughts always returned to his beloved Hearts and its moment of glory in the Scottish Junior Cup. However, that's another story.

The humble 'caboodle' was every bit as important as social clubs are today. These nondescript meeting places were the 'beating heart' of 1930s football and could be found scattered around the town in the most unlikely places. It was here that a player could manifest his loyalty, enjoy camaraderie and be part of a bonding process responsible for the extraordinary passion associated with the game at this time.

Clubs would often move premises, especially during a period of widespread demolition following the demise of the distilling industry. Kintyre had its 'caboodle' adjacent to the Argyll Bowling Club, a small lean-to building adjoining the rear of the now demolished Templars Hall. Last used by fishermen to store nets, it was gutted by fire and subsequently razed to the ground in the 1970s. Hearts occupied a ground floor flat in North Shore Street, now vacant land next to Davaar Laundry. Close to the wide expanse of Kinloch Green, it was perfect for training or simply for a kick about. The club moved to another location prior to the Second

World War, 'flitting' to a flat in the vicinity of the old school (Scout Hall) in John Street. The monumental tenements of North Shore Street, Princes Street and Queen Street were later demolished to make way for new Council flats in the mid-1960s.

Glenside Football Club – product of the Dalaruan Sunday School – utilised vacant ground created by the demolition of Dalaruan Distillery, later to become Parliament Place. The late Duncan McArthur witnessed these events and remembered the 'Glen's' caboodle as 'nothing more than an elaborate wooden shed'. However, the club had a major advantage over its rivals – it possessed an ash training area! The prized all-weather surface was the result of spent fuel left behind after the closure of Dalaruan and Glenside distilleries. A by-product of their boilers and stills, the same was stockpiled ready for use on farm roads etc. The coal-ash formed an artificial mound known locally as 'Cinder Hill', colloquially 'Sinner Hull'. Whether by chance or more intuitive means, Glenside FC became the recipient of a valued training ground, the unintentional gift of the area's industrial past.

Like his counterpart from earlier times, the 1930s player loved nothing more than to test his mettle against the 'big boys'. The vehicle of this ambition was the Scottish Junior Cup, a well-known proving ground for home-based talent. After rejecting £10 expenses – probably the cost of a bus – plus a share of the gate receipts, Campbeltown United retained their home rights and prepared to meet Irvine Victoria in the third round at Kintyre Park. The game was tied at 2-2 when referee W. B. McCallum disallowed a late United winner, an offside decision hotly disputed by all who saw it. It wasn't to be. The replay in Ayrshire the following week-end saw Irvine triumph by 2 goals to nil.

Campbeltown United v. Irvine Victoria, 1932/33: Dan McKiernan, Dougie McDougall and Angus Clark, Archie Lafferty, Malcolm Lang and Hector McDougall, Willie Ramsay, R. McNeill, Weir, N. Scally and Willie Black.

Changes for replay: McGeachy for McKiernan, and P. McMillan for N. Scally.

Campbeltown United once more represented the town in the following season's national cup, on this occasion drawn away to West of Scotland League and Cup winners Glenafton Athletic at New Cumnock. Confusion reigned as no-one had a clue where this particular town was, but a quick look at the map and a course was set for 'darkest' Ayrshire. Although 'United' suffered defeat by 4 goals to 2, the players were roundly applauded for their performance in a match described as a real crowd-pleaser. The same year, locally connected Robert Scott became the *Daily Record*'s leading sports writer under the well-known pseudonym 'Waverley'. After a number of years in abeyance, competitive football made a welcome return to Campbeltown in time for the 1934/35 season. Four teams entered the Scottish Junior Cup, Glenside, Hearts, Pupils and United, the latter's experience being enough to see them qualify to meet Dundee East Craigie in the fourth round at Kintyre Park.

On New Year's Day 1935, the Dundonians were beaten by 4 goals to 2. Two goals from John Ramsay, a Donald Gilchrist penalty, and an own goal by defender Simpson being enough give United a comfortable victory.[30] An unbelievable 5th round draw gave United a home tie against cup favourites Tranent Juniors, without doubt the tie of the round. A ripple of anticipation swept through the town as United prepared to meet a team bristling with top players. As on previous occasions, an attempt was made to persuade the local side to give up home advantage, however, United remained firm; 'come hell or high water', the match would be played at Kintyre Park. Undaunted by a day of heavy rain, a crowd of 2,700 – a record for the ground to date – paid £52 to see if the tide of opinion could be turned. The profile of the game persuaded Arthur Douglas, 'Lochee' of the *Daily Record*, to cover the match.

He saw the home side take the game to their more-fancied opponents and United opened the scoring in dramatic fashion when Donald Gilchrist hammered the ball home after a shot from Alex Caskie had been blocked – the same of Curran Buns' fame. 'The pace to me was amazing', declared the Glasgow-based critic. On a day of driving rain and the park little more than a quagmire, John Ramsay 'wormed his way through' only to see his net-bound shot strike the goalkeeper's outstretched leg on the goal-line. As United continued to attack, Chas McMillan's fine strike hit the post before skidding to safety – in the opinion of the correspondent, 'bad breaks which probably affected the course of the game'. The form book looked set to be torn asunder, but Tranent equalised just before the break when goalkeeper Houston carried into his own net under pressure. As the teams trudged off at half-time, things were certainly not going to plan for the favourites and the nervous newspaper hacks were hastily preparing to eat their words.

Campbeltown United 1935.

Back row, left to right: Neil McIntyre (Committee), Weir, M Lang, A Houston, A Clark. Front row, left to right: D McDougall, W Ramsay, T McGeachy, J Ramsay, D Gilchrist, W Black and C McMillan.

However, beaten finalists two years earlier, Tranent had too much class to 'give up the ghost.' The visitors emerged with renewed determination and, as the home side tired from their earlier efforts, Tranent were rewarded when coming from behind to win the tie by 3 goals to 1. In summing up, 'Lochee' waxed lyrical about the match. 'A great start is half the battle.' 'Maybe it can be bought at too great a price.'[31] Unbowed in defeat, United had taken the cup favourites down to the wire, a game remembered for years to come as the home side's finest hour. The match became part of local legend, one of many to join local football's role of honour. Regarded as the best junior side of the post-war era, Tranent marched on to claim its day in the sun. A visit to Ibrox Stadium in May 1935 saw them defeat Petershill by a record 6 goals to 1 to lift the Scottish Junior Cup in front of 22,000 spectators.

Complimenting the home side's efforts, 'Lochee' stressed that 'Campbeltown football has nothing to learn from others and others certainly share my opinion.' 'I have it on good authority that a Campbeltown United forward will be included in the next international team.' There was no mention of whom, but it was generally accepted the player in question was centre forward John Ramsay.

Campbeltown United: Arthur Houston, Dougie McDougall and Angus Clark, Archie Lafferty, Malcolm Lang and Weir, Willie Ramsay, Alex Caskie, John Ramsay, Donald Gilchrist and Chas McMillan.

For some reason, there was a misconception that Campbeltown teams would surrender home advantage for financial gain. Central Belt teams had little understanding of football in an isolated west coast community; where survival was important, but there was more to it than money. After the slog of town-based competition, the winner of 'the Scottish' qualifying rounds had the honour of representing the community as a whole. It was a chance to play in front of their 'ain folk' and test themselves against the best in the country. Given the restrictions of a small domestic league, these games should have been insurmountable, but the 'Wee Toon' always punched above its weight in 'no-contest' situations. The town has consistently produced players of a decent standard and, although unknown outside Kintyre, at this point local football was attractive enough to draw hundreds, if not thousands of people to Kintyre Park every week. Campbeltown football was a law unto itself, a remote microcosm of the game which mimicked the main stage, but exuded the intimacy and tribalism synonymous with local competition. In the 1930s, the street corners echoed with tales of battles won and lost – the stuff of which legends are made!

United's reputation had been enhanced by performances in the national cup. The early rounds of the Scottish Junior Cup were regionalised affairs, with the best of the qualifiers meeting in the 4th round proper, a difficult hurdle to clear as it brought together the cream of the geographical crop. The tie was normally played on the Saturday closest to New Year's Day and local supporters prayed for a home draw to make the game part of their holiday ritual. Advancing to the 5th round was a major achievement for a parochial club, a hurdle successfully negotiated on a number of occasions by teams from Campbeltown. Although falling to the mighty Tranent, 'United' claimed three of the four domestic trophies that season – 1934/35 – but the last competition, the Orr-Ewing Cup, was contested between two stalwarts of the period, Hearts and the Pupils. This tie highlighted the competitive nature of local football in the 1930s as it needed three games to decide the outcome – the Pupils finally claiming the trophy after two drawn matches.

Around this time, Campbeltown United found a new home at the far end of Argyll Street, a small industrial building adjacent to 'Hazelbank House', now 'Kirklea'. The club's caboodle was located on the site of the old 'Coal Ree', the depot of the Campbeltown and Machrihanish Light Railway Company. The railway ceased to exist in 1932, so the team was delighted to gain an impressive little clubhouse, probably a workshop in earlier life. From here it was a short walk to Stewart's Green, the setting for most of the team photographs. The former railway buildings were later used as a garage before finally becoming a base for building contractors 'Bud' McKay and Dougie McShannon in the 1970s. Some may remember the former engine-shed with its distinctive, corrugated iron-arched roof, a feature mirrored in the entrance to the present-day private housing estate, Hazelbank Court.

United honed their fitness at a venue called 'Wakeham's Hall', premises named after Canon C.T. Wakeham of nearby St Kieran's Episcopal Church. The hall was situated next to the church, in the backcourt of a small tenement building in Argyll Street, behind what is now Ramsay Place. The team contained a number of larger- than-life characters, none more so than Donald Gilchrist, better known as 'Rootie'. Donald was a ferocious striker of the ball, a man who had senior experience at Gillingham United, but it was the comical side to his nature that intrigued everyone. When shooting for goal he always shouted 'Gina!' No-one ever discovered the reason, but by all accounts his early warning system frightened the life out of goalkeepers.

Impressively consistent, United progressed through the local rounds of the 1935/36 Scottish Junior Cup, this before defeating Comrie from Perthshire in the third round of the competition. The victory set up a meeting with Dundee Arnot in the fourth round at Kintyre Park, a match which ended in a 1-1 draw. The replay at Dundee's East End Park attracted a crowd of 5,000, an amazing turn-out for a game of junior standard. The size of the crowd was even more impressive considering it had competition from a Dundee v. St Johnstone senior derby at nearby Dens Park. Support for the junior game was nothing short of phenomenal in the years leading to the Second World War, a period when communities the length and breadth of the country got behind their local eleven.

Unfortunately, the play on both sides was marred by defensive frailties, the main shortcoming in a game that failed to live up to its pre-match billing. Slack play was particularly true of the visitors, a gift-laden performance most were happy to forget. Dundee Arnot muddled through without ever impressing, with the bulk of damage self-inflicted by an over-generous 'United' rearguard. Nevertheless, it was a day to remember for centre-forward Jock Ramsay, the visitor's shining star in a disappointing 4-2 defeat. Watched by the international selectors and a host of senior scouts, his two superb goals kept United in contention to the bitter end. Well supported on the flanks by his brother Willie Ramsay – another under the international microscope – and Tarbert's Willie Black, it was a day of mixed fortunes as an impressive attack kept the game alive on a day of defensive blunders. The headlines managed to say it all: 'Easy for Arnot despite brilliance of Campbeltown centre-forward'.[32]

In line for a junior international call-up, John Ramsay's impressive display made him the target of a host of senior clubs. Awaiting the outcome of his performance were the likes of Hamilton Academicals, Fulham, Aberdeen, Portadown and Partick Thistle, but in advance of receiving a call to represent his country, John decided to join Partick Thistle, the nearest and most convenient place to home. Like many before, the call of his native Kintyre proved too strong and he failed to settle in a city environment. After a season in the

Campbeltown United v Dundee Arnot, Scottish Junior Cup, Kintyre Park, 1936.

Firhill reserves, he decided to return home to his trade as a cabinet-maker and resume his association with Campbeltown United. We have to understand that a career in senior football during the 1930s was significantly different than it is today. An untested player was normally offered a part-time contract, probably with a job on the side at his chosen trade. The wages of reserve players were unremarkable, in fact, in some cases non-existent. Perseverance and unshakable faith were absolutely necessary if a breakthrough was ever to happen. Given the circumstances, many decided the time spent away was a complete waste.

For whatever reason, John decided to return to United in 1936, a team regarded by many as the best side in Western Argyll. Among a host of fine players, there was one of the best centre-halves of the post-war era, the unassuming figure of Malcolm Lang. Malcolm was a stylish ball-playing central defender, a highly regarded player who was called upon to represent Mid-Argyll as well as his native Campbeltown. He personified composure and was renowned for his studied possession play. The exploits of this fine side inspired local poet Willie Mitchell to compose an ode, the words set to the music of the well-known Irish ballad 'The Mountains of Mourne'.

'Campbeltown United'

by Willie Mitchell
(1938 version)

Oh, boys, this United's a wonderful team,
In Campbeltown football they're always supreme.
They've won lots of medals and cups by the score,
And the boys that they've got now will win them some more.
There's Lamont in charge of the old 'onion sack',
And McDougall and Revie, two stalwarts at back.
They'll pull all together. They won't let us down;
But they'll keep old United the pride o' the town.

We've three sturdy half-backs, they've each made their name,
In attack or defence they are up to the game.
There's McLachlan and 'Peerie' and 'Chas' makes the third,
And about this wee fellow I must say a word,
For he's been with United since he was a lad,
And he's stuck to them fairly in good times and bad.
Oh, we're proud of ye, 'Chas', for the spirit ye've shown,
In putting your team in a class of its own.

We've five clever forwards with head and with foot,
If they once get an opening, they know how to shoot.
There's crafty wee Graham runs along the touchline,
And with 'Wilks' his big partner right well does combine.
Then there's Ramsay at centre, he's fast on the ball,
He's scored so many goals, we've lost count of them all,
And Robina and Chisholm make a team of renown,
The good old United – the pride of the town.

We've a bunch of supporters, who're loyal and true,
And they'll stand by the lads in the white and the blue.
And if they beat Benburb at the start of the year,
We'll stand all the players a big pint of beer.
We've a peerless tradition, my boys, to uphold,
And a hist'ry that cannot be purchased with gold,
So I'll give you the toast, lads, and then I'll sit down,
Here's to the Good Old United – the Pride o' the Town.

Published in 1948, *The West Highland Review* extolled the virtues of Campbeltown United, citing games against what was then the elite of the junior game. Clubs mentioned included Tranent, Scottish Cup winners in 1935; Irvine Victoria, St Ninian's, Renfrew, Dundee East Craigie (twice), Dundee Arnot, and Benburb. Players selected for special mention were Donald 'Rootie' Gilchrist, 'Wee Chas' McMillan, Angus Clark, 'Jock' Ramsay, Malcolm Lang, Willie Black and Dougie McDougall (the last two from Tarbert). I had the privilege of watching 'Chas' McMillan play in an 'old crocks' match at Kintyre Park in the late 1950s. He must have been in his mid-50s and was still capable of mesmerising runs down the left flank. If this was an indication of 1930s football, it was very special indeed. Although the days of the junior game have long since gone, Willie Mitchell's song conveys the passion for football in the period between the wars, a sport which gave supporters a sense of identity and pride in their 'ain wee place' during extremely challenging times.

Although the exploits of 'United' are indeed exemplary, quality football was not the preserve of a single club. The town had a number of outstanding teams during the closing years of the 1930s, a time when military storm-clouds were gathering across mainland Europe. Emerging from the shadows of their illustrious rivals, Hearts' star was in the ascendancy – across the Esplanade in Dalintober new legends were in the making. Winning through the local qualifying rounds, Campbeltown Hearts were drawn against Dundee East Craigie in the 4th round of the Scottish Junior Cup at Kintyre Park on Saturday 8 January 1938. A crowd of around 2,000 witnessed a drawn match, a game the locals should have won if territorial advantage had been converted into goals. Hearts now faced a tiresome journey to a notoriously difficult venue, the odds of success made longer by East Craigie's one hundred per cent home record. Hearts' casualty list mounted as the replay loomed, and the absence of 'star' inside-right Johnny Burgoyne through injury was a hammer-blow to their hopes of advancing. However, unlike today, even with key men missing, in-depth defence was never a consideration. The pack was simply reshuffled to include reserve winger Charlie Coffield on the left flank, with the mercurial 'Ned' Dewar moving across to inside-right to cover the duties of the absentee.

East Craigie was the best supported of the Dundee clubs, so it was no surprise when a capacity crowd of 5,000 greeted the men from the West to East End Park. A small contingent of around 50 Hearts supporters made the journey and the 'Wee Toon' diehards were determined to be heard. With home advantage, the in-form Tayside club looked more than capable of finishing the tie in their own back yard, an assessment only a rabid Hearts supporter would disagree with. Add a huge home support flooding the turnstiles, and the visitors' failure to win the previous weekend now appeared extremely negligent. Hearts were able to withstand the early onslaught, but alarm bells started ringing when the normally dependable Willie 'Dobbie' McIntyre misjudged a speculative cross. Luck favoured the home side, as the ball spilled to striker Hanlon who squeezed the ball home after a goalmouth scramble. A goal behind on the half-hour mark, it was a surprise when the anticipated siege failed to materialise. Hearts stalwart Robert 'Robina' Armour had somehow grabbed control of the mid-field and, with their top player running the show, a comeback was very much on the cards.

Coping admirably with the tricky underfoot conditions, the visitors pushed forward at every opportunity and caused untold panic in the home defence. An excellent passage of play brought the equaliser, this when an inch-perfect cross from Robert Armour found the eager Arthur Thomson on the edge of the box. The Hearts striker's first-time effort flew past the stranded home goalkeeper into the roof of the net, a wonderful goal to silence the home support. The tide had turned. Now in control of the midfield battleground, Arthur Thomson brought a superb save from Simpson in the home goal shortly before the break. The teams retired level at half-time, but the visitors were in the ascendancy after a remarkable recovery.

East Craigie's early second half efforts almost paid dividends when outside-left Dewar found space to send a vicious drive crashing off the underside of the crossbar. This 'let-off' encouraged Hearts to take the offensive and their best spell of the match was crowned by a precious second goal. A thunderous drive by Arthur Thomson was half-saved by a stunned goalkeeper, but the ball deflected into the path of 'Neilly' Hart who scored easily from close-range. Frustrated by the reverse, the home side launched forward in pursuit of an equaliser, a less than cautious approach which left acres of space at the back. The opportunity was quickly exploited by the ever-alert Robert Armour and a fine through-ball sent the strong-running Thomson free of his marker. Hearts' 'star' forward controlled the ball in one movement, sold the right back a 'dummy', then cut inside to send a blistering shot past goalkeeper Simpson from 25 yards – a goal fit to win any match!

The closing minutes of the tie produced a second goal for the home side, but by now it was little more than a consolation. Hearts easily ran down the clock to secure a place in the coveted 5th round of Scottish Cup, a victory achieved by outstanding teamwork and the individual brilliance of inside-forward Arthur Thomson. The game claimed banner headlines in the evening sports pages, although with over-ambitious expectations. 'Hearts heading for Scottish Junior Cup Honours' was the immediate reaction, followed by a more subdued sub-script 'Handicapped team beat Craigie at Dundee'.[33]

This victory will go down as one of the finest achievements in the history of Campbeltown football. The game itself was a personal triumph for inside-left Arthur Thomson, a performance widely acclaimed in the press. His form wouldn't go unnoticed by the game's ruling elite, as the same newspaper reported international interest with the headline 'Campbeltown Player May Be Capped'. The story related the comments of Pat Duffy of Wellesley Juniors – representing the junior international selection committee – who would 'sponsor the Hearts man for an international cap, provided the player is not called up by Shawfield'. However, the predication that Arthur Thomson could turn senior became a reality when he signed for Scottish First Division side Clyde FC. An all-round sportsman, later in life he proved his versatility by becoming a golf professional, a man well-known locally as the resident professional at his home course, Machrihanish Golf Club.

Hearts eventually lost 2-1 in the 5th round to former cup-winners Dundee Violet, in the opinion of many an inferior side to their city neighbours. Such is football. Nevertheless, for years to come, the East Craigie match remained firmly fixed in the psyche of local supporters, a tale retold many times to justify the standard of Campbeltown football in the 1930s.

Campbeltown Hearts v. Dundee East Craigie, 15th January, 1938: Willie 'Dobbie' McIntyre, Archie Thomson, Dougie McEachran, Duncan McLachlan, John 'Murphy' Riddell, Robert 'Robina' Armour, 'Neilly' Hart, 'Ned' Dewar, A. Fletcher, Arthur Thomson and Charlie Coffield (who replaced the injured John Burgoyne).

There seems to have been a host of quality players in Campbeltown around this period. Glenside goalkeeper Morris McSporran was

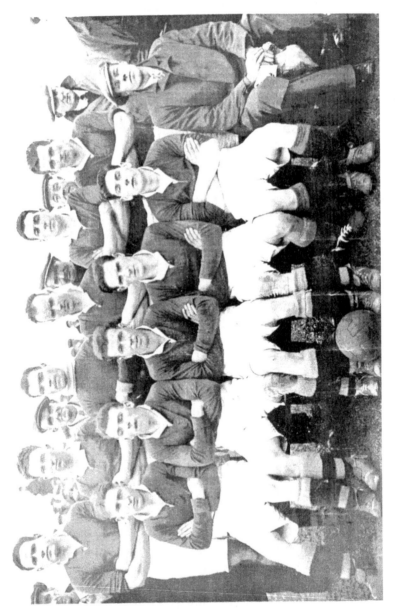

Campbeltown Hearts at Dundee East Craigie, Scottish Junior Cup, 1938.
Team only. Back row, left to right: Archie Thomson, Dugald McEachran, Willie McIntyre, Donald
McLachlan, John Riddell and Robert Armour.
Front row, left to right: Neil Hart, Ned Dewar, A Fletcher, Arthur Thomson and Charlie Coffield.

capped for Junior Scotland while playing with Dunipace, with fellow team-mates Willie Kelly and Dan McKiernan turning out for Clydebank and Vale of Clyde Juniors respectively. Senior signings from the period included Arthur Thomson (Clyde), John Ramsay (Partick Thistle) and Donald Gilchrist (Gillingham). Campbeltown Hearts' mid-field genius 'Robina' Armour was offered terms with Glasgow Rangers, but he had no interest in playing at senior level. Already making his mark in professional football was Dan McPhail from Drumlemble, Portsmouth's brilliant goalkeeper of the inter-war years.

The record of our next football personality cannot be regarded as local history, nevertheless it is impossible to leave this era without mention of Neil Hamilton Dewar, one of only five Argyll men to be capped for Scotland at full international level. He was born in Lochgilphead on 11 November 1908, and to his friends was known simply as 'Neilly' Dewar. He was a 'giant' of the game during the 1930s, a tall skilful centre-forward who had an intimate knowledge of the route to goal. Signing for Third Lanark in 1929, in separate spells at Cathkin he was top scorer in all but two of his seven seasons. His goal-scoring exploits – 120 in Scottish League games – made him immortal in the eyes of 'Hi Hi' supporters and he is included in the now extinct club's list of all-time greats.

Neil won the first of his international caps against England at Wembley Stadium on 9 April 1932, a match which Scotland lost by 3-0 in front of 92,180 spectators. He fared better in his second international against France at the Stade Olympique Colombes on Sunday 8 May 1932. In the stadium where Eric Liddell famously won his 400-metre Olympic gold, Scotland produced a much better performance and coasted to a 3-1 victory. For Neil, it was a day to remember, as he scored a first-half hat-trick to put the result beyond doubt. Goals in the 14th, 27th and 40th minutes were answered by a Marcel Langillier converted penalty, a fine performance to leave Scotland 3-1 ahead at the interval. There was no more scoring and the 'Dark Blues' eased to victory thanks to Neil Dewar's single-handed demolition of France. This performance was rated the best of his professional career.

Scotland v. France, 1932:

Jack Harkness (Hearts), James Crapnell (Airdrie), Joseph Nibloe (Kilmarnock), Alec Massie (Hearts), Rob Gillespie (Queens

Park), John Millar (St Mirren), James Crawford (Queens Park), Alex Thomson (Celtic), Neil Dewar (Third Lanark), Bob McPhail (Rangers) and Alan – 'The Wee Blue Devil' – Morton (Rangers).

Alan Morton's international jersey was part of the 'Kit and Caboodle' Football Exhibition at Campbeltown Museum in 2012.

Neil Dewar's full international record includes caps against England (1932), Wales (1932) and France (1932). He also received Scottish League honours against the English League (1933) and Irish League (1940).

His directness was a menace to defences, but he was hardly a 'battering ram' of a centre forward. Quite the opposite, by his professional peers he was termed a 'grand ball player', a skilful individual who, if he fancied, would take on a whole defence with his potent dribbling skills. He was the last striker to score past Celtic's ill-fated goalkeeper John Thomson in a 3-3 draw at Parkhead. The young goalkeeper tragically lost his life in an accidental collision with Sam English of Rangers in the very next game.

Neil was transferred to 2nd division Manchester United for the substantial sum of £4,000 in February 1933. Although at the club for nine months only, he still scored 14 times during his stay at Old Trafford, a scoring rate which alerted the leading clubs of the period. First division Sheffield Wednesday secured his services in December 1933 and he served the club faithfully for the next five seasons. He scored no less than 50 cup and league goals in a spell considered the best of his professional career and he was described in glowing terms as 'a great player in an era of great players'. He returned to Third Lanark in time for the 1937/38 season and, needless to say, finished top scorer in the next two campaigns with 18 and 25 goals respectively.

Neil Dewar's contribution to football didn't stop with his retirement, as in 1948 he edited the first magazine devoted to football in Mid-Argyll and Kintyre, *The West Highland Football Magazine.* Contained in the publication is a classic tale of a match between two rivals for the Mid-Argyll crown, Lochgilphead and Ardrishaig Khaki Rangers. This epic match was played during the early years of the 20th century and is saved for posterity in the following mirthful verse. The author, a tongue in cheek 'R. E. Swot', is supported in his observations by a 'side-kick' called 'Machker.' Enjoy.

'Twas Famous Battle'

(An Epic of the Long Ago)

Sit doon and I'll tell ye a story:
It wasna' a great big catch –
It wasna' a fight at the fit o' the lane –
It was only a fitba' match;
But Scotland rang wi' the story,
(Machkar'll tell ye it's true),
When the Point Boys won by the only goal
Scored as the whussel blew.

The Bank Park, boys, was crowded,
There were fifteen thousand there;
And Harvey sent six reporters,
And the 'Oban Times' had a pair.
Man, it was great, a' vallich
Man it was simply great'
An' the Kharkis swore they'd die before
They'd let themselves be bate.

Dugal kicked off for Ardrishaig;
And 'Fetty' and 'Geerach' began,
Like electric eels they went doon the wing.
And passed and dreebled and ran.
The ba' went across to 'Connie',
Who centred back to 'Cock' Bruce,
And 'Cock' let drive, but Cars'ell saved –
I could greet, but whit's the use?

It was then 'Hughie' Vean got excited –
'Hyug', the Lochgyeelipers pet –
And he off wi' the ba' at his toe
Till John Hamilton laid him flet;
But 'Jockie' got haud o' the ba',
And a dangerous man was he,
Till 'Sultan' cut over and cleared,
And that was sight to see.

Man, it was great, a vallich'
Man it was simply great'
The crood was wild wi' excitement,
And roared like bulls at a gate.
As the teams wan efter another
Pressed and struggled and tried,
But 'Phail' and 'Cars'ell' couldna be bate,
And every shot they defied.

Did I mention that I was playing?
I was one o' the backs, no less;
And 'Bowsie' and me were as steady as rocks,
And sherp as a bit o' gless;
And we needed to be, a vallich'
(there's 'Machkar' he'll tell ye it's true),
Fur Lochgilphead were pressing us hard at times
And twice they were nearly through.

But they never got time to aim at goal,
And same at the other end,
Where 'Fetty' himsel' could do nothing,
So strong did MacKurdy defend.
So half-time came wi' never a goal,
But man, the play was a trate,
And the Kharkis swore they'd die before
They'd let themselves be bate.

The second-half was a scorcher,
Man, but the play was fast,
And the Kharkis had a' the best o't
Till we thought we could score at last.
But Cars'ell was playing champion,
I must give Cars'ell his due,
For the shots went in like bullets,
But never a wan he let through.

'Connie' and 'Cock' and 'Geerach',
'Fetty' and Dugal' Law
Shot like a dozen maxims
Till they nearly burst the ba'.
The crood was mad wi' excitement

(Did I tell ye that before?)
It was only a meenit from time, my boy,
And still there wis never a score.

I spat on my hands a vallich'
On these two hands you see;
Says I to mysel' the'll be never a goal
Unless it's scored by me'
And just as I spoke the ba' came up,
Right to my feet it came;
For the half o' the half o' a second
I saw a big rud flame.

And then I up and started
(Machkar'll tell ye it's true).
I had less than a meenut to do't in –
But the deed I meant to do.
As I ran the length o' the field
I deedled a dozen men –
I was thirty yards from Cars'ell –
and then – and then – and then –

I shot, and no man living
Could have seen the ba' as it flew
Into the net like a cannon ball –
A goal Hurray – Hurroo'
Half a second before time up'
Man, if ye'd heard the crood'
If Cars'ell had tried to stop that shot
He'd been stiffened where he stood.

Who was he, Quinn o' the Celtic?
Who was McColl o' the Queens?
Who was he, Reid o' the Rangers?
There's non o' them worth two peens:
There's non o' them ever could shoot a goal
Like the goal that I put through,
When the Kharkis won by the only goal –
Just as the whussel blew.

As well as the excitement of a local derby, the author grasped the opportunity to celebrate the rich variety of nick-names that existed in the two villages around the turn of the 20th century. A little gem of a poem.

The 1930s will be remembered as a period of in-depth quality, of record crowds and unabashed enthusiasm for the game of football. Back then it was almost a way of life, a game that sustained the population through the dark days of economic depression. Its popularity knew no bounds, a fact illustrated by the world record attendance of 149,515 at Hampden Park for the Scotland v. England game in 1937. Nevertheless, for the second time in quarter of a century the playing fields fell silent as the young men trudged off to war. Competitive football was suspended for seven long years. Campbeltown, however, became a naval base and in lighter moments played host to a number of 'wartime internationals'. These games involved servicemen from all walks of life, some of whom had played at senior level prior to the outbreak of war. However, absence from the game brought many careers to a premature end, a sad fact when one considers the wealth of talent available during 'the skilful thirties'.

A New Beginning

At the end of the Second World War, Councillor Colin Campbell – president of the Campbeltown and District Junior Association – called together his committee to re-establish organised football in the burgh in May 1946. He was ably assisted by Walter 'Wattie' Paterson, a gentleman with 20 years of experience as secretary of the renowned Glenside Juniors. Also on board were Councillor Norman Cameron, Morris McSporran, James Gillies, John McDonald and 'Louie' McKechnie, the last two ex-members of the now-defunct Pupils FC. Also missing from the ranks was Kintyre FC, but this was no surprise as the club had struggled to survive in the years prior to the conflict. Five clubs applied for membership, Rangers, United, Hearts, Drumlemble and Glenside. Campbeltown Rangers returned to competitive football after an absence of more than twenty years and assembled a young, skilful side, with A. McKinlay and Jimmy McDiarmid in charge.

The league trophies were recovered from their war-time recesses and the first competitive football in almost seven years was resumed in August 1946. Campbeltown United was quickly into its stride, seeing off the nearest opposition to win both the Charity and Sutherland Cups, while Glenside awoke from wartime hibernation to claim the Orr-Ewing Cup. However, the main object of the exercise was simply to get the game up and running again. Major Duncan McCallum, the newly-elected Member of Parliament for Argyll, maintained a long-standing tradition by donating a cup to the local football association in 1947. The first winner of the new trophy was none other than United FC, and the same club proceeded to lift the MP's bright new trophy no fewer than four times in the first five years of its existence.

Kintyre Park had been used extensively by the armed services during the war years and the ground required re-laying to facilitate the resumption of domestic football. Excitement ran high as traditional rivalries were renewed and the streets once more came alive as people headed for 'the fitba' on Saturday. United maintained their dominance of local football by winning the Sutherland Cup for a second year in a row, but Drumlemble, with Tommy McPherson and Duncan 'Doachie' Johnston in charge, carried the Charity Cup along the winding road to the club's rural home.

Glenside were the surprise package of 1947/48, not only lifting the Orr-Ewing Cup for the second year in succession, but also by winning through the local qualifying rounds to represent the town in the Scottish Junior Cup. It was a first for the Dalaruan side and, as envious eyes looked on, it was Hughie McArthur's 'Black and Gold' to take on the 'foreign opposition' at the New Year's Day party. The draw produced far-flung opponents in the shape of Aberdeen Parkvale, but Lady Luck smiled kindly as the tie was scheduled for Kintyre Park. The men from the 'Granite City' decided to travel as far as Lochgilphead on Friday evening, a precarious decision given the unpredictable west coast winter weather; nevertheless, the morning of Saturday 3 January 1948 was crisp and dry and the onward journey was completed without a hitch.

The game attracted a healthy crowd of 1,800 spectators, less than in the halcyon pre-war years, but a sizeable crowd nevertheless. Refreshed by their overnight stop, the visitors started brightly and had easily the best of the early exchanges. With the lion's share of possession, the Aberdeen side raced to a two-goal lead in the opening 20 minutes of the match – the home side's day wasn't going as planned. 'The Glen' support suddenly found voice when inside-left Alex 'Tilta' Houston reduced the deficit with 15 minutes of the half remaining and as the interval approached, the same player scored again to complete an unexpected comeback. Honours even at the break, there was plenty to talk about as the home team's thrilling comeback had everyone anticipating the second half instalment.

The second half ebbed and flowed in classic cup-tie fashion, but in front of goal the day belonged to Parkvale. Two opportunist strikes ended the ambitions of Glenside, not the best of starts for football in post-war Campbeltown, as the home side slumped to a 4-2 defeat. Nevertheless, 'the beautiful game' was back on the agenda, the most important consideration, given the long absence of the war years.

Glenside v. Aberdeen Parkvale: Henry McGougan, A. Fletcher, Neil Gillies; Ewan Cameron, George Cook, N. McLellan; Pat McMillan, Hector Graham, John Dewar, Alex Houston, Adam Graham. (Fletcher, Cameron and Dewar from Lochgilphead).

Lack of housing created domestic unrest in post-war Campbeltown, the barren years of military confrontation bringing the country's construction programme to a complete standstill. Banner headlines in the local press graphically illustrated the desperate situation: 'House Hunters Besiege Housing Committee'.[34] Police presence was needed to restrain angry crowds outside the Council Chambers, a scene replicated across the country as people vented their fury. The new, post-war Labour Government moved swiftly to defuse the situation by introducing a nationwide programme of temporary accommodation known as 'Pre-Fabs' – Prefabricated Housing Units. These houses were very well equipped and lucky tenants even had the benefit of a refrigerator, an innovation unprecedented in municipal housing outside of the USA. Kintyre enjoyed its fair share of Pre-Fabs, the first units being built at Calton Hill, before spreading to other locations, including most of the surrounding villages.

The coal mine was reopened at Machrihanish in 1947, a massive shot in the arm for the area's depressed economy. The National Coal Board introduced key workers to train a new generation of employees: engineers, electricians, shot-firers, face-workers and the other skills necessary to get 'the pit' up and running. However, the influx of mining personnel once more highlighted the area's dearth of accommodation, a problem solved by the construction of the BISF houses at Meadows, known locally as 'the Miners or Steel Hooses'. In years to come, mine-workers would make a major contribution to the social and sporting scene in Kintyre, the famous Miners Welfare not only of benefit to employees, but to the wider community as well. Argyll Colliery, as the mine was known, would have football teams at both junior and amateur levels in the not too distant future.

Glenside's Scottish Cup exit brought the local league championship back into focus. At one point considered a two-horse race between Hearts and United, inspired by their recent cup form, Glenside unexpectedly beat Hearts by 4-3 to blow the championship race wide open. The main beneficiary was third-placed Drumlemble FC, but the chance of a surprise winner looked slim as the top two were in recruitment mode. Hearts and United were not averse to strengthening their squad with the occasional 'mercenary' or two. The Dalintober favourites recruited the services of Younger and Hamilton, respectively from Aberdeen and Kelso. Not to be outdone, Campbeltown United signed Newman, Tear and Alec Bruce, the latter an Ardrishaig man just returned from trials with Queens Park.

With the finishing line in sight, United emerged as firm favourites for the title, but there were still two matches against third-placed Drumlemble to negotiate. The first of these ended in a 2-2 draw, and a similar result or better was needed for the championship. For their part, Drumlemble had moved into second place and a win would see them overtake the long-term leaders. Everything now hinged on a last match. Against the odds, 'the Whites' turned the form book on its head with an emphatic 4-1 victory. The underdogs had pulled off the impossible, steering a course between the main contenders to win the 1947/48 league championship, a feat which looked impossible a few weeks earlier. These games show how evenly matched the town's junior sides were during the post-war era, a time when any one of our five clubs were within touching distance of the standard set nationally.

As previously mentioned, a favourite pastime of the people was ballroom dancing, but patrons at the Town Hall were slightly alarmed when the floor started to move to the rhythm of the beat. The *Courier* covered the story with tongue-in-cheek headlines: 'Swaying Dance Floor at Town Hall'; 'Council blame Canadian Barn Dance.' It appears the beams supporting the ballroom floor had been weakened by the weight of dancing feet and there were concerns for its possible collapse. A sum of £100 was set aside for repairs, but the Dean of Guild proposed the money be withheld and consideration given to constructing a new building. Mercifully, because of the building's historical importance this suggestion was rejected out-of-hand. Consequently, we still have our historic townhouse, presumably with the upstairs ballroom floor now Canadian Barn Dance-proofed![35]

Summer of 1948 saw a number of friendly fixtures between local clubs and their counterparts from the Central Belt. Campbeltown United travelled to play the famous Dennistoun Waverley, a game that spoke volumes for the popularity of junior football when an amazing 4,500 spectators turned out for a meaningless friendly. United surprised their hosts to lead 2-0 half-time, but a second half turnaround produced a narrow 3-2 home win. It was a similar story at Kintyre Park where Campbeltown Select led Maryhill Juniors at half-time, only to slip to a 5-3 defeat in the second half. Fitness rather than ability appears to have been the problem, as local football during this period was played in an 'off the cuff' fashion.

The town's Scottish Cup representatives, Glenside, salvaged local pride with an outstanding 2-1 victory over Central League

Champions, Strathclyde Juniors. Not content with the flurry of activity at club level, in August 1948 an ambitious league committee invited the Scottish Junior International team to Campbeltown. It was a bridge too far for the locals, as the national side ran out comfortable winners by 7-1. Nevertheless, the very fact that the SJFA were willing to visit the 'Wee Toon' was indeed a feather in the cap of local organisers. A crowd of 2,000 saw the teams line up as follows:

Scotland: Morgan (Shawfield), Paterson (Blantyre Victoria), Sloan (Kilsyth Rangers); MacKie (Bathgate), Graham (Dunipace), Middlemass (Petershill); Graham (Ashfield), Harris (Kilwinning), Ross (Yoker), Telfer (Benburb) and Wright (Royal Albert).

Campbeltown: Morris McSporran (United), Donald Shaw (United), William McConnachie (Drumlemble); Robert Armour (Hearts) capt, Dan Stalker (Drumlemble), Gordon McPherson (United); Alec Bruce (United), Hector Graham (Glenside), Alex Houston (Glenside), Duncan McIntyre (Drumlemble) and Pat McMillan (Glenside).

Right-half for Campbeltown Select was Robert 'Robina' Armour, a player who had spent most of his football career with the local Hearts Juniors. Arguably the most outstanding player of his generation, Robert was honoured with the captaincy of the local select against the best junior players in the country. Earlier in life – as mentioned – he turned down the opportunity of a senior career, preferring to stay in Kintyre and enjoy life on the coast. I have vivid memories of our many football discussions and learned much from this dedicated follower of the game. Robert continued playing until age became the enemy, and his last game was in the early 1950s.

Part of a sports week organised by the local YMCA, coaching was top of the agenda in July 1948. Campbeltown played host to a number of famous footballers, including George Young (Rangers and Scotland), Bobby Hogg (Celtic), Maurice Candlin (Partick Thistle) and the veteran goalkeeper Jerry Dawson (Rangers and Scotland). That same year, the community paid tribute to its 'stars' of the past with a veterans match between the Pupils FC and their old rivals United FC. Diplomacy at its best, the players were credited with having 'touches of sublime skill', although by the end of the match there were 22 extremely tired gentlemen only too happy to settle for a 4-4 draw.

Pupils v United, 'Old Crocks Match', 8 May 1948.

Pupils: L. McKechnie, A. Brown, D. Bannatyne; J. Riddell, P. McDougall, A. Mustarde, A. Graham, T. McGeachy, P. McMillan, A. Mathieson and W. Ramsay.

United: A. Houston, A. Clark, D. McEachran; H. McDougall, M. Lang, A. McMillan; D. Robertson, N. Scally, J. Ramsay, J. Burgoyne and A. Lafferty.

Campbeltown was still a favourite holiday destination in the days following the end of the Second World War. Clyde steamers the *Duchess of Hamilton, Duchess of Montrose* and the paddle steamer *Jeanie Deans* were always packed to the gunwales for trips 'doon the watter'. The opportunity to benefit from this vibrant holiday trade was not lost on the Town Council and they installed turnstiles at the Old Quay in an effort to cash in. A small cover charge was levied to access the pier before sailings, and records show that 54,000 people passed through the turnstiles in the period between June and September 1948. Busy times indeed! That year, Malcolm McCallum – head music teacher at the Grammar School – led Campbeltown Gaelic Choir to success in the National Mod. The event's premier choral award, the Lovat and Tullibardine Shield, was won for the fourth time in five years, the choir's 15th success in the competition to date. Three thousand people lined the streets of the town to welcome the choir home. The famous Campbeltown Gaelic Choir later recorded the soundtrack to the motion picture *The Bridal Path*, starring Bill Travis and Virginia McKenna, a film shown worldwide during the 1950s.

The fans besieged Kintyre Park for the Campbeltown United v. Cambuslang Rangers Scottish Junior Cup 4th round tie on Monday 3 January 1949. However, when the weather played its unpredictable hand, a game against one of the top sides in the country took an unusual twist. The park was declared playable after the usual early morning inspection, but the weather turned bleak with the opposition en-route to Kintyre. By mid-morning, things looked ominous when the town was hit by a massive fall of snow. The playing surface now resembled a Christmas card, which left the home officials with a major dilemma – do they intercept the bus or attempt to clear the snow? Although a massive task, the committee decided on the latter.

An appeal was launched for voluntary labour, and the fans responded in numbers. Wooden grain paddles were borrowed from Springbank Distillery and the park was gradually cleared in time for kick-off – a remarkable achievement. Unfortunately, the weather was the only thing conquered that day, as United 'slipped' to a 3-0 defeat at the hands of an excellent Cambuslang Rangers. *Campbeltown Courier* once more bemoaned the fact that a local club had failed to make the 5th round draw, but informed readers that the game had been 'An exhilarating and exciting tussle'. However, the newspaper was clear about the team's shortcomings, 'It was the old, old story of training tells, and it was just that and no more.'

The weather may have been beaten earlier in the day, but the gloom of cup defeat was hardly lifted by the choice of film at the 'Wee Pictures' that same night – *'Gone with the Wind.'*

Campbeltown United (v Cambuslang Rangers 1949): M McSporran; McMillan and Johnston; G McPherson, E Cameron and Cook; Mitchell, Hamilton, Fletcher, Bruce and Thomson.

As the final days of the decade approached, the professional career of another of the town's favourite sons was coming to an end, Alex 'Coogie' McMillan. He was one of a number of Argyll men to play for Third Lanark Football Club and wore the famous red jersey with distinction from 1947 until 1949. The news of his departure created interest south of the border, but despite the attention of both Preston North End and Gateshead, at this point a move to England held no appeal. He opted instead for a low profile move to East Stirling, a gentle conclusion to his time in senior football. At the end of his career, Alex returned home to work at Argyll Colliery and kept his football interests alive by playing with his old club, Glenside Juniors. Ironically, as one 'Wee Toon' footballer departed from Cathkin, another was set to take his place. Robert Mitchell – ex-Drumlemble Juniors – joined Third Lanark from Dunfermline Athletic in 1950, staying for one season only before moving south to play with Exeter City. Robert's final sporting days were spent with Headington United in the Southern League, a club eventually to join the Football League under the name of Oxford United.

An entry in the official minute book of the Campbeltown & District Junior Football Association refers directly to both players. Robert Mitchell returned home for a short period before his move to England, during which time he once more played in the colours

Campbeltown United (dark jerseys) v Cambuslang Rangers (striped jerseys), Scottish Junior Cup, 1949.

of Drumlemble Juniors. Alex McMillan and Robert Mitchell were then selected to play for Campbeltown against Mid-Argyll at Kintyre Park on 2 June 1952. In preference to listing the players under their respective local clubs, league secretary Walter Paterson chose to record them as ex-Third Lanark. Actions normally speak louder then words, but in using this method of identification, Walter's pride is there for all to see.

Youth football came to the fore with the birth of the Campbeltown Juvenile Association in the late 1940s. Charlie Duffy, along with his good friends Alex and Willie McLachlan, started the new league to promote the game among teenage boys. It was a long overdue initiative, as 20 years had passed since the town's last youth system – the Campbeltown Churches and Sabbath School Football League. The new organisation tried to fill the almighty chasm between schools' football and the heady heights of the junior league, a problem addressed a number of times through the years. There were two trophies on offer, the Juvenile Shield and Caskie Cup. The league produced a number of young players who would later grace junior football and the leading side adopted a name from the town's football past, Athletic FC.

Athletic Football Club (1949): Willie Gillespie, Alex McKinlay, Ronnie McCallum, Crawford Morans, David Graham, John Armour, Robert Duncan, Dan McCallum, Donnie Kelly (Capt), Peter Drummond and Alexander 'Sandy' Cunningham.

So ended a decade ravaged by conflict on a hitherto unknown scale. As a base for submarines and tugs, Campbeltown experienced war first-hand when enemy aircraft launched two separate assaults on the town with inevitable loss of life. However, although providing cover for the Clyde-based Atlantic convoys, the town emerged relatively unscathed in comparison to the devastation inflicted on Clydebank and Greenock. Rationing lasted until 1954, but even this failed to destroy the spirit of the people. Kintyre Park had been requisitioned by the armed services in the war years, and was badly in need of repair when handed back in 1946. Once this had been achieved, a dedicated committee set to organising a competitive structure. Teams were picked, old rivalries renewed and the townsfolk returned in their droves to the familiar surroundings of Kintyre Park. Football was back on the agenda...

The Fabulous Fifties: The Legendary 'Din from the Tin'

Given the luxury of choice, it would difficult to pick a better time than the 1950s for growing up. Despite post-war austerity, the world seemed a wonderful place crammed full of excitement and discovery. Our family lived a stone's throw from the local museum, a magical space with its red military uniforms, valuable coins and what in my imagination was a pirate's treasure chest. Living in Shore Street also had the advantage of being close to the town's two cinemas, the Rex and Picture House, both with regular children's matinees throughout the year. Saturday at 'the pictures' was preceded by a trip to R. S. McColl's in Main Street to surrender a few 'sweetie' coupons, then, suitably supplied, off to a land of Hollywood make-believe – gobstoppers at the ready!

For the more adventurous there were long summer days fishing off the quay, from memory a pastime which easily surpassed today's home-based electronic entertainment. Mischief was the innocent pestering of the putting green attendant, or an imaginary commando-style manoeuvre around the cinema floor. Raiding the nearby orchard was infinitely more serious, although from memory the ill-gotten fruit was hardly ever edible. These simple pastimes were enough to hold our youthful attention, but our habits changed when a new interest invaded our world. Around this time we were smitten by the 'football bug', a highly infectious condition and in most cases totally incurable. From here on, a ball was ever-present wherever we went – the start of a life-long obsession.

Forever on the look-out for a place to practise, our attention was drawn to a garage at the top of Fisher Row. It was perfect, as the entrance looked like an enormous goal. Needless to say, the wooden doors took a bit of a hammering, much to the dismay of the owner, Mr Smith. To our surprise, the anticipated repercussions never materialised and the reason for this gentleman's extraordinary patience only came to light many years later by sheer coincidence.

The garage belonged to the owner of a shop in Hall Street; however, more relevant to the story, in his heyday he was the 'star' centre-forward of the original Pupils Football Club, Hugh Smith. A kindred spirit, he fully understood our passion for the game and in kindness had acted accordingly. Thanks to the generosity of his niece, Moira McGeachy, Mr Smith's prized medals are now in my possession. It certainly is a strange, old world.

Discovering his youngest was smitten by 'the beautiful game', my father decided to give me a proper education. This involved regular visits to Kintyre Park to watch 'the juniors', more precisely, the one and only Hearts. Just seven years old, my recollections of the actual games are extremely vague, but my lasting memory is of people – lots of them! I'll never forget the good-natured banter of the crowd, in numbers which would put many of today's first division senior attendances to shame. Nevertheless, I found my first visit to the park seriously intimidating. Four foot nothing in height, the threat of being trampled underfoot was a real and present danger. Most of the action passed me by, but when a goal was scored, the celebrations were impossible to ignore. As the ball entered the net, a thunderous noise rose from the ground, the legendary 'din from the tin' as fans saluted their heroes by drumming with clenched fists on the corrugated perimeter fencing. A hangover from pre-war days, it was a trait of Hearts fans whose favourite meeting place was the side next to Limecraigs Road. A sea of people spilled from the ground at the final whistle, a tide of humanity moving as one up and over the Castlehill. What a sight – will we ever see the likes again?

The fans rolled up to see the likes of Hector and Adam Graham, Sammy and Robert Mitchell, Dan Stalker, Robert 'Robina' Armour, George Cook, Neil Campbell, Charlie Graham, Tommy 'Tucker' Galbraith, Alex 'Coogie' McMillan and James 'Roabie' Robertson. There were so many good players it was impossible to keep track. The games were hotly contested and supporters roared on their favourites bedecked in the colours of the Campbeltown elite: United, Drumlemble, Glenside, Hearts, Rangers and Argyll Colliery. Supporters of individual clubs had their own special areas inside the ground and a very noisy Kintyre Park it was! Never mind the South African Vuvuzela, post-war fans had their own method of producing noise, a wooden rattle used in wartime by air-raid wardens – an annoying contraption sometimes called a 'rickety'.

An unusual story from the period involved a very good player by the name of Jimmy Coll. This gentleman belonged to Rothesay, but

Hugh Smith in Sheffield Wednesday colours – circa 1912

after the war he was moved to Campbeltown where his employers, the electrical contractors Murray and Gillies, had a branch. Jimmy signed for Glenside Juniors and in time proved to be one of the best wing-halves of the post-war era. He came with excellent credentials, having played senior with Airdrie and previously represented the British Army. Many years later, in the early 1990s, a medal was found when a town-centre jeweller's shop was being renovated. The engraved letters 'JC' meant little, but a chance conversation with Dan Stalker produced a possible answer. 'If it's Glenside, then it must be Jimmy Coll from Rothesay.' I happened to be working on Bute at the time and, by sheer coincidence, the girl in the office was Fiona Coll. She quickly confirmed the gentleman was her Dad, so at long last, after a lapse of nearly 40 years, Jimmy Coll was presented with his winner's medal.

Large crowds were commonplace at Kintyre Park prior to and immediately after the Second World War. Attendances reached their peak during the 1930s, and continued at a reasonable level until the mid-1950s. However, with the exception of special occasions, at this point there was a steady decline in numbers through the turnstiles. Football had a greater significance in the lives of ordinary men and women during the inter-war years, and a higher profile in the community than today. The game flourished in the absence of home-based entertainment, only to decline with the coming of television and its mass coverage of sport. Town Councillors Colin Campbell and Norman Cameron held the reins of post-war football, an ideal arrangement, as any problems could be highlighted in the inner sanctum of municipal power. The licensing laws at the time also helped to swell the crowd, as public houses closed their doors between 2 p.m. and 5 p.m. This was a convenient interval for the pub's predominantly male clientele to attend the game. Add to this the passionate commitment of the ordinary fan to his or her district club, and a combination of these circumstances more often as not resulted in a healthy turnout.

There were five junior clubs in the membership during the 1949/50 season: Glenside, Hearts, United, Rangers and Drumlemble. There was little between the sides and the honours were evenly distributed. Drumlemble were league champions and Hearts claimed the Orr-Ewing and Sutherland Cups. Glenside won the Charity Cup and United was successful in the McCallum Cup. Treasurer John McDonald's annual balance sheet gave news of an association in a 'fairly healthy' condition. The general account held £71 - 1s - 9p,

Charity Cup Fund £47 - 18s and the savings account £53 - 7s - 3p. With the average earnings of an adult male then £5 per week, in today's money the total funds amounted to approximately £5,000. The association deducted 20 per cent from local gate monies, but it was responsible for the payment of parks and, in the case of injury and loss of wages, a player's one-off benefit payment from the Charity Cup Fund. The remainder of the money was then divided equally between the clubs. Campbeltown Rangers became the first casualty of the 1950s, withdrawing from competition in mid-season and the club eventually being wound-up.

Oblivious to the politics of the game, my education continued with regular visits to watch the Hearts Juniors. At this point, I had no idea a senior equivalent of 'the Maroons' existed, but my father's habit of checking his pools coupon from the radio sealed my allegiance to Heart of Midlothian – the 'Jam Tarts'. It was unusual to have a West Coast club adopt an Edinburgh name; in fact, since I cannot recall another, probably unique. This unusual anomaly gave Heart of Midlothian a sizable 'Wee Toon' support, something slowly eroded ever since the local club's demise in the early 1960s. So, why was the name chosen in the first place?

In the formative years, local clubs adopted the names of geographical features, like Kintyre, Kilbrannan or indeed Campbeltown. The fashion then changed to include classical, historical or patriotic names such as Corinthians, Albion or Victoria. Finally, they copied the names of famous senior clubs, something that came to pass with the birth of the first national league in 1890, the Scottish Football League.

The club known as Campbeltown Hearts was founded in 1899, a period prior to the dominance of Scottish football by the 'Old Firm'. While even in the early years, religious and cultural divisions made Rangers and Celtic the best supported teams in the country, they were not the 'giants' of the Scottish game like they are today. By pure coincidence, Heart of Midlothian – founded in 1874 – had grown to prominence around the same time as Dalintober's search for a football identity. The Edinburgh side had twice won the Scottish League Championship, had also been runner-up on two occasions and lifted the Scottish Cup three times in the closing decade of the 19th century. Therefore, it was hardly surprising the fisher folk of Dalintober picked the name of one of the country's most successful teams. As a present-day 'Jambo,' life has been rewarding at times, but after a bright start with a new owner and double Scottish

Cup success, the country's third force has found itself in financial difficulties. The club is embroiled in a late payments problem, in football terms a misdemeanour akin to playing 'Russian Roulette'. Hopefully, there will be a tomorrow to look forward to – with or without foreign influence.

The Scottish Junior Cup was always the highlight of the season in Campbeltown and Kintyre Park was packed to the gunwales as usual for a 4th round tie on Monday 2 January 1950. This time, it was Drumlemble's turn to host Lanarkshire Central League side, Thornliebank United. The game didn't get off to the best of starts, as both teams confused matters by turning out in the same colours; nevertheless, the respective jerseys were of different design, so recognition was just about possible. Given the circumstances, it was no surprise the ground was a sea of black and white as the large travelling support mixed freely with the home legions. What followed was a nine-goal thriller, a roller-coaster of a match from start to finish.

Drumlemble found themselves behind after only three minutes, Scally scoring in a goalmouth scramble to give the visitors the perfect start. It was a preview of what was to come, as the home side responded almost immediately when Robert Mitchell fired home from the edge of the box. Two goals scored and only eight minutes on the clock, the spectators were in for an interesting day. It was the cue for one of the most open games seen at Kintyre Park for many years, and defence was thrown to the wind as play raged from one end to the other. It wasn't always clever – according to the match report – but it certainly was exciting. A defensive blunder restored the visitors' lead mid-way through the first half, the ball driven home from close range by Telfer. There was hardly time to draw breath before a clumsy challenge resulted in a penalty kick for the home side. Winger Charlie Graham stepped forward to send the goalkeeper the wrong way, the execution picture-perfect from a man renowned as a dead ball expert. The interval was reached with the sides locked at 2-2 and there was plenty to debate after an incident-packed first half. However, it was only a shadow of what was to follow.

Thorniewood stunned the home support with a whirlwind start to the second half, a dejected home goalkeeper, Donnie McShannon, stooping to pick the ball out of the net twice in the first ten minutes. The first arrived courtesy of an angled header by inside-right Telfer, his second of the match. Outside-left McMeakin then doubled the visitors' lead with a shot off the underside of the crossbar. At this point the home side's confidence was severely dented, but in 'never-say-die' fashion they clawed their way back into the match. Inside-right Sammy Mitchell reduced the leeway with 20 minutes remaining, and the same player repeated the feat with minutes left on the clock. Pandemonium broke loose when the crowd invaded the park to celebrate the equaliser and unbelievable scenes took place as the game was stopped to clear the playing surface of delirious fans.

Normal service resumed, a draw looked inevitable as full time approached, but there was still one more twist in this remarkable tale. The home fans watched in disbelief as Drumlemble failed to clear their lines, the ball squared to the back post where visiting winger Moffat scored with the last kick of the ball. The euphoria of minutes earlier turned to despair. It was a cruel end to an absorbing cup-tie, the home side's epic fight-back rendered meaningless as Thorniewood claimed victory by 5 goals to 4. Lapses in defence proved Drumlemble's Achilles' heel, another glorious failure at a crucial stage of junior football's premier competition.

Although the result was ultimately disappointing, a crowd of 3,000 was regally entertained by an action-packed 90 minutes. Records tumbled at Kintyre Park, the biggest-ever crowd, the highest gate receipts and the highest scoring game in local junior cup history. However, for some reason the local sports correspondent saw the contest as 'a dreich game'.[36] Nine goals scored, an epic comeback, the pitch invaded by delirious fans, not to mention the trauma of a last minute winner – give me 'dreich' any day!

Drumlemble: Donald McShannon; Willie McConnachie, Jimmy Brown; James Graham, Dan Stalker, James Thomson; Tommy Mitchell, Sammy Mitchell, Robert Mitchell, Duncan 'Togan' McIntyre and Charlie Graham.

Thorniewood United: Cliens, Leith, Duffy, Robertson, Purdon, Davie; Moffat, Telfer, Scally, Ryan and McMeakin.

Referee: Mr W. Morrison, Clydebank.

A Campbeltown side had once more stumbled at the 4th round hurdle and the frustration felt in the town was palpable. A place in the coveted 5th round was proving more elusive than the Holy Grail! An independent writer under the pseudonym 'Armac' was scathing in his assessment of the game.[37] The correspondent berated the quality of both defences and, being local, was critical of the home side's rearguard in particular. Unwilling to shrink from what he saw as the truth, the anonymous contributor was feisty, controversial and every inch a critic. It made interesting reading. Nevertheless, expectations are always high prior to important cup-ties and it is understandable that disappointment often leads to bitter criticism. My own opinion, for what it's worth, is less critical and hopefully more realistic. At this stage of the competition, regional qualification had separated the 'wheat from the chaff' to leave the best teams from the various geographic locations. Due to its isolation, Campbeltown's part in this was somewhat unique. The town's football talent was spread across no fewer than five junior clubs, in terms of population a situation unparalleled anywhere else in Scotland. In no way is this excuse for defeat, but it certainly makes the difficulty more understandable.

Away from the woes of the Scottish Cup, Councillor Colin Campbell – President of Campbeltown and District Junior Football Association – was extremely worried about a unique situation at Kintyre Park. In his opinion, the newly constructed footpath leading to the Swedish-style houses at Limecraigs compromised the park's security. In his opinion, the height of the new pavement offered spectators a free view of the game. Town Surveyor, Mr David Kellock, was asked to appear at the next association meeting to discuss the problem. Did the association really expect him to re-route the footpath? No record of the debate exists, but the controversial footpath is still there today, so we have to assume that the football administration lost the argument. The gentlemen of the committee may have been over-ruled, but I certainly like their cheek.

Saturday 10th June, 1950, marked the beginning of Civic Week to celebrate the 250th anniversary of the Royal Burgh. As part of the programme, Blantyre Victoria – the Scottish Junior Cup holders – agreed to meet a Campbeltown Select at Kintyre Park. The newly-crowned kings of junior football beat the locals by 2-0 in front of 3,000 spectators, but – according to the press – the game failed to live up to its pre-match billing. 'The most entertaining feature of the afternoon was the half-time display of the Scottish Junior Cup'. Aberdeen's legendary centre-half Alex Young was at the time captain of Blantyre Victoria, a player remembered for his part in the Dons' famous half-back line of the 1950s, Allister, Young and Glen. Alex Young was inducted into the Pittodrie hall of fame in 2005. He died on 2 March 2010.

Campbeltown Select: Donald McShannon (Drumlemble), William McConnachie (Drumlemble), Neil Campbell (United), James Thomson (Drumlemble), Robert Armour (Hearts) capt, Callum Robertson (Hearts), Thomas Mitchell (Drumlemble), George Cook (United), Alex McMillan (Glenside), Angus McIntosh (United) and Richard Dewar (Hearts).

Blantyre Victoria: Warren, P. Allan and McCallum; J. Allan, Young and Wright; Gill, Herbert, Renwick, Lennon and Hughes.

Scorers: Lennon and Herbert.
Referee: W. B. Brown, SFA Grade 1.

There is a unique postscript to this story, as the Scottish Junior Cup was stolen on its return to Blantyre. Displayed in a local newsagent's shop window, it went missing about two weeks after its visit to Campbeltown. Before your thoughts drift in that direction, no one from the 'Wee Toon' was involved. Desperate for cup success we may have been – but not that desperate! Thankfully, the cup was recovered and is still the one competed for today. This is how the story was reported: 'The Scottish Junior Cup is back in circulation. Stolen a fortnight ago from a Blantyre newsagent's shop window, it was dug up 500 yards from the shop. Officials of Blantyre, apparently acting on information, decided to search a stretch of land (Blantyre Braes), and, after removing 30 tons of clay over the course of two days, the cup was found undamaged by two supporters, Frank Dunsmuir and Duncan McEwan.'[38]

The Blantyre Victoria game was part of Campbeltown Civic Week, an event preceded by a street parade and the re-enactment of the signing of the Royal Charter. At the time, my father was employed with the Kintyre Road Services (K.R.S.) – forerunner of the British Road Services – so, as a passenger in his lorry-cum-float, I was fortunate to have a privileged view of the proceedings. One of the highlights was the crowning of the Civic Week Queen, 18-year-old Miss Catherine Watterson. To mark the occasion further, Mr Alf Grumoli – proprietor of the Locarno Café – donated a new cup to the football fraternity. Named the Civic Week Cup by popular choice, it was played for annually from 1951 until the end of the KAFL during the late 1990s. The trophy was originally intended for inter-league competition, with the newly-formed 'Artisans League' playing the Junior Association on an annual basis, but the SJFA refused permission and it was gifted to the aforementioned amateur league. 'The Artisans League' – named after the skilled working-classes who made the game their own in the 19th century – was a forerunner of the aforementioned KAFL. Both leagues were bona fide non-remunerative organisations, the first football of a truly amateur nature played in the town for 40 years.

With eight clubs in its membership, the new amateur football league got underway in May 1951. The junior association still held centre-stage in the town, so it was no surprise to find the majority of amateur teams came from the surrounding villages. Clubs in the membership were Machrihanish, Laggan, Peninver, Carradale, Southend, NCB Strollers, NCB Athletic and Kilbrannan, the last-mentioned a team of shopkeepers. With outlets to cater for every conceivable need, the town centre was a vibrant place before the coming of supermarkets. However, for football-minded employees it was unfortunate that these shops were committed to Saturday opening. The new summer evening league provided the ideal solution, allowing some very fine players to have a kick at a ball after closing time.

Kilbrannan set the early pace in the league, and, just when it seemed that nothing could stop the ball-playing shopkeepers, a late surge from Laggan pinched the first amateur football championship. Laggan also added the inaugural Civic Cup to its list of honours, the first name engraved on the prestigious new trophy. The Artisans League was guided by secretary, John McAulay, but after only two years it was superseded by the Kintyre and District Amateur Football League. This respected organisation would control local football for the next 45 years, the saving grace of the local game after the demise of 'the juniors' in the early 1960s.

During long summer evenings, the amateur league provided excellent recreation and entertainment for players and spectators alike. Week-day fixtures suited everyone: shopkeepers, farmers and a variety of people unable to take part in winter competition.

The first president was Mr W.S. MacDonald – Rector of Campbeltown Grammar School – who provided astute guidance until his retirement in 1958. He was succeeded by the Rev Campbell M. McLean, minister of the Longrow Church and former player with Queens Park and Amateur Scotland. During the latter's tenure, a close relationship was formed between Queens Park and the Kintyre Amateur Football League. Campbell McLean would later gain prominence as Moderator of the United Free Church of Scotland and religious programmes presenter for BBC Scotland. He was assisted in his football duties by a man who would later become the cornerstone of the KAFL, the one and only Archie McCallum – 'Baldy'.

The redoubtable Archie McCallum wore a number of hats in the community, a respected Provost, Justice of the Peace, Argyll & Bute Councillor, Youth Club leader, KAFL Secretary, as well as being a well-known local character. He devoted the bulk of his life to the pursuit of worthwhile causes, but in a time when it seemed like everyone played football, 'Baldy' was the undisputed patriarch of the local amateur game.

One of his duties was drawing up the season's fixture list, the same conveniently displayed in shop windows for the benefit of interested parties. A number of new clubs joined the amateur league set-up as the 1950s progressed: the YMCA, Argyll Colliery AFC, Drumlemble Amateurs, ATC Athletic and Dalintober Hearts – not to be confused with the junior club of similar derivation. There was even a team representing the patrons of 'the Top Café'. Resplendent in red and yellow hoops similar to that of a certain team from Firhill, Mayfair Thistle were a skilful side that added a touch of quality to an already competitive league. Although it's a great feeling to be successful, in certain circumstances it wasn't a priority; at least that's how it appeared with the lads of the local Territorial Army. 'The Beagles' – who typified what amateur football is all about – had little chance of silverware, but they still managed to enjoy the experience anyway!

At the outset, the Kintyre Amateur Football League was dominated by the village teams, especially the men from the east, Carradale and Peninver. Carradale won three of the four competitions in 1953, the Macmaster Campbell and Miners Welfare Cups, plus the League Championship. Peninver had to be content with solitary success in the Civic Cup, but it was the last time an excellent Carradale side would have the upper hand. With Archie McCallum, James McNair and John Armour at the helm, Peninver dominated amateur football for the remainder of the decade. Archie McCallum – not to be confused with the league secretary – played in the side at left-back, where he was joined by his brother Donald, a goalkeeper. These people were the driving force behind the team. Peninver was equal to any of the local junior sides of the period, a well-run club that regularly represented the community in the Scottish Amateur Cup. The team had phenomenal success in its comparatively short lifetime and it seems inconceivable that it only existed for little more than a decade. Along with my brother Barney, I had pleasure playing for Peninver in the club's penultimate season, 1960/61, but the following campaign was the club's last and thereafter it slipped quietly into oblivion.

Here are a some of the players who played for Peninver between 1951 and 1961: Donald McCallum (G), Archie Simpson (G), John McPhee (G), Alastair McSporran, Archie McCallum, Hamish Miller, Robert Millar, Donnie Kelly, Neil Watson, Willie Anderson, Alastair Bell, Barney McKinven, David McGeachy, Neil McMillan, Malcolm McDonald, Ian Penman, Gavin Sinclair, Donald Armour, Pat McMillan, Duncan McIntyre, Jimmy McCrank, Richard Semple, Eddie Hughes, Donnie McLachlan, Neil Wardrop and 'Joannie' Sinclair. There were of course many more who pulled on the blue jersey and the aforementioned names are only a few of these who readily come to mind.

The highlight of the local amateur season was the visit of Queens Park Football Club, an annual friendly fixture which survived until the early 1960s. The Spiders' sent down their third string – Hampden eleven – to play a Kintyre Amateur Select each year on the September holiday week-end. Queens Park has always been a prolific organisation – at this juncture, a club capable of fielding no fewer than four separate teams. The first eleven were members of the nation's top league, the SFL 1st Division. Second eleven, the quaintly named 'Strollers', played in the Scottish Reserve League, with the third and fourth strings – Hampden and Victoria X1s – both members of the Scottish Amateur Football League, now the parent league of Campbeltown Pupils AFC. Queens Park brought a talented eleven to Kintyre Park in 1953, a season in which the same team won the SAFL 1st Division title. However, the home select were made of stern stuff and ended the day with a creditable 4-4 draw.

Kintyre AFL: Donald McCallum (Peninver), David McArthur (Largie), D. McMillan (Carradale), Murray Shaw (Carradale), Willie Anderson (Peninver) capt, H. Sharp (Southend), Jackie Bird (Largie), Gavin Sinclair (Peninver), Colin Galbraith (Carradale), Ian Penman (Peninver) and Archie McCorkindale (Southend).

Queens Park: P. Baxter, B. McLaughlin, G. Smith, W. McGregor, F. O'Hare, R. Smart, M. Kirk, R. Sturgeon, I. Johnstone, J. H. Devine and J. Geoch.

In 1950, Donald Dewar, secretary of Argyll Athletic, submitted an application for membership of the Campbeltown & District Junior

Football Association, but after careful deliberation the application was rejected. The recent loss of Rangers FC had still to be addressed, however, one year later the association expanded with the inclusion of Argyll Colliery FC. The boys from 'the pit' were organised by the affable Kenny McMillan, who was ably supported by his good friend and workmate, John Docherty. Kenny was a lifelong Motherwell supporter, so the famous 'claret and amber' was a natural choice of colours. Argyll Colliery initially had three separate sides: a junior squad supported by a couple in the amateur ranks – NCB Strollers and NCB Athletic. This was an ambitious but short-lived plan. The organisers eventually settled for a side in each of the grades, the amateur side arriving on the scene later in the decade. Extremely well organised, Argyll Colliery operated a carded membership scheme, with supporters contributing to the running costs of the two sides. Argyll Colliery Juniors was an instant success, the first eleven winning the McCallum Cup in its inaugural season – 1951/52. The final against Glenside was settled by two long-range efforts from Donald Paterson, and a third goal from centre-forward Sam Batey in a 3-1 win.

Drumlemble ruled supreme that season, winning the League, Orr-Ewing and Sutherland Cups, but the campaign could have been more successful but for an unusual turn of events. The team's strip went missing en route to a Charity Cup tie against Hearts! The hamper was dutifully loaded on to the service bus at Stewarton, but there was consternation when the kit failed to arrive. A slightly perplexed Hearts was given a walk-over, a game which turned into a poisoned chalice when the 'Reds' lost 6-1 to Glenside in the final. But where did the strip go? The bus was normally garaged at the end of its country run, the team strip then transferred to the office for collection later in the day. However, things went askew when the vehicle was commandeered by a party going to the opening of the Auchalochy Water Scheme. Drumlemble's hopes of cup success went with them, but despite local rumour, conspiracy was never a consideration. Although dominating local football, Drumlemble's Scottish Cup dream ended with a 7-3 defeat to Bridgeton Waverley in Glasgow on 4 January 1951.

Glenside's victory in the Charity Cup was a double celebration for their left-winger John McCorkindale, a young man on his way to Kilmarnock FC. The 17-year-old was an imposing six feet six inches in height and had a turn of pace to match a top club sprinter. Described in the local press as 'a man mountain', his outstanding sporting prowess made him Argyll Schools Athletics Champion for

1951. Pursued by both Newcastle United and Hull City, John decided to finish his secondary education at Campbeltown Grammar School and commute to Ayrshire to play for Kilmarnock. Manager Malcolm McDonald's new acquisition was rumoured to have received £200 for signing on, an extraordinary sum for one so young. However, as the average working man's wage was no more than £5 per week, it is safe to assume the inflationary tendencies of local gossip had been furiously at work.

After an inspection of facilities, the SJFA allowed Lochgilphead to gain membership of the Campbeltown & District Junior Football Association on 24 July 1952. It brought the number of clubs to six, an extraordinary figure considering the limited levels of population in Western Argyll. Many of the Mid-Argyll lads were already well-known in Campbeltown football, as they had previously worn the colours of one or another of the town clubs. Lochgilphead at this point was a hot-bed of talent, a club brimming with well-known names. There was Donnie McDonald, ex-Rangers, Alex Bruce, Campbell 'Kilberry' Fletcher, Ewan Cameron, Jimmy Stirling, Hughie Fletcher, John Dewar, Hugh McTavish, Willie Johnstone and Fraser McGlynn, the last mentioned a diminutive but highly acrobatic goalkeeper. The standard of their squad was endorsed by Glasgow Celtic, as the Parkhead club signed centre-forward Hughie Fletcher at the end of the same season, 1952/53. Hughie later converted to full-back and finished his professional career as captain of Carlisle United.

Lochgilphead won the Orr-Ewing and McCallum Cups in their first competitive season, a unique achievement, in as much it was the first time these trophies had travelled beyond the 'Mill Dam'. Glenside struck a blow for the town by securing the League Championship and Hearts added to the haul by winning the remaining two trophies – the Sutherland and Charity Cups. There was absolutely no problem sharing domestic success with a near-neighbour. However, it was another matter when the new order threatened the 'Wee Toon's' jealously guarded Scottish Cup 4th round place. The New Year game was a tradition dating back to the early years of the 20th century and for Campbeltown to lose such an honour verged on the unthinkable. However, there is no sentiment in football and a long-standing tradition was interrupted when Lochgilphead defeated Drumlemble by 5-2 on November 15 1952. The coveted 4th round tie against Blantyre Celtic was bound for Ropework Park in Lochgilphead. Drumlemble had been the area's representatives for

Argyll Select v Renfrewshire Select, Dunterlie Park, Barrhead, 1952.
Back row, left to right: Alex McMillan, Wattie Paterson, Willie McConnachie, Neil Campbell, Ewan Cameron,
Willie Hamilton, James Thomson, James Stirling, John Anderson and John McDonald.
Front row, left to right: John Dewar, Campbell Fletcher, Tommy Mitchell, Tommy Galbraith and Hugh
McTavish.

the previous three years without success, the last occasion being a 4-1 home defeat to Dundee side Jeanfield Swifts.[39]

The national cup tie missing from the town's holiday calendar, the association hastily arranged a friendly against Arthurlie Juniors, a fixture sensibly scheduled for the day after 'the Scottish.' Therefore, it was a unique scene acted out on 2 January 1953, for instead of the usual short walk to Kintyre Park, the Campbeltown public were faced with a journey to Mid-Argyll to support their 'local' team. However, the change of venue did nothing to improve the recent fortunes of Argyll clubs, as the spirited hosts were beaten by 4 goals to 2. There was little time to recover for three of the Lochgilphead team, as they were selected to appear in the association select the following day against Arthurlie Juniors, another narrow reverse by 2 goals to 1. Despite these results, the quality of the junior game in Western Argyll was still extremely useful, but since pre-war days the standard had fallen elusively short of the 5th round benchmark.

Campbeltown Select v, Arthurlie, 3 January 1953: Willie Hamilton (Drumlemble); Willie McConnachie (Drumlemble), James Stirling (Lochgilphead); James Robertson (United), Dan Stalker (Drumlemble), James Thomson (Argyll Colliery); Duncan McIntyre (Argyll Colliery), Tommy Galbraith (United), Hughie Fletcher (Lochgilphead), Duncan 'Togan' McIntyre (Drumlemble) and Alex Bruce (Lochgilphead).

In only its second season of competitive football, Argyll Colliery's progress was marked by a fine 4-1 victory over Glasgow first-class juvenile side Burnbank Swifts. This was followed by a creditable 1-1 draw against Shotts Bon Accord on 2 May 1953. Away from the playing side of the game, Campbeltown Town Council witnessed two stalwarts of junior football at loggerheads over a proposal to install hot water sprays – the terminology of the period – at Kintyre Park. Councillor Colin Campbell – immediate past president of the junior football association – said it was a waste of public money 'to install the extravagant and useless apparatus'. On the other hand, Councillor J. M. B. Anderson – serving president of the same association – argued that 'the health and well-being of sportsmen had to be considered'. The motion to install a single shower in each dressing room was carried by 11 votes to 2. In the event, a financial compromise was reached when two old-fashioned showers were fitted for the cheaper price of £48 10s. Unfit for purpose, the showers were largely ignored by the players, who continued to wash at home. Visiting sides were bussed to Argyll Colliery, where the miners' superb showering facilities were made available courtesy of the National Coal Board. Given the benefit of foresight, I wonder how our football predecessors would have viewed today's modern facilities with artificial grass parks, floodlights, and the recommendation of a shower for every competitor. More to the point, what would they make of a modern game in which tackling is frowned upon, 'diving' is an art form, injury is faked and time wasted? Would they even recognise the game entrusted into our safekeeping? I think not!

After a period of settling in, Argyll Colliery came to the fore when winning the league championship and three out of the four cups in 1953/54. Hearts were the only other side to claim a trophy that season – the Charity Cup. Well-known players registered with 'the miners' were: Ian 'Sleepy' McMillan, Henry McGougan, Jimmy Fowler, Don Thomson, Neil Campbell, Willie Colville, Dan Stalker, Joe Duncan, James Thomson, Stuart Hamilton, Tommy McIntyre, Donald Blue, Duncan McIntyre, George Cook, James Ford, Donald Paterson, Coventry Paton, Charlie McFadyen and James McMillan. There were a number of additions before the start of the new season, the squad further augmented with Dougie McArthur, Tommy Mitchell, Neil McLachlan and Archie McKerral.

Although empty-handed in domestic competition, Lochgilphead surprised everyone by progressing to meet Troon in the Scottish Junior Cup of 1953/54, this before falling to the Ayrshire side by 4 goals to 1. The following year saw Tarbert Football Club elevated to the heady heights of the junior ranks. The introduction of 'the Dookers' brought the association membership to seven clubs, its highest level since the First World War. Before being allowed to compete, the SJFA instructed Tarbert to have its ground enclosed behind a curtain wall – a facility overlooked by the bowling club, approximately where the industrial estate and bus stance are today. The club carried out the required work and maintained a junior presence for three seasons – 1954 to 1957. Here are some of the players who took part in the CDJFA during this period:

Tarbert FC: James McNab, McDougall, McQuilkan, Stewart, McLachlan, McFarlane, John Johnstone, James Johnstone, Willie Black, P Johnstone, Smith, McNeill, Campbell, Richmond, John McNab, Fraser McGlynn and Sutherland.

With the league flourishing and membership at its highest level in years, without warning, cracks began to appear in the fabric of the local junior game. The new campaign started brightly with a decent 1-1 draw between Campbeltown Select and Blantyre Celtic, but the CDJFA was again reduced to five clubs by the end of 1954/55 season. Lochgilphead disappeared from competitive football in March 1955, and, after a year's absence, the club was denied entry to the following season's competitions. A softening of attitudes saw the Mid-Argyll club re-admitted for the 1956/57 season, but the end of the road beckoned when Lochgilphead once more failed to fulfil its fixtures. Even more surprising was the demise of Glenside Juniors. Playing well and having recently won the McCallum Cup, 'The Glen' suddenly found it impossible to continue. It was the end of the road for this much-loved local football club, and after a life-span of forty-seven years 'the black and gold' was worn for the last time against Argyll Colliery on 15 August 1955. A shortage of manpower was the reason behind the club's demise, as many had left the area to find work in the steel industry at Corby, Northamptonshire. Founded in 1908, Glenside had survived the trauma of two world wars only to succumb to the town's age-old problem – the lack of jobs!

Nevertheless, there was little sign of panic in the minutes of the junior association, as the local game had experienced difficulties before and survived. Sadly, although unknown at the time, in a short five years the town's junior game was staring into the abyss. Oblivious to the situation, Argyll Colliery carried the flag all the way to Inverurie Loco in the 4th round of the Scottish Junior Cup on 3rd January 1955, but having passed on a number of gilt-edged chances they eventually lost the tie decisively by 4 goals to nil. However, with five clubs still in membership – Drumlemble, Argyll Colliery, United, Hearts and Tarbert – the attitude of junior administration remained upbeat and confident. There was concern when Hearts outside-left Hector Thomson broke his leg in a league match against Argyll Colliery on 16 April 1955. It was a particularly nasty injury, but Hector recovered fully to play his part in a famous Scottish Junior Cup victory in 1957. The end of a rather tumultuous season saw Argyll Colliery win the league championship and Sutherland Cup. Glenside made a successful farewell by claiming the McCallum Cup, and United lifted the Orr-Ewing Cup. While there was no trophy for Hearts or Drumlemble, at this point, both clubs were in the process of rebuilding and would soon prove a handful in the months ahead.

So it was that a young Hearts side made the early running in 1955/56, and, despite the close attentions of United, were good enough to clinch the first trophy of the season, the Orr-Ewing Cup. There then followed an uninterrupted run to the Sutherland Cup final, a game in which they demolished Drumlemble by 5 goals to 2. The referee for this match was Archie Mustarde ('Purba'), one of Campbeltown's greatest characters and a 'lion' of a man on the football field. No more than five feet in height, the 'man in black' was one the crowd loved to hate, but it mattered not, as he controlled the game in his own inimitable manner without flinching. Archie stood no nonsense and dictated the rules like a sergeant-major. To see him in action was worth the price of entry alone. The blast of his whistle was supported by exaggerated gestures to emphasis the decision. In his armoury was a catalogue of poses almost thespian in character. The crowd howled with anger and derision as he dropped on one knee to make his point. What a showman – just brilliant! His was hardly the easiest of tasks, but Archie was one the finest SJFA referees in the country and he shared the official duties with two other qualified 'whistlers', Ian Munro and Bert Morris.[40]

It is the opinion of modern experts that all football prior to 1966 was tactically naïve. TV pundits pour scorn on the old-fashioned opinion that attack is the best form of defence and are at pains to extol a brand of modern football, which borders on mechanical – but what have we sacrificed to inherit today's tactical monstrosity? Modern players are fitter than ever before and defending is now an art form, but people still love high-scoring games, even the ones riddled with defensive blunders. The 'old game' was never flush with defensive theory, but the absence of 'classroom tactics' often contributed to 90 minutes of pure theatre. This was evident when the season's two leading protagonists, Hearts and United, clashed in the Orr-Ewing Cup. Played on a home and away basis, no fewer than 24 goals were scored across the two fixtures – the results of 8-6 and 6-4 more in keeping with Wimbledon than Hampden Park. To labour the point, in 54 games played during the local 1955/56 season, a total of 331 goals were scored, an amazing average of 6.129 per game. Tactically naive it may have been, but in my opinion the old-fashioned attacking philosophy delivered a greater spectacle than is witnessed today.

This is not an attempt to compare the quality of modern football with that of the past, as the present era has produced some of the greatest players to ever walk the planet. It is a personal opinion based on entertainment value alone, not the impossible debate of who would beat whom if it came to the crunch. There are exceptions, the wonderful Barcelona of Messi and company in particular, but even the Catalans are beginning to suffer from the cold wind of defensive tactics. A prime example is Chelsea's win in the Champions League of 2011/12. Of course, this is a far cry from local football, and a speedy return to 1956 finds a young Hearts side rewarded with a winning haul of both the Orr-Ewing and Sutherland Cups.

Hearts (1955/56): A. McKinlay; Donnie Kelly, Clark Fulton; Jimmy West, Bobby Riddell, 'Maxie' McIntyre; Sandy McGeachy, Lawrence Robertson, Hector Thomson, Sandy Steele and Dick Dewar.

A season as 'nearly men' brought little domestic joy for Argyll Colliery, yet 'the Miners' progressed to meet Armadale Thistle in the 4th round of the Scottish Cup on 3 January 1956. Armadale Thistle – once a senior club, known as Armadale F.C. until 1935 – had won the East of Scotland Cup as recently as 1953, so the game at Volunteer Park was a major obstacle to the cup ambitions of the Kintyre side. Nevertheless, the boys in 'claret and amber' acquitted themselves very well, and, although losing the game by 4 goals to 2, were roundly applauded for their sterling efforts. Centre-half Dan Stalker was outstanding at the heart of the defence, and goals from Tommy Mitchell and Duncan McIntyre ensured the match was competitive from start to finish.[41] To compensate for the away draw, a friendly fixture was arranged between Campbeltown Select and Helensburgh at Kintyre Park and United's mercurial inside-forward Tommy Galbraith was man of the match as the home side ran out winners by 5 goals to 4.

It was fortunate these games had taken place when they did, as the following week Kintyre was hit by blizzard conditions. Four-foot snow-drifts crippled communications, closed roads and left stranded drivers to seek refuge in village halls. As well as highlighting the freak weather conditions, the *Courier* reported an attempt by the Town Council to persuade the Queen and Duke of Edinburgh to visit Campbeltown during their forthcoming West Highland tour. However, as a royal visit had already taken place as recently as August 1954, the invitation was politely declined. This story gave the local press licence to reflect on a much earlier royal visit, that of Queen Victoria and Prince Albert in 1847. The Town Council of that day asked the bellman – town crier – to go around the streets and announce the arrival of the Royal Yacht. Members of the national press, who were following the royal progress, were amused to hear the said gentleman call out, 'The Queen is in the loch!' This message was perfectly understood locally, but the images conjured in the minds of the mainly English-based media can be imagined.[42]

Campbeltown United recovered to dominate the remainder of the 1955/56 season, winning the league championship, Sutherland Cup and Charity Cup, the last-mentioned a three match marathon against Argyll Colliery. United had Hughie 'Delaney' Graham and Duncan McAulay at the helm, a team served by Donald 'Dolly' Cook, Willie Gillespie, Andy McShannon, Alexander 'Nicky' Campbell, Pat McMillan, Rab McCallum, Charlie McKerral, Donnie 'Flukes' McLachlan, James McEwing, Neil Campbell, Tommy 'Tucker' Galbraith, Charlie 'Feeney' Farmer and Alex McVey.

Alarm bells started to ring when Tarbert was unable to fulfil its remaining fixtures. The club's last competitive appearance was an Orr-Ewing Cup-tie on February 11 1956 – another club was about to fail. From here on, both Lochgilphead and Tarbert found difficulty in maintaining a presence in the junior association, possibly because of the number of away fixtures involved. In the league championship, there were six scheduled away fixtures when Tarbert joined in 1954. This figure could increase dramatically given an absence of luck in cup draws, possibly the reason for the club's eventual failure. Regarding Lochgilphead, club secretary D. McDonald made a case for his team competing in the McCallum Cup only, a scenario which would have allowed access to the all-important Scottish Junior Cup. This was rejected out of hand by the CDJFA. The saga rumbled on for months via the national association, but for Lochgilphead and Tarbert, it signalled their demise as junior clubs.

Although the CDJFA was technically correct in refusing anything but full commitment from member clubs, losing two teams was a devastating blow to the strength of the junior game in Western Argyll. However, nothing could have prepared the committee for the *coup de grace*. Hearts, the oldest club still in existence, was next to address the difficulties of survival. As recent winners of two competitions and with the youngest squad in the league, the collapse of the Dalintober club in February 1957 was the last thing expected by a now under-pressure administration. There were now only three clubs left, in the words of President J. M. B. Anderson, 'not sufficient to run a competition'. Falling crowds added financial difficulties to the equation, but at the eleventh hour, the committee decided to soldier on in the face of adversity.

Campbeltown's historic junior game was struggling for survival, but one club would buck the trend and bring a smile to supporters' faces. At the beginning of the season, six local clubs set out on their usual Scottish Junior Cup adventure, but a team with an historic cup pedigree once more came to the fore, Campbeltown United. Representing the area for the first time since 1939, even with local football in a state of flux, the players were intent on enjoying the experience. The local side was drawn at home to Aberdeen Mugiemoss in the 4th round and their opponents caused quite a stir by chartering a plane to fly direct to Machrihanish Airport – the first time flight had been used in Scottish Junior Cup history. The conditions at Kintyre Park on Saturday 5 January 1957 were simply deplorable. Heavy rain fell throughout the ninety minutes, an endurance test on a surface resembling a swamp. Good football proved impossible but nevertheless, the match remained exciting as both sides battled bravely for cup qualification.

Before a ball had been kicked, assurances were given that the tie wouldn't be all-ticket, something of a rash decision as bad weather played havoc with the anticipated turnout. Winning the toss, the visitors elected to kick towards the pavilion end and started much the stronger of the two teams. Midway through the first half, United's right-back Willie Gillespie handled the ball in the box. The ball appeared to strike his hand in the terrible conditions, but the visitors were delighted to be awarded a rather soft penalty kick. Left-half Bird drove the ball home with comparative ease, but his joy was short-lived as the kick was ordered to be retaken. A team-mate had inadvertently encroached into the box, leaving the 'scorer' to curse his luck when Donald Cook turned his second attempt over the top. What a let-off!

An unusually lethargic home side at last got to grips with the game, pinning the visitors back for the first time in the match. A through-ball at the Limecraigs end looked harmless enough, but in a frenzied effort to clear his lines, right-back Russell turned the ball into his own net. The home side were extremely fortunate to have a one-goal lead at the interval, but as the first 45 minutes had already shown, anything was possible on a quagmire of a pitch. Mugiemoss exacted revenge with two well-taken goals mid-way through the second-half. The first was a strike from the edge of the box by inside-left Duncan, and the same player repeated the dose with an angled drive from inside the box to put the visitors' in the driving seat with only 15 minutes remaining. With time ebbing away, the home side was badly in need of a hero. Then, in the closing minutes, up stepped a mud-splattered Neil Campbell to level the scores with a well-taken drive. The tie would go to a replay! [43]

The return match was played the following week at Linksfield Stadium, Aberdeen, on Saturday 12 January 1957. Failure to win at home had placed the boot on the other foot. Campbeltown United faced a long journey north by bus – the luxury of flight well beyond the local club's means. However, United prepared for the tie by travelling to Aberdeen on the Friday evening, and the short journey to the stadium was completed with everyone well-rested. A few loyal fans also made the long trek north to support their favourites, but unable to travel, the vast majority went to unusual lengths to get a blow-by-blow account of the match. A direct telephone link was set up between the stadium and Kinloch Bar in Main Street, but there was a problem, as the licensed premises closed its doors between 2 and 5 p.m. This was overcome by using the streets around the bar as an impromptu terracing, with news of the match relayed to fans by way of a runner. A touch of theatre saw the match details chalked on to the road surface, a novel idea if the messenger's body language hadn't already given the show away.

And so it began. The breaking news was less than welcome, as Mugiemoss scored early through inside-forward Johnson to take the lead. The next flurry of activity brought a great roar from the crowd – Hector Thomson had equalised for United! The scene was unbelievable as people milled around waiting for information. Without doubt, Tom Douglas's pub would never again be as popular with its doors closed. Joe McMillan, well-known local newspaper salesman, had volunteered to do the honours as go-between and scribe. Suddenly, there was another flurry of activity as more news filtered through. Mugiemoss centre-half Main was given as the scorer, followed by the words – 'own goal!' United were ahead by 2 goals to 1. I can still feel the excitement to this day.

Questions flew thick and fast. How long was there to go? Could the boys hold out? The crowd's silent prayers were answered with news of another crucial strike, this time from the previous week's hero, Neil Campbell. Two goals to the good and the clock running down, a celebratory atmosphere ran through the crowd. However, the joy was short-lived when Mugiemoss pegged a goal back right at the death. Time seemed like an eternity and an eerie silence fell as the crowd held its collective breath. Finally the side door of the Kinloch Bar opened and Joe's body language said it all. Game over: United had won by 3 goals to 2. The whole thing resembled a scene from *The Quiet Man*, John Ford's classic film of Irish community life starring John Wayne and Maureen O'Hara. Impossible to stage-manage, it was one of those days that will live in the memory forever. The 4th round hurdle had not been cleared since 1938, and Campbeltown prepared to celebrate long into the night. Times have changed since the halcyon days of junior football, but if we ever need an example of how important the game was and is to a community, this day certainly said it all.

Campbeltown United v. Mugiemoss (both games): Donald Cook, Willie Gillespie, Andy McShannon, Pat McMillan, James Robertson, 'Maxie' McIntyre, James McEwing, Tommy Galbraith, Neil Campbell, Hector Thomson and Charlie Farmer. The management were Duncan McAulay and Hughie 'Delaney' Graham.

Mugiemoss (both games): Cowie; Russell, Smith; Fraser, Main, Bird; Mutch, Baxter, Johnstone, Duncan, Shiach.

The prize for the winner was a 5th round tie at home to Loanhead Mayflower, a really tough fixture, but it was something for the fans to look forward to. The Lothian club arrived at Machrihanish Airport to become only the second team in junior cup history to use flight as a means of transport. After the Aberdeen success, hopes were high in the home camp of achieving something really special. The match grabbed the imagination of the public like no other in recent times and even the ex-pats of Corby sent a bus-load of supporters. It was the topic of conversation for weeks on end, so it was no surprise when a capacity crowd turned out for the fixture. Unfortunately, despite wonderful support, the game itself was an anti-climax. Loanhead Mayflower – a great name for a football club – proved too strong on the day and ran out worthy winners by 4 goals to 1. Loanhead reached the semi-finals of the competition, losing narrowly to famous Aberdeen club Banks O' Dee. In May 1957, the team from the 'Granite City' defeated Kilsyth Rangers by 1-0 at Hampden Park in front of 30,800 spectators to lift the Scottish Junior Cup.

Campbeltown United's success in reaching the 5th round was only the third time in more than 20 years that an Argyll club had reached

Campbeltown United, 1957:
Back row, left to right: A Campbell, W Gillespie, D Cook, A McShannon and M McIntyre.
Front row, left to right: J McEwing, T Galbraith, J Robertson, N Campbell, H Thomson and C Farmer. Missing from photo, P McMillan.

this stage of the competition. The record book shows the same club falling at this hurdle against the eventual cup-winners Tranent Juniors in 1935, and fellow-league members Campbeltown Hearts losing at the same stage to Dundee Violet in 1938. The reputation of Kintyre football had been established prior to the First World War with the Academicals, a standard maintained by Campbeltown United with a string of fine performances during the inter-war years. United's match against Loanhead Mayflower signalled the end of an era, the last time a major crowd would press the turnstiles at Kintyre Park.

However, the exploits of Campbeltown United wouldn't slip quietly into history, as local poet/songwriter Willie Mitchell was inspired to update his earlier tribute in salute of a new band of brothers. A football man through and through, Willie Mitchell's verse is a fitting tribute to this fine, old club. In the closing years of the junior game, he kindly revisited his original composition to honour the team of 1956/57. Like the original version, the words are set to the music of the Irish ballad 'The Mountains of Mourne.'

'Campbeltown United'

by Willie Mitchell
(1957 Version)

Oh, boys, this United's a wonderful team,
In Campbeltown football they're always supreme.
They've won lots of medals and cups by the score,
And the boys that they've got now will win them some more.
They travelled well over broad Scotland yestreen,
To meet their opponents in far Aberdeen,
How great was our joy when the message came through,
United victorious by three goals to two.

The critics all told us they hadn't a chance,
That the Mugiemoss lads would lead them a fine dance.
They were fast on the ball; they were sure with the pass,
And the Campbeltown boys weren't in the same class.
But they all determined to give of their best,
And final score shows how they rose to the test,
They caused a sensation, the critics looked blue,
With 'United' victorious by three goals to two.

All praise to the boys who earned glory and fame,
All praise to the courage in winning this game.
Tho' it's only a sport it shows what can be done,
When a hard road's to travel, a goal's to be won.
We hope that this victory will fire them anew,
To bring further fame to the white and the blue,
So I'll give you the toast friends, and then I'll sit down,
Here's to the good old United, the pride o' the town.

The song became a favourite of left-winger Charlie Farmer, a character if ever there was one. Blessed with a good singing voice, he never missed an opportunity to regale his audience with a rendering of the original song: 'Oh boys, this United's a wonderful team; in Campbeltown football they're always supreme.' Nevertheless, 'Feeny' at his mischievous best was not averse to a little poetic licence, sometimes adding his own words in a parody of the original. A player blessed with a sweet left foot, he was also acutely aware that his right 'peg' was merely for standing on. Numerically last on the team-sheet, having sung the praises of the rest of the team, his final words were – 'Last but not least there's 'Feeny' the wit, He's out on the left wing, he's only wan fit.'

Such were the days of junior football and the many characters that coloured the local scene. As I stared down at the result scrawled on the road outside Lipton's Grocery Store – now McKellar's shop – the euphoria of the moment masked the true state of our local game. There were a number of years still to run and there would be other Scottish Cup ties to see, but for me, this particular campaign marked the end of junior football as we had come to know it.

In an effort to stem the tide, a number of volunteers launched the Miners Welfare Youth League in 1958. The aim was to encourage organised football at boys' level, a structure designed as an aid to junior football. Unfortunately, it came too late to save an organisation which was more than a simple football league. Junior football had been the hub of community life in more difficult times, a structure that brought people together and allowed them to express their sense of identity. It is easy with hindsight to offer suggestions of what went wrong, but in the greater scheme of things, nothing could have saved junior football. Times were changing and it had simply run its course. It did survive in areas of population, a structure as strong today as at any time in its history, but the demands of modern living proved too much for smaller communities.

The new miners' boys' league clearly had plenty of support and six clubs were needed to satisfy the demands of 120 youngsters. The under-15s section was served by Glenside, Kintyre, Dalintober and Dalriada, with two clubs, Accies and Rovers, catering for the under 12s. Managed by Charlie Duffy, Glenside proved the strongest team in the first year of competition, winning the league championship and Caskie Cup. Bill Adams and Jimmy Stark's Kintyre FC were runners-up on both occasions. Players involved in the first year of competition are listed below. Memories are made of this:

Glenside: Willie McCormick; Davie Graham, Hughie Colville, Arnie Kelly, Sandy McPherson, Don Thomson; Leonard Gilchrist, Archie Cochrane, Wylie Hume, 'Mike' McGougan, Raymond Lafferty and Lindsay Brown.

Kintyre: George Simpson; Robert Barr, Wylie Connor; Archie Mathieson, Duncan McSporran, Eddie Keith; Jim McKiernan, Jim

Mathie, Alex McKinven, Billy Bruce and Willie McDonald. Young reserves were Alastair McLachlan, Alex Gilchrist, Kenny McKinven and Robert Johnston.

Dalriada: Douglas Hill; Eddie Brodie, Davie Livingstone; Ned McEachran, Malcolm McIntyre, Willie Munro; Alastair Cochrane, Jimmy Simpson, Davie Wilkinson, Malcolm Gilchrist and Robert McKinven.

Dalintober: Hamish Reid; Tommy Kelly, A Scott; J. Cox, G. McKay, J. McGougan; John Reid, Angus McGougan, Archie McPhee, Davie Brodie and Raymond Penman. [44]

Junior football still had a few years to run and in an effort to maintain momentum, United turned to a group of boys to act as a 'feeder team'. Campbeltown United Amateurs were gifted the famous blue jerseys worn against Mugiemoss, but the sudden collapse of junior football prompted the team to reinvent itself as Campbeltown Pupils Amateur Football Club. Hearts re-emerged in the final years of junior football, but the game was no further forward as, in turn, Argyll Colliery decided to 'call it a day'. Three clubs survived into the early 1960s, Drumlemble, Hearts and United, but when the latter was dissolved, the curtain was on its way down.

Unusual was the name of the game when extreme weather threatened to disrupt a Scottish Amateur Cup tie at Kintyre Park. It is a perfect question for a local sports quiz and simply a story too difficult to invent. Can you name the game when 14 were left on the field of play, and no-one was sent off? The answer: a match between Peninver and Saxone Youth of Kilmarnock in 1958. All was well at the start, but as the game progressed the weather deteriorated at an alarming rate. As any local will testify, an easterly wind in winter is a daunting experience in Campbeltown, but if rain is added to the equation, it can become unbearable. However, the players were coping with the conditions, that is, until the temperature dropped and the rain turned to sleet.

One by one, the scantily clad players surrendered to the Arctic conditions, but amidst the chaos one person was oblivious to the situation – the referee! It wasn't long before the ranks were depleted and the last of the spectators huddled in the pavilion watched in disbelief as the match official refused to abandon the game. There was no option but to 'tough it out,' and one after another the players returned to the dressing rooms to add to their clothing. It may appear something of an overstatement, but even the unfurling of a white flag wouldn't have stopped this game! A weird assortment of clothing made the scene more like Hallowe'en than a football match; having lasted this far, the survivors were now determined to complete the 90 minutes. At this point, one of the Peninver players hit on a splendid idea – Pat McMillan appeared wearing a waterproof plastic 'Mac', an almost obligatory piece of rain-wear in the 1950s, under his jersey. It wasn't long before most of the players had copied his example.

Fourteen of the original 22 players survived the ordeal, a match that always springs to mind when the word 'hero' is used with regard to football. So what about the villain of the piece? Having also survived a gruelling 90 minutes, the referee surely comes into the same category, without doubt, but given the circumstances, there was no rush to pin a medal on this man's chest. Although Saxone eventually won the match, after 90 minutes of madness, the result was the least of the players' concerns as they sought the refuge of the pavilion.

As the 1950s moved to their conclusion, local footballer Archie Nimmo signed professional forms with Partick Thistle. Drumlemble-born Archie had played for the local junior side of the same name before moving to Firhill. His new manager was the legendary David Meiklejohn, ex-Glasgow Rangers and captain of Scotland. Archie filled the centre-forward position and celebrated his arrival in senior football with a goal against Third Lanark on 2 January 1960. It was a performance well received by the leading sports writers, including an old friend from school days, Jock MacVicar of the *Daily Express*. He scored again the following week against Aberdeen, this before his third outing against Motherwell ended in a 1-1 draw. The highlight of his career was an appearance against Glasgow Rangers at Ibrox Stadium, against the likes of Eric Caldow, Ian McMillan, Jimmy Millar and Davy Wilson – all superstars of their particular era. Archie Nimmo completed his football odyssey with a spell at Maryhill Juniors.

By 1959, it was crystal clear that the town's renowned junior association was on its last legs, but there was still time for an event that was a first for a local club. Drawn away to St Andrews United in the 3rd round of the Scottish Junior Cup, Drumlemble Juniors chartered a plane to fly from Machrihanish to Fife. The club was always very well organised with Tommy McPherson and Duncan Johnston at the helm, but even by their own high standards, the journey was revolutionary to say the least. The tie was an extremely difficult one for a provincial club and it was no surprise when St Andrews United won the game by 6 goals to 1. Nevertheless, that season the Fife club managed to go all the way to Hampden Park, winning the coveted Scottish Junior Cup with a 3-1 victory over Greenock Juniors. St Andrews also dominated its domestic programme, winning the Fife League, and Fife and Rosslyn Cups in 1959/60. Given the standard of the opposition, the result wasn't that bad after all.

With regular defections taking place across the town's football 'divide', the amateur league and its member-clubs were growing in strength in the wake of the junior demise. A few years earlier – in 1955 – the *Courier* carried an independent view under the pen name 'Mill Dam', an opinion which was eerily prophetic given the circumstances. The anonymous writer bemoaned falling standards and was at pains to say there were too many clubs in relation to population.

Prior to the acceptance of Lochgilphead and Tarbert as members of the CDJFA, the leading players from these communities were already involved with Campbeltown sides. In his opinion, increasing the number of teams diluted the strength of existing teams and contributed to a fall in overall competitive standards. Given that the demise of the junior game corresponded with the gentleman's opinion, with hindsight it now appears an extremely accurate assessment. Nevertheless, although agreeing with the core principle of the statement, with hindsight there appears to have been other contributing factors. The junior association never regained its former status after the withdrawal of the aforementioned clubs, so obviously there were other influences at work. After years of excellent crowds, the junior structure became over-reliant on gate receipts and therefore a fall in numbers through televised sport and changing leisure patterns was financially damaging; participation also declined, more than likely for the self-same reasons. In a sparsely populated area, the changing social landscape destroyed a uniquely introspective and self-dependent junior association – the only one of its kind in the whole of Scotland. An army of armchair sports fans had the final say and, sadly, it was all too much for our historic Campbeltown & District Junior Football Association.

A Club Reborn

The Miners' Welfare Youth League, an initiative of Argyll Colliery workers during the late 1950s, produced a wealth of young players interested in advancing their football education. Unfortunately, all of this was too late to save a junior association now in a state of permanent decline. A combination of circumstances contributed to the creation of a new football identity in the town, the founding of which would have far-reaching consequences in the years ahead.

At a time when the town's historic junior game was racing headlong towards its demise, last gasp efforts were made to save one of its oldest and most renowned football clubs, Campbeltown United Juniors. Bernard McKinven Jnr. – 'Barney' – along with his brother Alex, the author, and brother-in-law Willie Gillespie, joined forces to form an amateur version of the same. A member of United during the 1950s, Willie considered it his duty to lend a hand in the club's darkest hour. The gift of a football strip was gratefully received, and the idea of bridging the gap between the two grades of football was set in motion. The new club was established as a nursery team for its senior counterpart and hopes were high of achieving a reversal of fortunes. Unknown at the time, these well-laid plans were destined to end in tears.

The fledgling club secured a base at St Kieran's Church Hall in Kirk Street, a building better known as 'The League of the Cross' – or 'The League' for short – now the Red Cross Hall. The team was a mixture of youth and experience, the emphasis placed on securing young players capable of making the transition between the two grades of football. Naturally, the team was keen to test its ability against what remained of the town's junior representatives and, surprisingly, the club's first match against Hearts at Kinloch Park produced an unexpected win by 4 goals to 1. The following week the new club achieved a creditable 3-3 draw with Drumlemble Juniors, but these were friendly fixtures and no one had illusions of the size of task that lay ahead.

As summer approached, an application was submitted to the Kintyre Amateur Football League and our club's attendance was requested at the AGM in the Town Hall Council Chambers. Our links to a junior organisation were discussed and although commended, was considered an infringement of the amateur code. We had no option but to dissolve our new identity and were suddenly faced with the dilemma of picking another name for the club – more difficult than it seems when suddenly 'put on the spot.' We struggled to make a decision, but Charlie McFadyen, then secretary of Academicals FC, offered the ideal solution: 'Call your team the Pupils.' He then explained that the Former Pupils had existed as a junior club until the Second World War and, being a well-known name from the past, in terms of identity would suit the purpose perfectly. Therefore, in the most unusual circumstances imaginable, the club known as Campbeltown Former Pupils AFC was reborn without as much as a second thought.

The club made its competitive comeback on 11 May 1961, its first meaningful fixture since disbanding prior to the outbreak of war in 1939. A team of mixed ages discovered a blend to overcome Dalintober Hearts by 6 goals to 1. However, at this point we were blissfully unaware of the new page just written in the history of local football. While restoring a famous name from the town's historic past was one thing, it was unimaginable that this was the start of an unbroken journey of 51 years and the birth of an organisation that in time would scale the heights of the Scottish Amateur Premier League.

Campbeltown Pupils v. Dalintober Hearts, 11 May 1961:

Hamish Colville; Duncan Black, Willie Gillespie; Duncan Hart, Hamish Paterson, Robert Armour; Alex McKinven, Charlie Morrison, Barney McKinven, Harry Maguire and Jim Ingram.

In June 1961, the club progressed to meet Lochend Amateurs in the Civic Cup Final at Kintyre Park. The opposition was organised by Alastair McKinlay, a gentleman better known in recent times as a local Argyll & Bute Councillor. A keen amateur footballer, Alastair was player/manager of a team representing Lochend Church, an impressive building then dominating the skyline at the end of Kinloch Park. The final wasn't memorable by any stretch of the imagination, but the Pupils' 3-1 victory gave the club its first silverware since winning the junior league championship in 1937/38.

Civic Cup Final 1961:

Pupils: Hamish Colville; Duncan Black, Robert Armour; Murray Shaw, Hamish Paterson, Malcolm McDonald; Alex McKinven, Charlie Morrison, Duncan Hart, Barney McKinven, and Jim Ingram.

Lochend: Eric Ireland; Alastair McKinlay, Donald Urquhart; M. Murdoch, Tom McCorkindale, Willie Kelly; David Wilkinson, Arnold Kelly, Dan Galbraith, Richard Dewar and Angus Nimmo.

The 1960s were exciting times, a period christened 'the Swinging Sixties' by a star-struck media. Liverpool became the unlikely capital of 'pop music' and the 'Mersey Sound' took an unsuspecting music world by storm. It was a period blessed with great Scottish football teams, with home-grown players of the highest quality and hardly a foreigner in sight. European trophies found their way to Parkhead and Ibrox – 1967 and 1972 – and an equally brilliant Dundee side reached the semi-final of the European Cup, only to lose to AC Milan. Scotland was the place to be if you wanted the very best in football, something that has changed dramatically over the years.

Like the rest of the nation, football supporters from the 'Wee Toon' revelled in the halcyon days of Scottish football, but all was not well at home. The junior game stumbled towards its demise, hardly earth-shattering when compared to human tragedy, but nevertheless, it was a bitter blow for those who had fought long and hard to retain a game of semi-professional standard in Campbeltown. For many it was the end of a way of life and, after a period of more than half-a-century, the town's ferocious appetite for junior football had been sated. The final chapter was written by the oldest club still standing, Campbeltown Hearts. A troubled organisation since its initial collapse in the mid-1950s, attempts to restore the club's former glory ended in calamitous defeats to both Kirkintilloch Rob Roy and Dundee St Josephs. These two games signalled the end of the town's junior football. The historic Campbeltown and District Junior Football Association had been unceremoniously laid to rest.[45] The magic of junior football at Kintyre Park was now reduced to nostalgic conversations in pubs and clubs, distant memories of leaner times when life was made a little more bearable by the simplest of games.

However, life went on, and there were six amateur clubs still operating in the aftermath of the junior collapse: Peninver, Lochend, Dalintober Hearts, Southend, Academicals and Pupils. All stood to gain from an influx of reinstated talent, but this proved a complex process and clearance was not available until the following season. Meanwhile, Peninver FC was still the team to beat after completing a clean sweep of the trophies in 1960.

The time of Campbeltown Pupils AFC had begun, with an encouraging start by winning the League Championship and Civic Cup in its very first season – 1961/62. The other honours, the Macmaster Campbell and Miners Welfare Cups, went respectively to Charlie McFadyen's Academicals and the ever proficient Peninver FC. The season progressed with the Scottish Amateur Cup, the 'new' club's journey into the unknown put on hold when paired with Peninver in the zoned first round draw. The usual tongue-in-cheek innuendo preceded the tie, not least that the referee had received his normal quota of potatoes, a bit of fun and standard repartee when country faced town in days of yore. Peninver rescued a hard-fought match at Kintyre Park with a last minute penalty kick, and the tie ended in a 3-3 draw.

The replay proved surprisingly straightforward, when in strength-sapping conditions, a much younger Pupils side won the match by 5 goals to 1. Success brought a home tie against Moorpark Amateurs from Govan and another comfortable victory by 4 goals to 1. We now faced our first away tie against Eglinton Amateurs from Kilwinning, a long journey to play one of Ayrshire's top 1st Division sides. We were soundly beaten by a much better side, a sobering experience and our first taste of top grade amateur football. The learning process had just begun.

During the early 1960s, the ever-popular Clyde steamers were still to the fore and the town was a popular destination for summer visitors. The Clyde coast had a special resonance with city-dwellers, and trips 'Doon the Watter' were all the rage until the now imminent coming of the foreign package holiday. Meantime, the town's entertainments officer was still actively involved arranging open-air dances and pop concerts on the Quarry Green, events which were moved to the Victoria Hall when the weather refused to co-operate.

Football held centre-stage three nights a week at Kinloch Park, an area quickly surrounded by spectators when the 'gladiators' appeared. Glasgow Fair brought its own brand of humour to the touchlines: stand-up comedians drawn as if by magnetism to the edge of the playing surface. While it was the era of the mercurial wide-man, the likes of Jimmy Johnstone, Willie Henderson and wonderful Gento of Real Madrid, the wingers' union was alive and well in the less salubrious surroundings of the 'Big Green.' Whether professional or amateur, members of this elite band had one thing in common – a reluctance to share the ball with anyone else. As an 'Old Firm' look-alike shimmied down the wing, his ego was quickly deflated with 'haw wee man, the baw's naw fur eatin'!' Eloquent, certainly not, but a better criticism of the greedy winger is yet to surface.

Kinloch Park was ready-made for the touchline 'wag' and a veritable paradise for practical jokers. The humour was always light-hearted, nevertheless the absence of a barrier contributed to some weird and wonderful happenings. Players in full flight were often sent sprawling by 'ghost tackles' from the depth of the crowd. Frustrated defenders complained bitterly as wingers' became adept at the deft one-two off spectator's legs. Then there was the amazing elastic ball, the one that defied logic by refusing to go out of play. Great fun for the crowd, but complete frustration for participants as the game raged on. Without fail, there was always a stray dog with ball skills infinitely better than his human counterpart, or a posse of people claiming right of way across the playing surface, when the fairer sex was involved – prams included! The backdrop to this chaos was Stringfellows Funfair. Opening hours were accompanied by a constant stream of 'Top of the Pops', and the referee's whistle went unnoticed in an environment better suited to semaphore than his standard issue 'Acme Thunderer'.

At the time, changing facilities were non-existent 'Doon the Green', so the pre-match ritual involved a frantic search for somewhere to leave your clothes. Favourite venues were the Civil Defence Hall in Bolgam Street, the Pipe Band Hall at the Diamond Vault or, if extremely lucky, the Kinloch Mission Hall immediately across from the park. In the case of Peninver, it was the cellar of the Kilbrannan Bar – 'Mitchell's – where an upturned beer case served as a seat.

Young and with plenty of energy, football continued after the match with a game of 'buddies' or 'three and in'. We had no need for a watch, as the descending gloom and acute hunger drove us to nearby 'Glundies' for a fish supper. However, Friday evenings were a different matter completely. The park cleared quickly as our predatory instincts drew us towards the Victoria Hall, the last of our energy spent dancing the night away to chart-topping groups such as Manfred Mann, the Tremeloes or a host of Irish Show Bands, not forgetting local favourites Jay and the Zodiacs. Crowds of 1,000 were commonplace at the 'Vic' during the halcyon days of British pop music. Happy days indeed ...

The absence of Peninver at summer roll-call was a major blow to local amateur football in 1962, but league membership actually increased with the resurrection of Carradale and the appearance of a mixed team of teachers and students from the Grammar School. The long-awaited integration of ex-juniors began and the inclusion of the town's top players improved the standard of competition overnight. At this point, Campbeltown Pupils decided to re-align with the past and restore the club's historical colours – white jerseys, white shorts and red stockings. As older members retired, they were replaced by players from the now defunct junior ranks. Two sets of brothers were the first to arrive: Archie and Alistair McKerral, followed by Leonard and 'Sonny' Gilchrist; a third brother, Malcolm ('Shorty') joined at a later date. The squad was further enhanced by Archie McLellan and 'Nicky' Campbell, bringing the total of ex-junior signings to six. An excellent centre-half was recruited from the now disbanded Peninver FC, the reliable Willie 'Wuff' Anderson. The committee's industrious off-season was immediately rewarded as the club completed a clean sweep of the silverware and were undefeated during the course of 1962/63.

It should have been a memorable year, but personal disappointment followed when I was made redundant from Argyll Colliery. It was the start of staff reductions and five years later the inevitable happened when 'the pit' finally closed its doors. However, it is not my intention to dwell on the negative, only to highlight a place of employment that was unique in its interaction with the local community. It certainly wasn't the best environment in which to work, but there was always a strong sense of camaraderie and cheerfulness among the miners, commendable given the conditions they faced every day. My two short years as a surface worker at Machrihanish gave me an insight into the workings of the wonderful Miners' Welfare, an organisation wholly financed by contributions from employees' wages. Money was of course essential to its survival, but it was the commitment and dedication of individuals that really made the whole thing work.

Nothing was too much for this unique organisation – at its heart the well-being of employees and their dependents. It also embraced the local community, running gala days, picnics and festive parties for the children. It had many other facets, like sport, drama and the arts, coupled with a host of socially-orientated activities. Entertainment was high on the agenda and the Miners Welfare Hall in Bolgam Street was equipped to show live televised football, beamed on to a large screen, as far back as the late 1950s. The 'Miners' Hall' was originally the old Town Court House in Bolgam Street, now in a sad state of dereliction and a shortcoming that reflects badly on our modern day administration.

With the construction of the NATO fuel depot at Glenramskill and the refurbishment of the air base, Campbeltown was a busy place in the early 1960s – all in preparation for the opening of RAF Machrihanish in 1964. Life without junior football was a strange experience and wrestling on 'the box' featuring Mick McManus and company was a poor substitute. Nevertheless, the dark days of winter passed and there was relief all round when the summer fixture list appeared in McIlchere's shop window. Campbeltown Pupils started where it had left off the previous season, adding the Civic Cup to its ever-growing list of trophies. While a 5-2 victory over Glenside Amateurs in the final wasn't unexpected, it heralded the start of a recurring statistic in local football. Like Peninver the previous decade, the Pupils dominated local football in the 1960s, but without fail, a challenge to their supremacy occurred every other year.

After the initial set-back, Glenside A.F.C, a team blessed with a famous old name from the past, set about creating a record or two for themselves. The Dalaruan club never looked back after its early season loss in the Civic Cup Final, maintaining a rich vein of form to win the Macmaster Campbell Cup, Miners Welfare Cup and the KAFL Championship. For reasons unknown, the team was a one-year wonder and failed to reappear after its only season in amateur football. Glenside's make-up was similar to most clubs of the period – a solid base of ex-juniors, interlaced with young players of future potential.

Glenside 1963/64: George Simpson, Dougie McArthur, Duncan Brown, Charlie Morrison, Malcolm 'Maxie' McIntyre, Alex Kennedy, David Wilkinson, Arnold Kelly, Duncan McSporran, Sandy Steele, Peter McPherson, John McMillan, Ian McLellan and Lawrence Robertson.

The Royal Air Force opened its new camp at Machrihanish on June 1 1964, an installation staffed with personnel from far-flung corners of the globe. The military build-up breathed new life into the local economy, with an injection of revenue that sustained the community in the years following the demise of Argyll Colliery. Numbers were few at first: an advance party of trades, security and administration charged with bringing the camp to operational standard. Although 'thin on the ground', the RAF still managed to enter a team in the local football league and, as the base expanded, new faces became well-known around the town. A few made Campbeltown their home in years to come, marrying local girls and settling down to a life in Kintyre. Some of the lads were accomplished players, others unbelievable characters and often a combination of both. Here are some well-known personalities who graced RAF Machrihanish, the majority arriving from the mid-1960s onwards: Bill Hunter, Dick Potts, Alan McGillivray, Bill Young, Frank Blake, Al Laurie, Eddie Fletcher, Ron Bainbridge, John 'Rip' Cord, Matt Dillon, Charlie Stewart, Willie Hepburn, Tom Cummings, Eddie Flood, Alan Terry, Dick McFadzean, Bill Andrew, Pete Todd and Harry Hutchison.

One name is missing from the group, an unbelievable character I have chosen to call 'Bertie'. This gentleman was the most unorthodox serviceman you could ever imagine, a man who epitomised the rebellious fun-loving 1960s. In the days when it was fashionable to wear long hair, he was determined to follow the trend irrespective of his vocation. Military discipline was at a loss when it came to 'Bertie', because he managed to serve 'Queen and Country' with tresses fully intact. Football-mad and a player of real quality, he was someone you would rather have on your side than playing against you. The only flaw in his character was a dislike of authority, quite unusual for someone serving in Her Majesty's Forces.

We 'crossed swords' with 'Bertie' and his RAF buddies on the field of play, but away from the park we were all as 'thick as thieves'. The Junior Ranks Club would organise a bus whenever a 'big match' was due and the transport was used by a cross-section of the town's football fraternity. Of course, we chipped in to help with the costs – an outrageous half-a-crown per head (twelve and a half pence). Heavily subsidised, no wonder these trips were extremely popular. One trip in particular sticks in my mind, a day out to a European match in Glasgow. Everything was running like clockwork and suitably fortified we set off on the return leg home. We had only travelled a few miles when there was consternation at the back of the bus – someone had been left behind! After a few well-chosen expletives, we returned to our departure point in search of the missing passenger, who, as you have probably guessed by now, was the inimitable 'Bertie Boy'. Needless to say, the search proved fruitless.

His absence wasn't appreciated when the bus returned to base, but a few days later, the happy wanderer returned. Being a few miles from home and unable to resist the temptation, he decided to pay his folks an unexpected visit. As expected, 'Bertie' was disciplined and grounded. No more visits to the city for him! A few weeks later another trip was organised for an international match at Hampden Park. The same travel arrangements applied, so we made our way to the base to catch the bus. We were saddened by the absence of 'the wee man', but we realised being in the forces was to learn the hard way. As the bus approached the junction of the 'Drome' road and the A83, the driver was flagged down by a hitch-hiker, well-covered for the rainy weather. Needless to say a great roar went up when we realised who was boarding – sure enough, it was the man himself, 'Bertie'. It may not have been the 'Great Escape', but the best efforts of Her Majesty's Armed Forces were simply not enough to keep this colourful character down.

Campbeltown Pupils once more swept the board in 1964/65. That year the club welcomed a couple of our own characters to the fold, Duncan 'the Laird' McSporran and Tommy 'Iron Man' Kelly. At 16 years of age, Duncan was one of the youngest to play at junior level, but despite his tender years he was a talent that couldn't be ignored. His ability soon alerted Motherwell FC, where he had an extended stay and rubbed shoulders with the legendary Ian St John, Bert McCann, John Martis, etc, a team of stars known collectively after their manager as 'the Ancell Babes'. Duncan had the misfortune to be plagued by a knee injury and a recurrence at a critical time finished his hopes of senior football. With a clean bill of health, many believe he would have carved out a considerable career in the professional game. Although small in stature, he was fast, tenacious, and had skill in abundance. Duncan McSporran was arguably the finest local player of his generation and even his time in amateur football was cut short by injury.

Tommy Kelly, as his nick-name suggests, was a player in the mould of Tommy Smith of Liverpool or Norman Hunter of Leeds United. While he was more than happy to wear the label as a badge of courage, nevertheless, there was a lot more to his game than mere strength. Part of a football-minded family, his brothers Donnie, Willie and Arnie were similarly-accomplished in their own right. Tommy's claim to fame was to attract the attention of the inimitable Brian Clough, one of the greatest managers of the modern era. At the time in charge of Hartlepool United, Brian invited Tommy for trials and he set off with high hopes of making the grade. He exceeded expectations by scoring twice for the reserves in a 4-2 win and was immediately offered amateur terms with the North-East club. However, Tommy was a man on a mission and his straightforward response was echoed in the following week's local newspaper – 'It's Professional or Nothing'.[46] In the end, it didn't work out, but there are few who can say they played for the irrepressible Brian Clough!

Another fine player to join the club around the same period was Archibald 'Mike' McGougan. Comfortable on either side of the mid-field, you could describe him as a strolling player reminiscent of the style of the famous Jim Baxter of Glasgow Rangers. Mike was a class act, a man who could place the ball on a sixpence for your convenience. He was one of a number of fine players from Campbeltown never to come under the scrutiny of the senior scouting system. Mike tragically died in a boating accident, a young man whose talent lives on, if only in memory of happier times. Angus McGougan – Gus, a brother of the aforementioned – was also a fine player for the club. Gus was one of the 'stars' of the school team and progressed seamlessly into amateur football.

Unashamedly biased, for me the 1960s was a fabulous decade to watch football, starting with one of the greatest spectacles ever witnessed – the European Cup Final between Real Madrid and Eintracht Frankfurt at Hampden Park. It was an unbelievable performance by the Spanish champions, a glorious attacking display reminiscent of an age soon to disappear. Ten goals were scored as the legendary De Stefano and Puskas destroyed the Germans in a 7-3 victory, a performance ably assisted by a team of the highest calibre, including a genius of an outside-left called Francisco Gento.

Another fantastic memory was the Scotland v. England match at Hampden Park on 2 April 1966. Unshackled by modern tactics, it was attacking football at its very best. Joined by my friends Charlie Morrison and Leonard Gilchrist, we watched with 130,000 others as the game ended in England's favour by 4 goals to 3. While the sole purpose of the visit was to see the 'Auld Enemy' beaten, football was the winner long before the final whistle sounded. The presence of great players dissolved the barriers of bias and, on a wet Saturday afternoon at Hampden Park, the pick of the bunch were Bobby Charlton, Bobby Moore, Denis Law and the effervescent Jimmy Johnstone. However, my patriotic blindfold was removed for 90 minutes only, as like every other Scotland supporter, it was firmly back in place for the World Cup later that same year.

This period was a watershed in modern football, as until now no-one had heard of a 4-4-2 system. If it was on view at Hampden Park that afternoon, it certainly wasn't obvious to me. However, after an uninspiring opening draw against Uruguay, the England manager Alf Ramsey switched to the new system and won the World Cup with his 'Wingless Wonders'. It was the beginning of defence-minded counter-attacking football, but there were notable exceptions such as Glasgow Celtic's swashbuckling style when winning the European Cup in 1967 and the exploits of a wonderful Brazilian team in the World Cup of 1970. The day of the super-coach had arrived and players became efficient in the art of denying space. Fitness was honed to hitherto unknown levels, creating the athleticism needed for tactical domination. Numbers behind the ball became the name of the game, and safety was followed by lightning-quick counter-attacks – the sign of things to come.

There were, of course, extremes such as Helino Herrera's infamous 'Catenaccio', an ultra-defensive system employed by Inter Milan. Reviled throughout the world, in terms of defensive tactics it was the equivalent of opening 'Pandora's Box'. However, speaking as a member of the Tartan Army, it was a joy to watch Alf Ramsey's revolutionary system destroyed by unadulterated skill. It may have been good enough to win the World Cup, but in the interest of southern fans of a nervous disposition, no mention will be made of the score at Wembley in 1967.

Although deserting local football for a moment or two, I feel it's important to mention the sweeping changes taking place in the professional game. But what was happening in Campbeltown with all this modernisation? Very little is the simple answer. Football in Kintyre was comfortably cocooned in the past and had no intention of following the latest trends, at least not for the time being anyway.

The new season set the stage for a young side called Kinloch Thistle. Most of the team had cut their teeth the previous year at Southend – winning the Macmaster Campbell Cup in the process – but a year older and physically stronger, it was time for a new club to make its mark on local football. Playing an attractive brand of attacking football, Kinloch Thistle deservedly won three of the four competitions in 1965/66. It was a lean season for the town's most successful club, a year in which the Pupils had to settle for winning the Miners Welfare Cup only. In different circumstances, the lads of Kinloch Thistle could have gone on to bigger and better things, but the club surprisingly disbanded a few games into the new season. It was extremely disappointing to lose such a good young side and lack of off-field organisation appears to have been at the root of the problem. I'm sure the mention of this particular team will bring back a few memories.

Kinloch Thistle (1965): George Simpson; Archie Johnstone, David Livingstone; Jim Martin, Robert Campbell, Charlie Morrison; Calum McLean, Alistair McLachlan, Duncan Hart, Leonard Gilchrist and Robert McKinven.
Club colours: White.

Around this time, news arrived from Australia of an ex-pat who had just become the *Soccer News* player of the year for 1965. Well-known in local football, Tommy McPherson had originally played for Drumlemble Juniors and, on moving to Glasgow, turned out for Bellshill Juniors, Blantyre Victoria and Linlithgow Rose. He then moved to Australia where he signed on at George Cross, a club of Maltese extraction competing in the Victoria State League. He was part of a side which won the Australian Cup and twice finished runners-up in the league championship.[47] Tommy was also awarded the '*Maltese Herald* Best and Fairest Award' in recognition of his contribution to football 'Down Under'. He returned home to play and coach at Campbeltown Pupils, bringing with him some revolutionary ideas gleaned from his time abroad. He later became a founder-member of Campbeltown Boys Football Club, a team whose origins lay in the association of the same name.

The roots of the McPherson family are firmly planted in the soil that is Campbeltown football. Tommy's brother Sandy McPherson also left his mark on the game by signing for Morton and St Mirren. He then became Head of Physical Education at Campbeltown Grammar School, replacing the popular figure of Johnny Burgoyne, a star performer at inside forward with Campbeltown Hearts in the 1930s. Sandy's commitment to the game was further evidenced when he introduced a number of local school boys to the ranks of Drumchapel Amateurs. He was personally involved driving the boys to and from Glasgow every Saturday for their games and without his dedication, many would have missed out on an experience of a lifetime.

Of course, all of this didn't happen by chance, as their father Tommy McPherson Senior, along with good friends Duncan Johnston, Donnie Paterson and Angus Munro, were inspirational in running the post-war Drumlemble Juniors. Tommy McPherson Senior played as a member of the original Campbeltown Grammar School FPs in 1919.

After a period of settling in, RAF Machrihanish was now producing teams of a very good standard, but Campbeltown Pupils AFC were back on top form and by late summer of 1966 had secured the first three competitions of the season: the Civic Cup, Miners Cup and League. Now 'done and dusted', another clean sweep looked on the cards for the local champions, but a fast-improving RAF fancied their chances in the last competition of the year – the Macmaster Campbell Cup. The teams came face-to-face in the semi-final of the competition, a perfect opportunity for the airmen to justify their new-found confidence. It was a tie of mixed emotions, often explosive, sometimes controversial, but at all times fiercely competitive. It was a marathon affair of four matches, not forgetting a period of extra time, and, more disturbingly, some unwanted front-page headlines. However, football back then was a game of passion as well as skill – a spectacle more carnivorous than its modern 'thespian' counterpart.

Played on a 'home and away' basis, the first match at Kinloch Park produced a narrow 2-1 win for the Pupils. The second game at RAF Machrihanish was also a tight affair, this time ending in a 3-3 draw. Both ties were fiercely-contested, but the end result was an aggregate 5-4 win for the Campbeltown side. That appeared the end of story, but the tie escalated to another level when the RAF lodged a protest over an ineligible player. The problem involved the disbanding of Kinloch Thistle and the subsequent distribution of club players. According to the RAF, the transfer window of four weeks had been breached by the signing of an individual from aforementioned. It was controversial to say the least, as the rule clearly referred to operational clubs and Kinloch Thistle no longer existed – all of their players having been snapped up by other league sides, RAF included. However, the protest was upheld on the basis of the unintentional use of an ineligible player. The Pupils were stunned by the decision.

In fairness, there was probably a feeling of injustice in both camps and the replay promised to be a real grudge affair. What followed could only be described as a 'battle with boots on', a cross between 'Custer's Last Stand' and 'The Gunfight at the OK Corral'. Although the game was never dirty, as a spectacle it was a firecracker – not for the faint-hearted – as tackles flew in from start to finish. Further problems materialised when the match ended in a 2-2 draw and confusion reigned when the referee insisted on playing extra time. An explanation that the aggregate score was 4-3 to the Pupils went unheard and the official insisted on playing an extra 30 minutes. At that, the players reluctantly returned to the park.

Campbeltown Pupils AFC v Viewfield Rovers, Scottish Amateur Cup, 1967.
Back row, left to right: T Scott (Trainer), W Monteith, T Kelly, A Brodie, J McKinnon, M McGougan, D Brown and B McKinven (Manager). Front row, left to right: A McKinven, C Morrison, D Wilkinson, D McKinnon and C McLean.

A few minutes later, Bill Hunter – the hardest striker of a ball in local football – scored a tremendous goal to put the RAF deservedly ahead on the night. From the restart, the Pupils launched forward and were immediately awarded a corner-kick. The atmosphere crackled with a feeling of injustice and tempers began to fray as players jostled for position inside the box. A phalanx of bodies attacked the in-swinging corner-kick, a forward rush that carried the goalkeeper, a few strategically-placed defenders and the ball into the back of the net. The match descended into chaos and all hell was let loose. As both teams scrapped it out in the congested goal net, the referee made a quick exit from the park, his best decision of the night – Match abandoned and front page ignominy awaited![48]

A meeting of the league committee agreed that the controversial extra-time should not have taken place. Was that the end of story? Certainly not – the game was ordered to be replayed for a second time. The biggest crowd of the season turned out to watch the never-ending cup-tie, but this time round it was a bit of a damp squib. Pupils won a tame affair by 5 goals to 2 – thankfully, after 367 minutes the cup-tie eventually had a winner. Friendship survived these moments of on-field madness, but there was a distinct feeling of anti-climax among the spectators when the anticipated bloodbath never materialised. The Pupils later defeated Lochend in the final of the competition.

Pupils: Angus Brodie; Les McMillan, Davie Livingstone; 'Mike' McGougan, Jake McKinnon, Willie Watters; Alex McKinven, Leonard Gilchrist, Tommy Kelly, Duncan McKinnon and Malcolm Gilchrist.

RAF: Ron Bainbridge; Archie Johnstone, T. Williams; Larry Kinsella, Robert Campbell, H. Swanson; Alastair McLachlan, A. McBain, D. O'Neill, Bill Hunter and Danny Brady.

It was a remarkable year, as Paul McCartney caused a sensation when he bought High Park Farm. He later paid a visit with actress/girlfriend, Jane Asher, the perfect opportunity for Kintyre's equivalent of the Paparazzi to get on the case. Enter ace reporter of the *Campbeltown Courier*, the indefatigable Freddy Gillies. When the promise of an interview failed to materialise, Freddy decided to do what reporters do best – he invited himself. The journey to the farm had the hallmark of a military operation and, accompanied by

RAF Machrihanish – 1967/68

two friends, he set off to try to get the story of a lifetime –'Through Bogs and Bracken'.[49] However, things came unstuck when they fell foul of the irate farmer. The party was reduced by one when the driver of their vehicle beat a hasty retreat, leaving the remnants of the expedition to walk the rest of the way. Their determination was rewarded with not only the treasured interview, they also secured a meal in recognition of their sterling efforts. The *Courier* was a colourful read during Freddy's time as reporter, especially his descriptive coverage of football. He also was a bit of a player, a flying winger with Dalriada Thistle and the Youth Club. 'A regular scorer of spectacular goals from impossible angles', he was first to admit that writing the reports himself was a major advantage!

RAF Machrihanish gained revenge when a rejuvenated eleven won the first two trophies of the new 1967/68 season. Team manager Joe Beals had the foresight to strengthen his squad with the signings of 'Mike' McGougan and Leslie McMillan, both men joining 'forces' with the other civilian in the squad, Archie Johnstone. The RAF gained its first ever domestic success by defeating the newly-formed Caledonia AFC in the Civic Cup Final by 4 goals to 1. The Miners Welfare Cup also found its way to the Base and both trophies were displayed in the guardroom at the station's entrance, a clever piece of psychology as teams entered the "Lion's Den". Playing football on a calm summer's evening at 'the Drome' was a joy, with pitches maintained to the highest quality and hospitality every bit as good. While there was a host of social clubs at the station, the Junior Ranks Club or NAFFI was our normal port of call after 90 minutes' exertion.

RAF Machrihanish: Dick Potts, Ron Bainbridge, J. Weir, J. Richardson, Gary Williams, Leslie McMillan, 'Mike' McGougan, Archie Johnstone, Bill Hunter, Al Lawrie, Danny Brady and Willie Hepburn.
Manager: Joe Beals.

As mentioned previously, the dominance of the Pupils FC was regularly challenged during this period, but for some reason these efforts were extremely short-lived. This was particularly true of Glenside, Kinloch Thistle and, at a later date, Caledonia Athletic, all with life-spans of no more than two or three seasons. Despite this anomaly, the closing years of the decade were the most competitive the Kintyre Amateur Football League had ever experienced. The new season 1967/68 was as competitive as ever, probably too much, as after a spate of abandoned fixtures, the league's management committee called for sanity with a simple but direct message, 'Keep it clean or Go'.[50]

The RAF failed to reach the next cup-final, their place being taken by the season's shock troops, Campbeltown Youth Club. The boys from the Christian Institute produced the upset of the year with an unlikely 2-1 victory over the Pupils in the Macmaster Campbell Cup Final. Holding their own in a seven-team league, the Youth Club's victory demonstrated the competitive nature of local football at this time. Nevertheless, a few days later the Pupils claimed their fifth league championship in seven years with a thumping 8-0 win over Largieside at Tayinloan. The West-Kintyre village would in time become an extremely difficult place to visit, the club revived with a new generation of talent in Duncan Johnstone, John Rennie, Murdo Thomson, John Smart, Campbell MacDonald and the Mitchell brothers from Muasdale, to name but a few of a very good squad.

A designated NATO installation, the presence of RAF Machrihanish helped to broaden the horizon of local football. Countless military exercises brought a flood of overseas personnel to the base, a presence that gave local football a cosmopolitan feel. Dutch and Norwegian personnel were particularly fond of their football and a number of 'internationals' were played on the wide expanse of the Laggan Moss. There was also the occasional week-end tournament to add to the excitement – one in particular springs to mind, a four-cornered event involving RAF Kinloss from the Morayshire Junior League, Johnstone Burgh of the Central Scottish Junior League, Campbeltown Pupils and the hosts, RAF Machrihanish. RAF Machrihanish beat Kinloss 2-0, a shock for the much larger air base, but there was another upset when Campbeltown Pupils defeated Johnstone Burgh by 4 goals to 1. It was great to see the two local sides qualify for the final, the score somewhat irrelevant as Kintyre football had already proved its point.

There were seven entries for the following season's competitions – 1968/69 – Dalriada Thistle, Largieside, Southend, Youth Club, Pupils, RAF and Caledonia Athletic. The emergence of Caledonia as a serious contender for the trophies coincided with an unlikely merger of interests, the club's association with local businessman, Jack McKinven. He was a colourful character, a man of intelligence and versatility who had a great love for his home town. Jack's talents were legion; he was a storyteller, columnist, historian, sign-writer, amateur film-maker, entertainments promoter, as well as an outspoken critic in the columns of the local 'rag'. He also ran a small grocery business at 11 Saddell Street, and in his 'spare time' organised the charity Bingo in the Good Templars Hall.

It was a complete surprise when Jack became involved in local football, but he went about his new task with enthusiasm. He helped to put the club on a better financial footing; once achieved, he lambasted the Town Council for failing to provide changing accommodation at Kinloch Park. A lengthy eighty plus years had elapsed since the area's recovery from the old 'Mussel Ebb' and still nothing had been done to provide basic changing accommodation. Jack was a compulsive writer of letters to the press and a dictionary was prerequisite to deciphering his educated text. He constantly hounded the Council on the subject and his efforts were instrumental in highlighting the problem.

After the centralisation of local government in the early 1970s, new changing accommodation was provided at the park. Given the time spent in trying to get these facilities, it's always a source of annoyance to witness the mindless vandalism inflicted on this building.

Caledonia Thistle won the inaugural Dalriada Cup in 1968/69, the club's first success since joining the amateur football league. Donated by Alex McMillan of the Man's Shop in Main Street, the cup replaced the Sheriff Macmaster Campbell Cup, now returned to the newly-reformed Country League. The Macmaster Campbell Cup is actually called the South Kintyre Sports Council Challenge Football Cup, a trophy won by Auchencorvie United in the first two years of competition, 1921 and 1922. Campbeltown Pupils continued on their merry way winning the League Championship and Civic Cup, with the Youth Club making its mark by claiming the Miners Welfare Cup.

Under the management of Jimmy Taylor, the team affectionately know as 'the Caley' came into its own during the summer of 1969, nevertheless, the RAF got off to a 'flier' by beating them in the Civic Cup Final by 1-0. The 'Caley's' progress was rapid and those of a nervous disposition covered their eyes when the local 'big guns' went head to head – not surprising, the Caley v. Pupils derbies were not for the faint-hearted. When these two flexed their muscles, the *Courier* always had a field-day. The teams met in the Miners Cup Final, a fractious affair which went the way of the Caley by 3 goals to 2 – 'The Angry Cup Final'.[51] Both teams then made it to the Dalriada Cup Final, predictably another 'Titanic' struggle with the Caley

Auchencorvie United with Macmaster–Campbell Cup, 1921.

once more edging it by 5 goals to 4. A bone-crunching league game followed – the score reversed as the Pupils claimed victory by 5 goals to 4. The destination of the league championship now hinged on the last meeting between the clubs, with only a win good enough for the 'Caley.' However, the crucial encounter ended in a 2-2 draw and the Pupils claimed their seventh league title in nine years.

Caledonia: Angus Brodie (G), Brian Watters (G), David McEachran, Robert Anderson, 'Mike' McGougan, Leslie McMillan, Ronnie Brown, Willie McMillan, Jim McEwing, Calum McLean, Charlie Morrison, Leonard Gilchrist, Jack McGeachy and Neil McGeachy.

Pupils: Ron McLean (G), Ian McGregor (G), Duncan McSporran, David Livingstone, Jim Martin, Jake McKinnon, Ronnie McCallum, Alex McKinven, Andy 'Jap' Campbell, Robert 'Choc' Campbell, Duncan McKinnon, Wylie Hume, Peter Thomson, Robert 'Doodie' Cameron and Archie 'Goochie' Cunningham.

Andy Campbell and Archie Cunningham hailed from Ardrishaig. Robert Cameron and Ian McGregor were from Lochgilphead.

Both clubs had considerable success against teams from outside Kintyre, but one match in particular would prove unique, Campbeltown Pupils versus Clydebank in the 1969/70 Scottish Amateur Cup. This match gave an old acquaintance the chance to revisit the scene of his playing career, as the manager of the visiting club was none other than Jimmy Kinloch, one-time player with Campbeltown United Juniors. As junior football neared its end, Campbeltown United decided to strengthen their squad by signing two players from Clydebank Juniors, Coyle and Kinloch. Both played for Campbeltown United in the club's last appearance in the Scottish Junior Cup, a narrow 3-2 defeat to Kirrie Thistle in 1958. Jimmy's sentimental return to his old stamping ground was of course coincidental, but it was a reminder of the level of ambition that existed in our own junior set-up and the surprising lengths it would go to achieve success.

As the 1960s neared their end, Kintyre Park hosted a special match in which a town select provided the opposition for Drumchapel Amateurs under-18s, a team which had just won the Dutch International Tournament. In the days prior to professional

Drumchapel Amateurs – 1969

youth teams, Drumchapel Amateurs was the country's main source of emerging talent. The club became a Europe-wide phenomenon, an amateur organisation that represented Scotland against the very best the Continent could muster, a 'who's who' including the likes of Benfica, AC Milan and Barcelona. In other words, the task facing the local select was daunting to say the least. League President, Alastair McKinlay, acted as team manager for the day and quite an experience it turned out to be.

The reason for the visit was simple: Douglas Smith – the founder of Drumchapel Amateurs – had a strong affinity with Kintyre, in particular Neil Watson's Ardnacross Farm at Peninver. It was here that the 2nd Glasgow BB Company had held its camp every summer since 1952. The camp became a halfway house for a cross-section of the Drumchapel youth team, extremely talented boys from 15 to 18. However, this was the real thing, the best the club could muster. A large crowd turned out for the occasion, a game in which the home players were determined not to be over-run by their illustrious opponents. It also was a day when 'the hatchet was buried' and Campbeltown's two main protagonists – 'Caley' and 'Pupils' – joined forces to keep the town's football reputation intact.

If the visitors thought it would be easy – they were in for a major shock. The Select drew first blood when a through-ball sent Robert Campbell free behind a square defence, and drawing the advancing goalkeeper, he sent an unstoppable shot into the bottom corner for the opening goal. Minutes later the visitors should have been further behind. Jim McEwing – later to sign for St Johnstone – raced clear on the right to send a thunderous drive off the outside of the upright. Playing tidy possession football, Drumchapel dragged themselves back into the match when inside-left Hendrie equalised from close range at the Pavilion end.

The game was played like a cup-tie and the action swung from end to end as both teams tried to gain the initiative. The second goal was almost identical to the first, Robert Campbell racing on to a through-ball to slam the ball past the stranded goalkeeper and restore the home side's lead. Back came Drumchapel in a terrific game of football, Hendrie notching his second of the match with the equaliser 15 minutes from the end. Chances were missed at either end as both teams refused to settle for the draw, but a touch of pure class won the match in the dying minutes – gathering the ball on the attacking left, Hendrie cut inside to curl a magnificent shot into the far corner of the net, his hat-trick and a goal fit to win any match!

Defeat for the home side was hardly deserved, a sickening feeling only experienced by players who have given everything. However, there was some consolation in the after-match reaction of the visitors' management. Drumchapel's Doug Smith remarked that, 'Campbeltown has very good players – they surprised us'. The local newspaper repeated this sentiment in the following week's sports headlines 'Select Surprise Glasgow Stars'.[52] The 1960s was a particularly strong period for local amateur football, and it's safe to say a number of combinations could have been picked to carry the banner of local football. Man of the match was the home side's centre-half Les McMillan. Three of the visitors later signed for Glasgow Rangers, namely McWilliams, Morrison and hat-trick hero Hendrie.

Campbeltown: A. Brodie (Caley), R. Anderson (Caley), and C. Morrison (Caley); M. McGougan (Caley), L. McMillan (Caley) and R. Brown (Caley); A. McKinven (Pupils), J. McEwing (Caley), R. Campbell (Pupils), J. Martin (Pupils) and P. Thomson (Pupils).

Drumchapel: McWilliams, Campbell and Savage; Sweeny, Henry and Monteith; Banks, Morrison, Tytler, Hendrie and Chisholm.

Drumchapel Amateurs, in tandem with its founding satellite organisation, the 2nd Glasgow Boys' Brigade, made regular trips to Kintyre over a period of 30 plus years, circa 1952 to 1985. It is fitting, therefore, that our story continues with a tribute to a man whose mission in life was to provide a finishing school for young amateur football players. Under his guidance, many matured to become icons of the professional game, first as players with the country's top sides, and later in management with success on a spectacular level. I refer to Douglas Smith – Mr Drumchapel Amateurs.

A Man For All Seasons

A milestone in Scottish football was created when the redoubtable Mr Douglas Smith decided to take the reins of the 2nd Glasgow Boys Brigade Company in the early 1950s. You can walk through the hallowed halls of Hampden Park and never trace a single footprint of this unsung hero, but I believe this is the way he would have wanted it. Writing about some one from Cardross on the banks of the Clyde may seem strange when relating a story of Campbeltown football, but this man and his remarkable club were inextricably linked with our community at the time of their successful journey through the world of youth football.

Invalided out of the army in 1949, Douglas Smith was handed the job of reorganising the local BB football team, a task he undertook with the same missionary zeal that would later be a feature of his life organising the finest youth team in the country. He soon discovered a latent talent among the younger members of the group and immediately laid the foundations of a club that would later become a well-spring of talent for the professional game. No Murray Park or Lennoxtown in these days, just hard work and a burning ambition to breed success and have young charges move on to greater things.

A 'wha's like us' attitude existed in post-war British football and, at a time when our Continental 'cousins' were planting the seeds of future success, we were firmly rooted in the mire of our own self-importance. We were top of the world and didn't need a FIFA-sponsored tournament to prove it – or so we thought! As ever, the streets provided a limitless supply of talent and there was no reason to change something that had been successful for generations.

British football failed to recognise that as post-war living standards improved, greater choice would alter the leisure patterns of the people. Television brought entertainment into the home – for families, an opportunity to spend their free time in front of 'the box'. Cars dominated the tarmac and the sound of laughter disappeared from streets that were once the playground of the nation. Football was the biggest loser and, as never before, the future of the game depended on organisation.

Douglas Smith was a visionary, an ambitious, single-minded man who set about creating a system unrivalled in post-war Britain. He gathered together a group of trusted 'lieutenants' and joined the SAFA in 1950. It was a far-sighted plan involving no fewer than four separate teams of under-15, 16, 17 and 18 years of age. His club became a force to be reckoned with and as senior football slumbered, he produced a football entity recognised and respected throughout Britain and mainland Europe, the once famous Drumchapel Amateurs.

Of course, all of this was a far cry from the club's humble origins, the 2nd Glasgow Boys Brigade and its association with Neil Watson's Ardnacross Farm at Peninver. This idyllic setting on Kintyre's eastern shore became the site of the company's annual summer camp, a popular destination for countless youngsters from 'new Drumchapel', a post-war public housing estate on the western edge of the city. The BB contained players from many of the team's age groups, but the camp also welcomed the 'stars' of tomorrow, a bunch of talented youngsters with no brigade connection. Campbeltown benefited from this association and during the 'Glasgow Fair Fortnight' many a future household name cut his teeth 'doon the Green' or on the wide swathe of Kintyre Park.

On the club's first visit to the town in 1952, Drumchapel played an experienced Drumlemble Juniors at Kintyre Park and won by 3 goals to 2. It was the beginning of a close relationship with the town which lasted almost 50 years. Kintyre had its very own reservoir of football talent, an untapped supply often used by Douglas to our mutual advantage. Through the years, a number of local players made the journey to Glasgow to wear the colours of Drumchapel Amateurs and one in particular made a lasting impression, Wylie Hume. His commitment to the cause is remembered in the club's 50th Anniversary Magazine, an accolade better delivered in Douglas Smith's own words. Recalling his favourite moments he said: 'This lad came from Campbeltown and used to make his way to our games by a wonderful variety of routes and transportation. Wylie would get a lift from a fish lorry that left Campbeltown every Friday at noon. He would stay overnight with relatives in Glasgow, play for us on the Saturday, and leave to return home on Sunday morning on the bread van. And do you know something? – he never once asked us for expenses.' Wylie's expeditions to Glasgow were labours of love, journeys which were more difficult in the 1960s than now. A stylish performer, he had balance, pace, and skill in abundance, some of the attributes that carried him to Newcastle United on trial.

In the same magazine, the story of Drumchapel Amateurs continued with an honourable mention for another local man, Sandy McPherson, Head of Physical Education at Campbeltown Grammar School. His profession was ideal for gauging the strength of emerging talent and he kindly gave up his own leisure time to drive the boys to and from Glasgow to augment the ranks of the famous youth team. He was also a member of the club's coaching staff on regular trips to Iceland, a travel experience shared by a number of players from Campbeltown. These expeditions could be regarded as missionary work, as the Icelandic FA was in its infancy and obviously delighted to have assistance from the famous Glasgow 'youth academy'. This relationship resulted in a second Viking invasion of Kintyre, this when the Icelandic youth champions Keflavik Throttur played here in 1975. It was a particularly strong period for local under-age football and Campbeltown Boys Football Association played host to both the USA under-16s national team and a top quality Canadian club in the space of a few weeks.

A few years later, Campbeltown Pupils AFC had good reason to be grateful for the support of Douglas Smith. The local club's original application for membership of the Scottish Amateur Football League fell on deaf ears, so it was very clear that some one needed to champion the cause. That person was, of course, Douglas Smith. He immediately offered to back our application as a character sponsor and the rest, as they say, is history. His support had far-reaching consequences for football in Kintyre, as the breakthrough allowed other clubs to follow a similar path. In the coming years, Carradale, Tarbert and Campbeltown Boys also gained membership and it is almost certain that none of this would have happened without the intervention of Douglas Smith.

As the years passed, Drumchapel went from strength to strength – the under-18s breaking all records to win the Scottish Cup no fewer than 10 times. Although a tremendous achievement, it paled into insignificance compared with the under-16s. The youngsters won the national trophy no fewer than 17 times in 20 years, an astonishing achievement. The number of players who turned senior soon reached legendary proportions and the last count was around 300. Here are some of the better-known names: Alex Willoughby, Jim Forrest, George McLean, Archie Gemmill, John Robertson, Asa

Hartford, John Wark, Eddie McCreadie, Stevie Archibald, Andy Gray, Tommy Craig, Alex Miller, David Moyes, Jim Cruikshank, Iain Munro, John McCormack, Bobby Hope, Paul Wilson, Tony Green, John O'Hare, John Colrain and, lest we forget, Sir Alex Ferguson. Thirty of 'the Drum' went on to play for Scotland at full international level.

At a time when the future of Scottish football was left in the hands of the 'butcher, baker and candlestick-maker', Douglas Smith designed a successful system to be copied in years to come by professional clubs. It is hard to believe this was an amateur organisation, albeit the most famous unattached boys' club in Europe. Football in this country failed to recognise the sweeping changes taking place in the game, a coaching revolution that destroyed the myth of British superiority. The leading continental clubs had their own professional youth academies, harnessing talent at an early age and coaching it to the highest level. An academic education was also provided by the top European clubs, a system that still bears fruit for great names like Barcelona and Real Madrid. It is little wonder football in this country fell behind.

Unable to match the financial clout of such illustrious company, working within its means, Drumchapel flew the flag for British football. The club was invited to international youth tournaments the length and breadth of Europe, to Holland, Germany, Denmark, Sweden, Iceland, Italy and Yugoslavia. Household names provided the opposition: Inter Milan, Torino, Roma, Lazio, Napoli, Fiorentina, Benfica, Panathanaikos, Partizan Belgrade, Eintracht Frankfurt and Gothenburg, a list which also included the national sides of East Germany, Algeria and Senegal.

Drumchapel crossed swords with some of the world's greatest clubs and the pride of Glasgow and Scotland was more than capable of holding its own. The Scots youngsters won 11 international tournaments on their travels, a feat unlikely to be repeated by any other domestic club in the foreseeable future. True ambassadors, Drumchapel Amateurs were the only football organisation, apart from the 'Lisbon Lions' of 1967, to win the coveted Glasgow Lord Provost's Trophy for meritorious athletic achievement. While all this was taking place, unbelievably, senior football in this country was still without a professional youth system. When this eventually happened it was the end of Drumchapel as we had come to know it.

By the 1980s, boys' teams started to appear under the banner of senior clubs, many from the English Football League. It was a well-intentioned exercise, but at best a token gesture compared to the giant strides taken across continental Europe. Nevertheless, the lure of playing for clubs associated with their idols, especially Rangers and Celtic, would prove irresistible. Drumchapel found it impossible to compete with the charismatic names of the senior game, the best players entering the controversial government Youth Training Scheme. It was a bitter-sweet end to the club's involvement in youth football, realisation that professional football was moving in the right direction, but still without the commitment needed to reinvent our domestic game. Unable to influence the game at youth level and after a period in the SAFL, Douglas Smith introduced his latest brainchild – the Caledonian Amateur Football League.

In 1983, he created a system to improve conditions within the amateur game. Players could now play on the best grass surfaces and enjoy proper changing facilities. His idea was initially frowned upon as elitism, but it soon attracted a host of the best organised clubs from around the country. Campbeltown Pupils were invited to join his revolutionary set-up, but as members of the Scottish Amateur Football League, we wanted to remain faithful to the organisation which had given us our chance in competitive football. The success of the new system forced others to have a hard look at their product and almost every other league in the country used Douglas Smith's template to improve – our own SAFL included.

Drumchapel Football Club celebrated its 50th anniversary at the Moat House Hotel Glasgow on 7 October 2000, a glittering occasion attended by a 'Who's Who' of Scottish football. The occasion was originally planned for the White Hart Hotel in Campbeltown, but arrangements went slightly askew when 600 applied to attend. It was a chance to honour not only the most famous youth club in Scottish football history, but also the man who helped so many youngsters to scale the heights. Campbeltown was represented by a group of ex-players who travelled to take part in the club's special day, but there was also a real desire to honour the commitment of its founder, Douglas Smith.

That night, his life's work was reflected upon by his greatest ever protégée, a man who had himself attained the status of football legend – Sir Alex Ferguson. He considered his former mentor to be 'indefatigable' ... unflagging or tireless. He also referred to him as a football purist, a man who insisted that the game was invented for a single purpose – to entertain. Sir Alex paid tribute to his learning years at Drumchapel and gave thanks to a man who, above all others, had shaped his future. He remembered, as a boy, that 'Douglas Smith cut an impressive figure and was a character who wanted his team to be the best at everything. If we had been a tiddlywinks outfit, we would have to be the best in the land. I realised this was the right way, and would like to think that I have not let him down' – definitely the understatement of the century!

Formalities completed, I managed to have a few words with Douglas as the night came to an end and, as usual, he deflected the attention away from himself and let the spotlight fall on the club. After a few moments of quiet reflection he suddenly said, 'Do you know I really miss our summer trips to Campbeltown and the great times we spent at Ardnacross Farm.' It was the last time I ever spoke to him, as Douglas passed away in February 2004 at the age of 76. A few months later, in May of the same year, his beloved Drumchapel Amateurs won the Scottish Amateur Cup at Hampden Park – the club's first major trophy as an adult organisation. It was a proud day for everyone at 'the Drum', no less for a member of the squad from the 'Wee Toon', Paul McWhirter. Our community's long-standing association with Drumchapel Amateurs had been maintained on the club's day of days, and I know of one person who would have approved!

The Journey: 'Chips with Everything'

The future looked bright for football at the beginning of the 1970s, as an all-time high of nine clubs applied for membership of the KAFL: Southend, Largieside, AD Rovers, RAF, Tarbert, Phoenix, Grammar School, Youth Club and Pupils. The Campbeltown Boys Football Association was launched the previous year in 1969 and the new youth organisation promised much in the way of maintaining the standard of football in the burgh. Leading lights of the organisation were Willie McLachlan, Malcolm Lang, JMB Anderson, Willie McKerral, Roddy Girvan, Archie McCallum, Iain McMillan, John McLachlan, Willie Paterson, Alastair McKinlay, David Brodie, Wylie Hume, Hughie Mitchell and Robbie Robb, of course, supported by a host of willing volunteers too numerous to mention. There were various age groups in which the children could take part, from under-10s through to the almost adult under-17s. A leading light from senior football was engaged annually for the presentation of trophies – an array of silverware to take your breath away.

Changing accommodation was provided for the first time at Kinloch Park, albeit in the shape of a wooden caravan minus running water. Nevertheless, it was a start, and a few years later the Council at last constructed modern changing facilities at Lochend. Campbeltown Pupils continued their dominance of local football, enhancing their reputation with fine wins against 'foreign' opposition. Visitors to the area included Anniesland College, Vale of Leven, Notre Dame College, East Kilbride Rovers, Greenock HSFP, Bishopbriggs and Strathkelvin. Scottish Cup duty saw the club travel to Strathclyde University, Greengairs and Gartlea, all of which produced positive results – this before the predictable demise at the hands of one of the leading lights.

New Year's Day 1971 will not be easily forgotten, as the match between Rangers and Celtic at Ibrox Stadium ended in disaster. A late goal as the crowd left the ground resulted in a stairwell crush in which 66 people lost their lives. The accident occurred in an area usually frequented by the local branch of the Rangers supporters club, but as only 17 members applied to go, the bus was cancelled on Friday evening by secretary, Peter McKinlay. It was the first time a local Rangers supporters' bus had ever been cancelled.

Two league clubs fell by the wayside before the start of the 1972/73 season – Grammar School and Phoenix. Last-mentioned was a group of boys originally drawn together by Jimmy Shaw and local Sheriff Clerk, Frank Shanley. The club's name was cleverly chosen, a legendary bird associated with rebirth being used to describe the remnants of the recently defunct Youth Club. However, the following year the same club underwent a second metamorphosis and re-emerged as Campbeltown United, this time under the guidance of Alex Russell. The loss of the School and Phoenix did little to affect the strength of the league, as the pack was simply reshuffled to include Ardrishaig and A&B Lochgilphead. It was the Mid-Argyll clubs' first foray into Campbeltown amateur football, although a few years earlier both teams had been involved in the Oban & District Amateur League.

At this point, Campbeltown Pupils had just completed a winter season in the Mid-Argyll Association, winning the SNP and Possil Cups. First mentioned was a comfortable 4-0 cup final victory over Ardrishaig, but the Kintyre club's second success was not as clear-cut. The Possil Cup Final against Lochgilphead Thistle at the old Kilmory Football Park was nail-biting affair, a match refereed by the inimitable Reverend James Callan. This gentleman was a stickler for impeccable behaviour and would punish even the slightest hint of foul language. The game after 90 minutes was tied at 3-3, a headed goal in the final seconds by Alex McKinven taking the match to extra-time. Dougie McTavish put the home side back into the lead, only to see Ronnie Brown and Malcolm O'May score to win the cup for the visitors. Lochgilphead had a number of excellent players on show, one in particular drawing the admiring glances of senior scouts, Kenny Crawford. On target for the winning side was a young man who would later break all sorts of goal-scoring records for the Pupils, Malcolm O'May.

Campbeltown Pupils (circa 1971/72): Angus Brodie, Robert Anderson, Les McMillan, Jake McKinnon, Duncan McKinnon, Ronnie Brown, Douglas Gillespie, Robert Millar, Malcolm O'May, David McArthur, Tommy Kelly, Duncan Ritchie, Robert McGougan, Robert Campbell, Duncan McSporran, Jim McEwing, Tommy McPherson and Alex McKinven.

Being heavily involved in running the club, it is impossible to have an impartial view of things close to the heart. Nevertheless, I would agree the departure of the Pupils to the Mid-Argyll Association encouraged a resurgence of football in Kintyre. The club's long term ambition was to play at a higher level and, as such, its organisation was geared to making the transition from provincial football to a recognised national league. With this in mind, the club tended to have the strongest squad, therefore, it was no bad thing when the team moved on and allowed the KAFL to once more become a competitive environment. The Mid-Argyll Association was a structure that comprised a single team from each community or similar, a perfect stepping-stone for the club's ultimate ambition. RAF Machrihanish followed the same path and for a few seasons the league provided a strong competitive environment. Member-teams were Lochgilphead Thistle, Ardrishaig, Tarbert, Inveraray, Argyll & Bute Hospital, RAF Machrihanish and Campbeltown Pupils.

Around this period, a number of young players started to make their presence felt. First to make the break-through was a gifted forward by the name of Sandy Glendinning. He was part of a very talented Grammar School team and, along with his good friend Ian McAlister, was offered trials at Partick Thistle. He soon became a fixture in a strong Pupils side, a skilful forward with searing pace and a ferocious striker of the ball. In time, he formed a lethal partnership with Malcolm O'May and it is difficult to think of a better combination when it came to scoring goals. Another youngster to become a future club 'star' was David Martin, the hardest striker of the ball I have ever witnessed. A mid-field stalwart, 'big Davie' dominated the 'boiler house' with strength and aggression, a sight to see as the opposition melted in front of his single-minded pursuit of possession. Such was his strength, a throw-in was as good as a free-kick. However, he also weighed in with his fair share of goals and was no slouch with ball to feet. Then there were the supreme skills of Duncan McAulay, arguably the most talented individual to colour the local football scene since the early 1960s. Norman O'May joined from Campbeltown United Amateurs, a speedy 'no nonsense' defender who was a powerhouse at full-back, but also possessed the finesse of a tricky winger. While at this point the future looked promising, in time it was to get even better.

Deciding to invest in youth, the club found a breeding ground in a team called Campbeltown Rangers. A football strip was provided, and, completely oblivious to implications, its colour just happened to be bright orange. The leader of this group was a boy named Campbell Robertson, a player who later made his mark as a fine central defender with Campbeltown Pupils and, in time, became secretary of the club. The core of a future team was completed with sweeper Stewart McSporran and, at a later date, mid-field anchor man Michael Donnelly. Add Finlay Wylie at left full-back and the 51st Highland Division would have difficulty breaching this uncompromising rear-guard.

Another member of the team was an intelligent youngster named Jimmy Lay, a 'Rangers' player who followed a similar path and joined the parent club. A born organiser, Jimmy became a PE teacher and was well-known in basketball circles as the head coach of St Maurice's Basketball Club, Cumbernauld. He also coached the Scotland under-16s ladies' squad and won BBC Scotland's Unsung Hero Award in 2007. It's fair to say he loved sport, particularly football, and quite literally spent his life encouraging youngsters to better themselves. Jimmy died suddenly in 2012.

The midfield was blessed with a Billy Bremner-type character, a ball-winner with skill and tenacity in equal measure, Jimmy McCallum. There was also the immaculate skill of striker Duncan 'Crusoe' Robertson, another proven goal-scorer who was different in style to his frontline running mates. The squad was augmented a few years later with a fine left-sided fullback in David Campbell and an all-action dynamo of a player, Tommy Finn. There was also the assured presence of John Cord and the emerging talents of William McKinven, Alan Glendinning and Archie McMillan. Playing behind this dependable crew was goalkeeper Hughie McDonald, an athletic shot-stopper well-known for his acrobatic displays as last line of defence.

They arrived from different directions to reshape Campbeltown Pupils in readiness for an adventure – membership of the Scottish Amateur Football League in 1977. The average age of the team was lowered in hope of progressing through the divisions with the same squad. Character sponsors were found in Douglas Smith of Drumchapel and George Frame of Millerston Thistle, this before an inspection of facilities by members of the league's management committee. I think they were pleasantly surprised with what they found at Kintyre Park. The final hurdle was an interview with the match secretary and president, respectively, Joe Paterson and Angus McConnell. At the end of an extremely nervous night, our application had been accepted. It was a dream come true – we were members of one the top leagues in the country and a memorable period in the life of the club was about to begin. A Campbeltown club was set to become the furthest-travelled team in Scotland and in 35 years has accumulated close on a quarter of a million road miles.

It wasn't long before we became acquainted with a trio of top class performers, Palombo (Balloch), Al Pacini (Paisley) and Pepe (Renton) – not some foreign inside-forward line, but the people who kept us alive by serving chips with everything.

A 4-3 away win against Vale of Leven at Alexandria set the course for a successful first season in the SAFL. In 1977, amateur football was alive and well, our league system alone having no fewer than 10 divisions of 12 teams – 7 first-team and 3 reserve divisions. The match secretary must have been superhuman to cope with this amount of fixtures, but he did so in a calm and dignified manner. The first season flew past, but there was celebration when the club won the SAFL 7th division title without losing a single game. It also claimed the Top Score Trophy with 122 league goals, a record still intact to the present day. Centre-forward Malcolm O'May deserves a mention for an incredible 49 goals, the biggest contribution by an individual to a brilliant first season in the SAFL. Sponsorship in football was still in its infancy, but the club managed to secure a deal with Jack Horn, the owner of the Argyll Hotel in Main Street. The team became associated with the Captain's Cabin, a forerunner of the present-day Wee Toon Bar in Cross Street. It was a popular 'watering hole', a pub renowned for its bi-annual trips to Wembley for the England v Scotland internationals, memorable excursions run by Neil Kennedy and Derek Sandler.

Campbeltown Pupils AFC 1977/78:

Hugh McDonald, Norman O'May, Finlay Wylie, John Cord, Duncan McAulay, Campbell Robertson, Stewart McSporran, Michael Donnelly, Jimmy Lay, William McKinven, Malcolm O'May, Jimmy McCallum, David Martin, Sandy Glendinning, Archie McMillan, Duncan Robertson, Alan Glendinning and Alex McKinven, player/manager.

An excellent committee guided the administration of the team, unsung 'heroes' who deserve their place on the rostrum as much as the players. Here are a few of a less well-known, but nevertheless

Campbeltown Pupils AFC – Winners of SAFL 7th Division and Top Score Trophy, 1977/78.
Back row, left to right: P Ferguson, D McArthur, C Graham, M Donnelly, D Robertson, D Martin, H McDonald,
S McSporran, D McAulay, B McKinven, B Glendinning and J Lay.
Front Row, left to right: A McKinven, F Wylie, J McCallum, S Glendinning, A Glendinning and N O'May.

important squad: Don McIvor, Bill Glendinning, Barney McKinven, Dougie McArthur, Peter Clow, Bill Hunter, Charlie Graham, Jamie Stimpson, Elizabeth Stimpson – now McKillop – Peter Ferguson, Donnie Kelly, Hugh Little and Lawrence Ferguson.

Our path to the 6th Division was shadowed by County neighbours Lochside, a club also in its first year of membership. The Furnace-based outfit had fought 'tooth and nail' to gain one of the promotion places and rightfully joined the Argyll bandwagon as it rolled onwards and upwards. It was great to see some well-known faces progress: good friends like Mungo Sinclair, Kenny Crawford, Billy Luke and Alan Johnston – the last two destined to wear a Pupils jersey in the not-too-distant future.

We never lost a fixture against Lochside, but every match was an extremely testing affair. One match in particular springs to mind, a day I could hardly forget. The game in question was played at Goatfield Park, a farmer's field opposite the village of Furnace. A sizable crowd had gathered by the touchlines and the usual seismic confrontation commenced. Although well past my sell-by date, on this occasion I was called upon to play, thankfully something that didn't happen too often. It was a torrid match with nothing spared in the tackle, in football terms a rather 'meaty affair'. As luck would have it, my opposite number was swift of foot and in the full flush of youth, so it seemed fair to remind him that he was still in a game. I 'nailed' him with a tackle next time round and momentum carried both of us into the crowd. Next thing I remembered was a cold sponge in my face. On seeing her son flattened, his mother was overcome by the irresistible urge to introduce me to a family heirloom – a rather large wooden-handled umbrella which she deployed to maximum effect over my head! Now that's what I call a real woman.

The Sixth Division campaign brought us into contact with another of our Argyll neighbours, Oban Saints. David Buchanan's 'Saints' had gained membership the year previous to our own entry and this unique breakthrough allowed other Argyll clubs to gain a foothold in the Scottish Amateur Football League. Champion of our cause was a gentleman by the name of Joe Paterson, at the time match secretary of the league. Joe was held in high esteem and when he died, a cup was presented to commemorate his tireless work for both the league and football in Argyll. The Joe Paterson Memorial Trophy was the brainchild of our own Jimmy Lay – an annual fixture between teams representing Argyll and the SAFL. The first of these

Campbeltown Pupils AFC. Winners of SAFL 4th Division, 1980/81.
Back row, left to right: B Hunter, J Stimpson, D Martin, M Donnelly, S McSporran, C Robertson, A Terry, J Lay, T Finn, D Campbell and D McArthur. Front row, left to right: F Wylie, M O'May, J McCallum, S Glendinning, D Robertson, D McAulay and A McKinven.

games took place at Kintyre Park in 1981, but the match now makes its rounds to various locations throughout the county. After many years, the success rate is surprisingly close, so it's possible our good friend has used his influence with a much higher authority!

Around this time, a young and skilful Pupils' side was preparing to sweep through the lower divisions at break-neck speed. The initial success was followed by runners-up spot in both the Sixth and Fifth Divisions. In 1980, the club crossed paths with Greenock High School FP, like itself, a team in the ascendancy. It gave everyone a chance to renew old acquaintances, as prior to the league membership the boys from the 'Tail of the Bank' had been visitors to Kintyre Park. Previous winners of the Scottish Amateur Cup in 1922 and 1949, the club's fortunes had been restored under the guidance of Willie Wright and Ronnie McKay, the latter a holidaymaker for countless years at 'sunny' Bellochantuy.

Two points were all that separated the teams as Greenock claimed the 5th Division championship in 1980. It was frustrating for the Pupils, as an outstanding run to the quarter-finals of the Scottish Amateur Cup left too much to do in the closing weeks of the season. Unbelievably, the Kintyre boys needed to play 14 games in nine weeks to catch up, five week-ends playing on both Saturday and Sunday – and they say professional football players are over-stretched!

However, the situation was reversed the following year when the Pupils stormed to the SAFL 4th Division title in 1981. This time, Greenock finished five points adrift in fourth place and, after another fine run in the Scottish Cup, the Pupils went 10 games undefeated to pip Eaglesham by one point on the last day of the season.

It's unusual for the winners of a competition to feel sorry for a defeated manager, but on this occasion even a heart of stone would feel remorse. At the beginning of May, Eaglesham sat proudly at the top of the division with their programme complete and a cushion of 12 points between them and their nearest rivals. There was only one team left that could catch them. With seven games to play in four weeks, it looked an impossible task for the Pupils, but week by week the margin gradually eroded. The Kintyre side stuck tenaciously to its task, well aware that one defeat would give Eaglesham the title. The run-in –including three double-headers – was negotiated with the loss of single point. It was a remarkable achievement, a record that gave the club a shot at the title on the last day of the season against Thornliebank. It was one-way traffic from start to finish. A release of tension after weeks of catch-up swept the Pupils to a rousing 6-1 victory and more importantly, the SAFL 4th Division Championship. After faithfully following our away games during the closing weeks of the season, it must have been agonising for the Eagles' manager to have failed. A few weeks earlier his team was on the verge of the championship, only to have the trophy ripped from his grasp by two late goals in a last gasp Pupil's win over Glasgow Wingate. Although his prayers went unanswered, he had the grace and humility to congratulate our boys on their championship success.[53]

Campbeltown Pupils v. Thornliebank, May 1981:

Alan Terry, Jimmy Lay, Tommy Finn, Davie Campbell, Davie Martin, Michael Donnelly, Stewart McSporran, Campbell Robertson, Finlay Wylie, Malcolm O'May, Jimmy McCallum, Sandy Glendinning, Duncan Robertson and Duncan McAulay.

Winning the SAFL 4th Division title coincided with a particularly fertile period in local football, as Campbeltown Boys Football Association was in full flow and producing a regular supply of talent to augment an already strong Pupils squad. You could say it was easier to pick the winner of the 'Grand National' than our team on a Saturday afternoon. The 'boys' league' produced Kevin Gilchrist, Archie Millar, Douglas McCallum, Iain McGeachy, Jim Lang and Thomas Maguire, the latter an irrepressible talent returning after a spell as a senior with Aberdeen FC. These bright young men were brilliant players whose collective talents added to our selection conundrum. The club also secured a couple of players from Tarbert, a quality striker by the name of John McGregor and full-back John MacAlpine – now an Argyll & Bute Councillor for North Kintyre. These lads joined one of the best Campbeltown squads in decades, and the club was rightly proud of everything they achieved.

Local football was on the crest of a wave during the early 1980s and the Kintyre Amateur Football League would also benefit from the town's productive youth system. Leading lights were Campbeltown Fishermen and Campbeltown Boys, the latter formed from the boys' league over-aged players. It was exciting times and 1982 proved a watershed year for the younger members in the Campbeltown Pupils squad. The club missed promotion for the first time since joining the SAFL, finishing just outside the qualifying positions behind Netherlee Church and Clairmont. Nevertheless, compensation was at hand in the form of the Colin Munro Cup. Among the fancied teams for the cup were Bellarmine and Eastern Villa, two fantastic sides that gained membership a few years after our own inclusion. Like the Pupils, both clubs had made a major impact since joining the league and with quality in abundance, either looked capable of lifting the cup. Nevertheless, our own form had been excellent throughout the season and, given the luck of the draw, we quietly fancied our chances.

There is no easy route to success and our 'make-or-break' game arrived in the quarter finals against the favourites, Eastern Villa. Thankfully, it was the cue for an outstanding Pupils performance. Leading by a Jimmy McCallum strike at half-time, the local favourites dominated the second period before running out comfortable winners by 4-0. The game was decorated with a Jimmy McCallum hat-trick, although the goal of the match was scored by the youngest man on the field, a scorching effort from substitute Kevin Gilchrist.

Campbeltown Pupils, March 1982: Alan Terry, Davie Martin, Finlay Wylie, Stewart McSporran, Campbell Robertson, Mike Donnelly, Duncan McAulay, Sandy Glendinning (Capt.), Dougie McCallum, Jimmy McCallum and Tommy Maguire. Subs: Kevin Gilchrist and Duncan Robertson.

Alan Terry had a quiet day in the Pupils goal, almost a spectator as his team mates guaranteed cup success. Alan was a fine goalkeeper, a player who progressed to represent RAF Great Britain at under-23 level. He also appeared for the same representative side against the might of Tottenham Hotspur, but his absence in a Pupils shirt was well-covered by a clutch of young pretenders. The club had the likes of Graham Marrison, Ian Hill and the soon-to-be first choice goalkeeper, Campbell MacBrayne, waiting in the wings. A journey to Lochwinnoch for the semi-final followed and it was a day to remember for a side containing many of the club's younger players. They slotted in seamlessly, winning 2-0 against North Kelvin to take the club to its first league cup final. It was a learning experience for the youngsters on the day they met Viewfield Rovers' long-serving club secretary, the inimitable Willie Turner. They looked at one other sheepishly as they were banned from a pre-match kick-in. No use of the goalmouths before the start of the game was his command! Willie ran a tight ship at the host venue, an attractive junior-standard ground supported by a small social club. In patriotic fashion, the Union Jack was hoisted before each match and everything that followed was undertaken with military precision. It was the old-fashioned way and for me the exact recipe for running a successful football club.

The Colin Munro Cup final against Dalmarnock loomed large on the horizon, and an exciting few weeks passed as we planned our big day out at the home of Giffnock North. It was the ideal venue for an amateur cup final, as the club from Glasgow's south side had excellent playing facilities and a fantastic social club with all the usual amenities. The Pupils travelled with a full-strength squad, probably the strongest gathering of players to pass the 'Mill Dam' since the 1950s. The unenviable task of selecting a team fell as usual to Bill Hunter and yours truly – without doubt the hardest task we had ever undertaken. Everyone was excited about playing in the cup final and to say it was gut-wrenching to leave out some excellent players summed up our feelings. A perfect playing surface 'screamed' for front-runners who were small and quick on the turn, especially against a team known for its physical approach. After deliberation, we opted to play possession football from the back and out-pass the opposition. The die was cast. We played excellent football in the first period, but doubts began to surface when the game remained goal-less at the break. Should we have gone for a more direct approach? We needn't have worried, as the team ran riot in a one-sided second half. A Thomas Maguire penalty opened the scoring, this before further goals from Duncan McAulay, Kevin Gilchrist and Douglas McCallum put the game out of sight. Dalmarnock scored at the death from a penalty kick, but it was consolation only for the valiant losers. [54]

The Pupils had a large travelling support and they needed little encouragement to join the celebrations. These people were part of the club's success and sizable crowds once more became a feature of home games at Kintyre Park, not in the same numbers that existed in earlier times, but encouraging enough for the club to produce season tickets and supporters' scarves. Amazingly in amateur football, the club had 400 registered season ticket holders and there were times when attendances reached as high as 700 for a normal Saturday fixture. This was the case in a cup-tie against Gourock Athletic, a day when we even had the services of Campbeltown's legendary piper, Tony Wilson. Senior scouts arrived at our games to follow one player or another, in particular Duncan McAulay, who was tracked by no less than Glasgow Celtic and Liverpool. Duncan was a precocious talent who at the tender age of 14 became the club's youngest-ever player. In the end, it was Greenock Morton who took a chance on the Pupils skilful mid-fielder and he signed on at Cappielow Park. There is a post-script to this story, in that Morton had no obligation to recompense an amateur organisation for the loss of a player. Nevertheless, a few weeks after his departure, a cheque arrived in the post for £25. Duncan must have been the bargain of the century, more so in the knowledge that the cheque has never been cashed.

You would have been spoiled for choice if you fancied playing football in Kintyre during the early 1980s. Not only was there an active KAFL winter league, but also an adult Sunday league and an excellent boys' league during the summer months. There was also indoor football for adults and youths at the Victoria Hall, all of which sustained the town's Scottish Amateur League team, the Pupils. With so many people playing the game, it was only a matter of time before other sides applied for membership of the Scottish Amateur Football League. This duly happened when both Campbeltown Boys and Carradale gained admission to the SAFL. Tarbert followed and the gates of competitive football were thrown open as an all-time high of nine Argyll and Bute clubs claimed membership of a national league system. The quality of Campbeltown football in the early 1980s was highlighted by the success of the Grammar School under-13s team. With PE master Sandy McPherson in charge, the youngsters swept the board in the Argyll Schools Cup, winning 2-1 against Rothesay, 5-1 against Oban, 5-0 against Lochgilphead and 4-0 against Dunoon. At this point, there was little doubt which was the strongest football community in Argyll and after a run of convincing victories it was pleasing to see the cup travel the long road to Kintyre. 55

That very week, Campbeltown Pupils AFC won the SAFL Third Division Championship, a level of success never anticipated at the beginning of the exercise. Picking the best memories from this magical period is difficult to say the least, although if forced to make a choice, it would have to be our record-breaking run in the Scottish Amateur Cup of 1979/80. There is something special about the 'Scottish', a competition with so much appeal it tends to mesmerise players and supporters alike. An infatuation with the cup has been a trait of countless generations of Campbeltonians and the feeling is just as strong today as it was more than a century ago. When the draw for the Scottish Cup comes around, everything else pales into insignificance.

With up to 800 teams taking part each year, the Scottish Amateur Cup was at one time Europe's largest domestic football competition. Numbers have diminished in recent years and, although still considerable, it has been overtaken by the annual Norwegian International Youth Tournament. Nevertheless, to win the blue ribbon of amateur football requires a team of the highest quality, coupled with a monopoly on the whims of Lady Luck. The benchmark for Campbeltown clubs prior to 1979/80 was the fourth round of the national cup, a realistic target for teams operating outside of the main league systems. However, this Pupils squad was toughened by three seasons of SAFL competition and competitive football had shaped the team into a match for the elite of the amateur game, and so the adventure began!

The first round of the competition produced an away tie against Cartside Athletic from Johnstone, a team languishing in the lower reaches of the Paisley & District League. No wish to be disparaging, the draw had been kind, and a 9-0 away win allowed the club to proceed without too much trouble. The second round was a home draw against Arthurlie from Barrhead, a team which benefited from watching our previous game courtesy of a 'bye' in the competition. Far from being complimentary about the demolition of their near neighbours, Arthurlie vowed to make the forthcoming game a much closer encounter. These threats proved wide of the mark and the Pupils raced to a third round place virtue of a convincing 8-2 victory.

Avoiding the leading lights in the early rounds was a blessing, although it was only a matter of time before the 'big guns' came calling. The blue touch paper of competition had been ignited and the club found itself on a collision course with the elite of the amateur game. It was a journey full of surprises and not a little excitement.

Next on the agenda was Fenwick Thistle from Ayrshire, previous winners of the coveted Scottish Cup and as difficult a tie as could be imagined at this stage of the competition. As the club prepared for its biggest challenge to date, the players were consoled in the knowledge that the game was at least on home soil, a major advantage considering the distance involved.

Nevertheless, when the big day came, the club's best-laid plans were thrown into disarray. At the eleventh hour the game became a victim of the elements, the worst of the weather setting in as the visitors made their way to the town. Thankfully, the committee were well prepared for this eventuality and the game was moved at the eleventh hour to RAF Machrihanish. Playing conditions at the base were nigh on perfect, as the park was seated on sandy soil and could resist everything 'Mother Nature' could throw at it. The only drawback was the open nature of the ground, ideal for the Atlantic blast to create its own particular brand of mischief. It was extremely wet, but the prevailing wind was good enough to hold its breath for the duration of the game. Nevertheless, the change of venue gave the management an unusual problem for an amateur club. Blessed with a loyal support, the club made provision to move the home crowd as well as the football team. A few urgent phone calls to the Station Officer at Machrihanish and West Coast Motors Service brought the desired result; with military precision, the 'Kintyre Park bandwagon' was transferred lock, stock and barrel to the new venue.

Our disappointment at losing the home advantage was short-lived, as the visitors' resolve deserted them in the bitterly cold, wet conditions. Facing the winter blast at Machrihanish is not for the faint-hearted, and our knowledge and acceptance of the elements acted as a twelfth man. Anticipating a close game, the supporters watched in disbelief as Fenwick capitulated. The home side ran out easy winners, goals from Sandy Glendinning, David Martin and a brace from Duncan 'Crusoe' Robertson making the result a foregone conclusion long before the referee's whistle brought play to a halt.

Being part of the Scottish Amateur Football League committed the club to thousands of miles of travel each and every year, so fund-raising efforts had to expand in keeping with the additional costs. There was very little that wasn't tried in order to meet the outlay. There were annual raffles, summer celidhs, dances, coffee mornings, race nights and jumble sales, not to mention the weekly football accumulator. The search for money was non-stop and almost a way of life. Everything was organised prior to our Scottish League adventure, although a close eye was kept on expenditure by the treasurer's department, ably managed at different times by Charlie Graham and Don McIvor.

Constraint on spending was a normal state of affairs, which brings to mind an instance in a Johnstone restaurant prior to one of our far-flung cup-ties. The committee decided that the club should pick up the tab, a gesture loaded with strong overtones to take it easy on the treasurer. No problem – it was only a light pre-match meal and the responsibility of controlling costs fell to me – in other words, I had drawn the short straw. The menu was quickly scanned in the hope of finding a bargain or two and my reaction was predictable – whatever else, no steak at that price. It was comforting to see a number of affordable options further down the list and, being self-service, while we waited it seemed a good tactic to open a conversation on healthy eating. No-one had the slightest interest in carbohydrates, but it was worth the effort to steer them towards the cheaper pasta dishes. The moment of crisis arrived when the first of our motley crew reached the service point.

After giving the menu careful consideration and clearly disappointed with the fare on offer, he asked a very profound question – 'Hae ye any mince?' My spirits soared: cottage pie with a side-service of vegetables – the cheapest thing on the menu. The euphoria lasted about 30 seconds before he changed his mind. 'Naw, don't bother. A'd prefer chips, so A'll jeest haev steck instead.' – a chain reaction followed! It was a devastating experience – not a macaroni and cheese in sight. My tactics had failed miserably, so, as the 15th order for the best sirloin was taken, it was time for me to capitulate. I never liked pasta anyway. 'Make mine medium to well done – with chips on the side please!'

Luck was still on our side when we drew Arden Villa from Glasgow in the 4th round of the cup at home. Everyone was well aware of the importance of this particular fixture, as one more victory would push us into hitherto unknown territory – the first time a Campbeltown side would reach the 5th round of the Scottish Amateur Cup. Our form was good and fortune seemed to be holding. It was a day to remember – a pulsating cup-tie with goals galore.

The game started at a frantic pace and the visitors made their intentions clear by grabbing the lead after 10 minutes, McConville scoring from the edge of the box after a corner kick. Michael Donnelly equalised for the Pupils when he got on the end of a Jimmy Lay 'knock-on' to squeeze the ball home at the near post, the opposition falling foul of the home side's secret weapon, a David Martin long throw.

Minutes later, Sandy Glendinning gave the home side the lead when he volleyed the ball home after a corner kick, a sound piece of skill from the home side's mercurial forward. Arden looked to have a mountain to climb when Malcolm O'May scored on the stroke of half-time. A 3-1 advantage at the break had the home side dreaming of a new record, but this tie was far from finished.

Within six minutes of the re-start Arden Villa had drawn level. The fight-back began when Graham scored an absolute beauty with his head and the visitors' joy was complete when Cunningham drove the ball home from close range to 'put the cat among the pigeons'. The Pupils' dream looked in tatters, but another wayward pass-back sent Duncan Robertson on his way and the striker 'kept his cool' to round the stranded goalkeeper and restore the home side's lead. Goalkeeper Angus Brodie was called upon to keep Arden Villa at bay with a number of fine stops, this before a mesmerising run and cross by Jimmy McCallum left the incoming Jimmy Lay to complete the scoring from point-blank range. Arden were worthy opponents and the visitors had the final say when Stewart pulled one back in the dying minutes. It was a nerve-wracking cup-tie, but the Pupils survived the ordeal to win a difficult game by 5 goals to 4. The headlines said it all: 'Pupils Triumph in Tough Tie'.[56] The fourth round barrier had been broken and it was now a question of how far the team could go.

There was a certain resolve about this group of players, a team spirit created by the familiarity of travelling hundreds of miles in one another's company. It was helped by a number of colourful characters and laughs were legion as we travelled the length and breadth of the country. Some incidents verged on the unmentionable, the rest, innocent fun that had to be seen or heard to be believed. To while away the miles, we often turned to a quiz or playing cards, but it was a complete surprise when a few of the team became proficient in the art of storytelling. Superstition ranked high on the agenda and with fishermen 'on board', many a tale was of the 'salty' variety. Football and fishing are definitely from the same mould, as they are both theatres in which ritual abounds. This, then, was the source of our introduction to the 'Cara Broonie', a fully paid-up member of the little people. Local fishing legend dictates that homage must be paid to 'the wee man' and only then will you be blessed with good fortune. Well, if it was good enough for the fishing fleet, it certainly was good enough for our football team. The small gentleman from Cara was immediately signed up and so it was that on every away journey a bus-load of grown men waved in unison as we passed Tayinloan – acknowledgement of the power of local myth and superstition. All-in-all, 'the Broonie' played a blinder – so reliable, even the sceptics were won over.

Inexplicably, with three home-draws in succession, we now expected the ballot to favour our cause. Sure as fate, round five produced another home game, this time against Auchenheath Hearts from Lesmahagow. The tie turned into a marathon affair and it took three games to separate two evenly matched sides. In the first meeting, a goal from David Martin with nine minutes remaining appeared to have sealed a home win, but the Pupils were caught by a sucker punch when Prentice equalised for the visitors in the closing minutes. Star of the game was Auchenheath goalkeeper Dewar, a fine last line of defence who simply defied everything sent his way. The replay at Lesmahagow was more of the same: a goal from Stewart McSporran giving the Pupils the lead, only to be pegged back by an Ellis equaliser to take the tie into extra time. A spectacular strike from John McGregor should have won it for the visitors, but Ellis equalised once more for a determined home eleven. A toss of the coin was needed to decide the next venue, and drama began to unfold as the two captains were called forward for the vital decision. A certain gentleman from Cara now held the Pupils' fate in his hands and when David Martin executed a more than reasonable impression of a high jumper, we knew the 'wee man' had done his stuff. The following Saturday the game returned to Kintyre Park.

A large crowd turned out to watch the second replay; one way or another the cup-tie had to be decided on the day. Dewar, the visitors' diminutive goalkeeper, was in sparkling form and threatened to 'put up the shutters' with one of the best displays witnessed at Kintyre Park for many a day. Both sides' play had now become familiar, so the home team tried to pull a tactical switch by moving Sandy Glendinning to right midfield. The idea was to free the Pupils' striker from the tight marking of earlier games, a move which seemed to be working, only to founder on the end of brilliant goalkeeping. The Pupils dominated possession for the first time in the tie, but the elusive winner was nowhere to be found. Suddenly, Glendinning broke free on the right flank and sent a ball to the near post. The visitors' defence faltered for a split second, just enough time for a fearless Malcolm O'May to launch himself forward and head home a sensational late winner. The Pupils centre forward disappeared under an avalanche of ecstatic team-mates – this time, there was no way back for brave Auchenheath Hearts.

It had been an epic struggle and after a number of weeks on cup duty everyone was happy to resume the league programme. A daunting prospect lay ahead; now massively behind with fixtures, it was a case of 'catch up.' This comes with the territory in amateur football, as success in the cup creates more pressure on the league programme – normally to the detriment of the achieving club. The position was even more difficult given our remote location. Unable to play in mid-week, the club faced the prospect of two games every weekend. The pressure was on, but there always seems to be one person in a group who is able to take everything in their stride when the chips are down. The Pupils had such a person, a practical joker who kept everyone going through 'thick and thin.' He also was a bit of an amateur philosopher, a man with a strong opinion on just about everything; so it was, as we travelled to and from Glasgow, a completely irrelevant issue began to dominate the conversation: what were the cages in the water between Tarbert and Ardrishaig?

First of their kind in the area, the general opinion sided with the obvious – it's a fish farm. This view was accepted by the majority, that is, with the exception of a mischievous personality who decided that there was mileage in the subject. There was a fair amount of leg-pulling going on, but as time passed the cages became the centre of heated discussion. One suggestion after another was voiced as to their use, each one as far-fetched as the last. The topic exhausted and everyone bored to tears, the bus approached the area for the umpteenth time in a few weeks. Everyone slumped into their seats in anticipation of the next instalment, but not a word was spoken. Suddenly, the peace was shattered and a voice shouted: 'There, I told you so – look at the sign!' As everyone jostled to catch sight of the notice board, his punch-line was delivered in a slow and deliberate manner: 'This is not a fish farm!' Final score: Wit 1, Passengers 0.

Events surrounding our Scottish Cup 6th round tie against Anderson Strathclyde can only be described as unbelievable. Our luck continued with another home draw, our fifth on the trot. By now, any doubts about the influence of the Cara connection had disappeared. The day began with an unusual occurrence – our visitors arrived minus their football strip. Their coach developed mechanical problems en-route and the team's equipment had been removed from the boot at Inveraray. It was only when they arrived in Campbeltown that the kit was posted missing. The police recovered the said item, but there was no chance of getting it delivered. Sympathetic to their predicament, we managed to kit the visitors out in our white change strip. Before the final whistle this tie would have more twists than a corkscrew.

The Pupils' soon discovered their opponents for a 7th round place were top quality, but little else could be expected at this stage of the competition. The game was one of the hardest contests I have ever witnessed. With the match on a knife-edge, emotions were raw as both teams chased the elusive goal that would put them among the country's elite. Eight minutes remaining, we conceded a free kick in a dangerous position on the edge of our 18-yard box. A cleverly disguised pass found Cox in space, and the forward's angled

Campbeltown Pupils AFC – circa 1982/83. Back Row, left to right, D McAulay, S McSporran, A Terry, M Donnelly, C Robertson, D Martin and N O' May. Front row, left to right: J McCallum, W McCallum, J McGregor, J Lay and D Robertson

drive powered its way into the bottom corner of the net. It was a magnificent late goal and looked a match-winning strike.

The ground emptied as the large crowd resigned itself to home defeat – no shame after a fantastic cup run. What happened next was straight from the realms of fantasy. A last gasp effort was made to disrupt a rock-solid visiting defence, all change as full back Jimmy Lay moved to centre forward, with centre half Campbell Robertson supporting from the mid-field. Jimmy's 'no nonsense' approach forced the Anderson rearguard to concede a corner kick and, as the unsettling tactics continued, Stewart McSporran appeared in the six yard box to score a priceless equaliser. Not the best goal he ever scored, but certainly the most valuable. A storm of protest followed, but the score stood and a lost cause was saved at the death – and the fairy tale didn't end there...

With the game already deep into injury time, the visitors made the fatal mistake of giving the ball away cheaply from the kick-off. Back in possession, a simple through-ball sent Jimmy Lay forging through the middle, his determination carrying him beyond the last defender to send a shot against the goalkeeper's legs. The strike rebounded into the path of Campbell Robertson, who controlled the ball casually before lashing it into the roof of the net. It was coolness personified and an unbelievable finish to a fascinating cup tie. The final seconds seemed like a dream. We had played 90 minutes without a sight of goal, only to score twice in the last minute of injury time. As the whistle sounded, players, officials and supporters celebrated in an outpouring of emotion seldom witnessed at this level of the game – sheer theatre and simply the best moment I can remember in football!

The decision to throw caution to the wind had won the day, but the lasting impression of a memorable occasion was the abject desolation on our opponents' faces. Victory had been torn from their grasp in such cruel circumstances – a sobering thought in our moment of celebration. The result was greeted with disbelief when we returned for the after-match hospitality. An almost empty ground had witnessed one of the most dramatic moments in the old venue's history, and needless to say, the supporters were roundly chastised for lack of belief. In honesty, most of the players were pinching themselves as well!

The competition now in closing stages, it was no surprise when one of the favourites came out of the hat. In the quarter finals we drew West of Scotland Cup holders, Newarthill Hearts, away from home. The game was played at Newmains in Lanarkshire and the home team's management was astute enough to move the tie to a red blaise surface. Although well within their rights, it was a blatant attempt to unsettle their rural opponents, but all is fair in love and war. Unbeaten on their home patch in three years, Newarthill Hearts presented an almighty obstacle, a team installed as firm favourites for the cup. Nevertheless, although unhappy with the choice of surface, the visitors weren't here simply to make up the numbers. Another match would go down to the wire.

Satisfied with the dimensions of the park, the Pupils opted to play a 4-4-2 formation, a system to deny the home side space in the opening stages of the game. It also allowed time to adapt to unwelcome playing conditions and gradually the visitors began to exert pressure on the cup favourites. Newarthill were soon under siege from the long-throw of David Martin, riding their luck on a number of occasions when efforts from Campbell Robertson and Jimmy McCallum were blocked en-route to goal.

It was a good start by the visitors and the home side seemed genuinely surprised by the quality of the Pupils' play. After being on the receiving end of the early exchanges, totally against the run of play, the home side drew blood. Although fortunate to be in front, the execution of the goal was excellent. Right winger Clark – a recent acquisition from Queens Park – raced clear and sent a pin-point cross to the far post for McCutcheon to score with a well-placed header. The Pupils held their game plan together, being rewarded when a David Martin 'special' crashed off the underside of the bar and Duncan Robertson scored with his chest from the rebound. Minutes later the visitors should have been in front, another thunderbolt from Martin striking centre half Connelly on the goal line after an inch-perfect cross from John McGregor. It was a major incident in the game, as the defender knew little about the goal-bound strike. However, unfortunately for the visitors the ball spun agonisingly over the bar.

Relieved to be level, the home side started the second half on the front foot and scored within six minutes of the restart. The scorer remained anonymous, as a Clark cross was scrambled over the line in rugby fashion – but they all count! The game was poised on a knife-edge, and play swung from end to end as both teams chased their cup dream. The Pupils strained every muscle to regain a foothold in the game and were nearly rewarded when a speculative shot from the edge of the box was spilled by Davidson in the home goal. The ball trundled agonisingly along the goal line, and as the visiting forwards closed in for the kill, it was driven to safety by centre half Connelly.

With the game on a knife-edge, luck finally deserted the visitors when a long ball turned their rearguard. Confusion reigned as the Pupils defence stood motionless in anticipation of an offside whistle that never came and 'star' of the show, Clark, ran clear to loft the ball over a stranded Sandy Ronald to clinch the tie. It was a controversial ending to a highly competitive match and there was a few minutes' delay as the visitors conveyed their displeasure to the referee. Nevertheless, the score stood and a journey that promised so much finally came to an acrimonious end. As the home side celebrated in an unrestrained manner, it was an indication of just how close the Kintyre side had come to 'upsetting the applecart'. It was an unbelievable experience and if you believe in superstition, all made possible with a little help from a friend.

To the victors go the spoils and an excellent Newarthill Hearts moved on to defeat former cup-winners Dumbarton Academy FP in the semi-final. They then marched to their day of destiny at Hampden Park in May 1980, defeating Star Hearts from Fife decisively by 4-0 to lift the Famous Grouse Scottish Amateur Cup. As previously mentioned, any team that succeeds in this mammoth competition thoroughly deserves its victory. It remains one of Europe's most difficult competitions and will continue to be for some time to come.

Returning to league duty, the club could hardly fail to notice the long line of talent being produced by the Campbeltown Boys Football Association – known locally as the 'boys' league'. Earlier teams had come from the traditional breeding grounds of town and country football, but now for the first time, new arrivals were direct from under-age sources. These lads made their presence felt during the early 1980s, in fact, numbers were such that other local clubs began to entertain ambitions of joining the Scottish Amateur Football League. The Kintyre Amateur Football League was still producing fine players like David Campbell and John McDonald, only two of many good enough to grace the SAFL.

Team selection should have been straightforward, but the complete opposite was the case. There is no denying the club was spoiled for choice, but it was no easy task picking 11 players from a squad bursting at the seams with quality. Not a bad complaint, but every week-end we faced the same dilemma – selecting the right team for

Campbeltown Pupils AFC. Winners of SAFL 3rd Division, 1982/83.
Back row, left to right: T Finn, C Russell, D Martin, T Maccrine, C Robertson, C MacBrayne, T Millar, M Donnelly,
M O'Hara. Front row, left to right: T Maggire, D McCallum, S McSporran, M O'May and J Lang.

the occasion. Match day was full of nervous tension and not only for the players. In the end decisions had to be made and a player's worst fears were realised when he was called from the dressing room prior to the team announcement – an indication he hadn't made the starting eleven. It was only right to explain our decision to the individuals concerned. I speak in plural, as around this time I was joined by good friend Bill Hunter in management of the team. In his playing days he was centre-forward for RAF Machrihanish and 'Big Bill' is best remembered as the owner of a thunderous right 'peg'. He quickly became a great favourite with the players and owing to a likeness with a well-known American screen actor, was affectionately named 'Bronson'. Then, as the result of fertile imagination, the players made us a double act, 'Redford and Bronson', although you can rest assured the names we were called were a lot less complimentary in the wake of our regular weekly team selections.

In 1983, Campbeltown Pupils won the SAFL 3rd Division with three games left to play and although the job was complete, the home programme ended with a flourish when the lads defeated Duncanrigg from East Kilbride by 7 goals to 1. The 3rd division promised to be the most difficult challenge to date, with Greenock – including 'our own' Duncan McAulay in its line-up – Gourock Athletic and Bellarmine as opponents. However, it proved the team's most successful campaign to date and was won by a comfortable seven-point margin. Old rivals Greenock finished runners up and followed the Kintyre side into the league's second tier. It was unusual to line up against a former favourite of the home crowd, as Duncan McAulay had returned to amateur football after his spell with Morton FC. Still employed in the ship-building industry, Duncan turned out for a good Greenock side that contained his cousin, Gordon Parker, an excellent player with league representative experience. Duncan followed a similar path in the not-too-distant future and, surrounded by many of his Campbeltown Pupils team mates became captain of the SAFL Select team. The championship-winning side, at least the one which appeared in the last home game of the season minus a number of regulars, was as follows:

Campbeltown Pupils AFC, May 1983:
Tommy Finn, Chris Russell, David Martin, Campbell Robertson, Campbell MacBrayne (G), Tommy Millar, Michael Donnelly, Kevin Gilchrist, Tommy Maguire, Douglas McCallum, Stewart McSporran Malcolm O'May and Jim Lang.[57]

At this juncture, the home favourites were capable of producing two separate sides so, with the league won, it was all-change the following weekend for the corresponding fixture at East Kilbride. Seven changes did little to upset the rhythm of the team, and a Kevin Gilchrist first half hat-trick saw the youngsters through to victory by 6 goals to 2 – halcyon days indeed! The return journey was usually accompanied by a song or two, Paul McCartney's 'Mull of Kintyre' or the less familiar 'Allez la Rouge', a Jimmy Lay-inspired song influenced by the club's all-red strip. Long-suffering driver Willie McDonald accurately summed up his feelings thus: 'Thank goodness they can play fitba, if they were singing for fish suppers they wunna get a chip.' Frankly, this was an extremely kind assessment of their vocal abilities.

The SAFL 3rd Division was won without losing a single home game, something today's team could well do with emulating. However, a bigger fish was set to swim into our pond later that same year. Argyll Bowling Club had the misfortune to have its premises destroyed by fire, so the Pupils made a conscious decision to help the fund-raising effort to replace the building. David Hay, then manager of Glasgow Celtic, agreed to send a team to play at Kintyre Park on 14 August 1983. The game attracted a crowd of 1200, probably the last major gathering at Kintyre Park for the foreseeable future. A few years earlier, the local favourites lost 3-1 to a top-class Celtic Professional Youth team captained by David Moyes – now Manager of Everton FC. This was a far harder proposition, as the Celtic team contained Derek Whyte, Peter Grant, Owen Archdeacon, Jim McInally, Lex Bailey and the legendary 'Lisbon Lion', Bobby Lennox. Needless to say, we were proud of the boys that day, as they produced a massive effort to deny Celtic the space to cause damage. The locals were, of course, beaten in the end, but it took a couple of long-range 'specials' from Peter Grant to separate the sides. Nevertheless, the home team had its moment of glory, a story told and retold down Princes Street way; similar to the tales of fishermen, this one also gets more elaborate with age.

Our substitutes were desperate to take part in the match, none more so than Duncan Robertson, a dyed-in-the-wool Rangers man. It was a blow to his spirits when he was listed on the bench as he saw the match as some sort of personal crusade. The big fellow perpetually paced up and down the line and hounded us every minute of the match with the same question: 'When will I get on?'

As the clock ran down, he made a final desperate effort to take part in the match: 'Put me on and I'll get a goal!' This was quite a promise considering the class of team we were playing. We decided to save our sanity and make the change. With Celtic leading 2-0, we forced a corner kick at the pavilion end and Duncan was immediately marked by a well-known Parkhead personality. His moment of truth had arrived. True to his word, Duncan slipped his marker and sent a powerful header raging into the roof of the net. Not content with fulfilling his lifetime's ambition, he turned to the disconsolate Celtic defender and delivered the now immortal line, 'If I were you, son, I'd get a trade – you'll never make it at this game.' He certainly got the last part wrong as his marker, who will remain anonymous, went on to play for Scotland. Celtic won the match 3-1, but every one was a winner on a memorable day at Kintyre Park.

Campbeltown Pupils v. Celtic, 14th August 1983: Campbell MacBrayne, Tommy Finn, Tommy Millar, Stewart McSporran, Michael Donnelly, Campbell Robertson, David Campbell, Finlay Wylie, Jimmy McCallum, Thomas Maguire, David Martin, Douglas McCallum, Sandy Glendinning, Malcolm O'May, Archie Millar, Kevin Gilchrist, Duncan Robertson and Willie Luke.

In 1983, Campbeltown Boys made their bow in the Scottish Amateur Football League. The club was founded in the late 1970s and brothers Tommy and Sandy McPherson were the driving force behind the venture. The team was an initiative of the local boys' football association, but the name was sensibly shortened for administration purposes. A very well organised club, Campbeltown Boys would in time create its very own niche in the history of the local game and for a lengthy period the town was fortunate to have two top class sides in the SAFL. Around this period, the league expanded to eight senior and three reserve divisions, and considering only five remain today, it is an indication of how much the game in Scotland has gone backwards in the last 30 years. Many of the great names of amateur and junior football have simply disappeared and our national game is much poorer for their absence.

As a reward for their efforts, Campbeltown Boys AFC claimed the SAFL 6th Division Championship in 1985/86. A second championship came their way on the creation of the Premier League. Two separate sections now existed, and the 'new' first division title – equivalent to the SAFL 4th Division – was won in 1993/94. Campbeltown Boys eventually gained membership of Premier Division Two and the club's finest hour was winning the division in 1996. Campbeltown Boys survived well into the new millennium, but owing to a shortage of players in and around the town at this juncture, they eventually merged with Campbeltown Pupils AFC. The 'new' identity tried to maintain two adult sides for as long as it could, but unforeseen circumstances made it an impossible dream. With the reorganisation of local football, teams are now operating at under 16s and 17s levels, extremely important cogs in the development wheel. The message is loud and clear – watch this space!

As Campbeltown prepares to embrace a brand-new era, it faces difficult challenges. The organisers recognise the importance of youth in maintaining our local game, and a quick look over their shoulder to the days of the prolific boys' league will show the way forward. The erosion of football standards is nationwide, but not replicated on the world stage. Therefore, is it safe to assume that the old excuse of modern technology interfering with the game is a myth? We have our own long-standing problems in Campbeltown, as the demise of industry has resulted in a reduction of population. However, on a much larger stage, numbers were not a hindrance when a tiny nation like Uruguay won the World Cup. Small nations continue to punch above their weight, including the aforementioned, so perhaps we should spend time learning from the successful minnows, rather than attempting to mirror the unmatchable sharks?

Football is a working-class game, something the administrators have lost sight of in recent times. The main ingredient in the modern football recipe is cash, the unfortunate pursuit of which discourages participation; for example, is it really necessary for local authorities to charge so much for public facilities, especially in the case of all-weather parks? People fully understand the maintenance and staffing theory, but charging less could mean more usage and a greater chance of producing the 'stars' of the future. Another proposal to really rankle is a registration fee for amateur players, the ones who derive nothing more from the game than pleasure. How out-of-touch with reality can you get! If you want to discourage participation, this is definitely the way forward. The game used to be inexpensive to play, the very reason for its popularity and mass participation in the first place. Is it only me, or is there a lesson to be learned from history?

For those with aspirations of playing first division football, 1984 would prove a watershed year. The SAFL 2nd Division had just been won by old adversaries Eastern Villa, but for Campbeltown Pupils the other promotion place was still theirs for the taking. It had been a successful campaign to say the least, as the club had lost only one league fixture during the entire season, but still finished second by virtue of five drawn matches. The journey towards the top division had been eventful and now there was only one game separating the team from its original goal, a place among the elite of the Scottish Amateur Football League. The match in question was against old friends and keen rivals, Greenock High School FP. The players knew a place at the top table wouldn't come easy – it was a day when the team would have to give its all. *Campbeltown Courier* managed to capture the mood in the opening paragraph of the match report: 'A potent combination of ambition and adrenaline carried the Pupils on the crest of a tidal wave into the First Division of Scottish Amateur League.'[58] There had been some memorable performances from this squad of players, but this must rank among the very best. The blue touch paper of possible success had been ignited and the team simply exploded like a sky-rocket.

Four goals ahead after 20 minutes, a hat-trick each from Jimmy McCallum and David Martin, plus a single from Duncan McAulay, had the game won before an hour was on the clock. It had been a memorable run, a tale of perseverance, tenacity and talent, a journey through the divisions from the seventh to the first in only eight seasons. Really, there is little more a management team can ask of its players!

Campbeltown Pupils v. Greenock, 20 April 1985:

Sandy Ronald, Bruce McNab, Stewart McSporran, Campbell Robertson, David Campbell, Jimmy McCallum, Michael Donnelly, Duncan McAulay, Jimmy Lay, David Martin, Kevin Gilchrist, Kenny Brown and Archie Millar.

For Campbeltown Pupils, the dream of lifting 'the big one' nearly came true, as in their second season of first division football the championship was lost on goal difference only. It was a painful experience as the players had set up a grandstand finish by defeating league leaders Knightswood on their own ground. Everything looked set for a perfect ending and a home win against lowly Giffnock North would seal the deal. However, it was not to be and a disappointing no score draw gave the championship to the Glasgow-based side.

The team even had to endure the disappointment of a disallowed winner, but such are the 'highs and lows' of football. There was no way of knowing that the future had a much bigger prize in store. In the meantime, the club consoled itself by winning the Baird-Lindsay Trophy in three consecutive years – the pre-season sevens tournament of their great rivals, Oban Saints. Over the years there has been a healthy rivalry between the Argyll teams, something that works in our favour when coming together to select a County team to play the might of the Scottish Amateur Football League. On paper Argyll should have little chance, but an unwritten code tends to galvanize the 'Gaels' into a fighting force and the competition is still finely balanced even after many years of competition.

There was unrest in the amateur game during the 1980s, as many of the better organised clubs hungered for an improvement in their opponents' playing facilities. There were threats and counter-threats, suggestions of break-away leagues and general disillusionment with the status quo. Although the SAFL discussed the matter, to many it smacked of elitism, and they were prepared to say so, but given the state of the public parks in and around Glasgow, in the end it proved the right way forward. As a friend of Campbeltown football, Douglas Smith of Drumchapel Amateurs invited the Pupils to join the impending revolution, but the club declined his offer to stay faithful to the SAFL. Nevertheless, in preparation for what the club saw as inevitable, the Pupils applied for the lease of Kintyre Park to improve existing facilities. The anticipated restructuring of our own league system duly happened and the SAFL Premier section was launched in time for the 1991/92 season.

It was exciting times, as a refurbished Kintyre Park was reopened in 1988 and the occasion celebrated with a marvellous 1-1 draw against Greenock Morton. Morton was coached by two club legends, manager Allan McGraw and his assistant John McMaster, the latter famous for his heroics in an Aberdeen side which beat Real Madrid to lift the European Cup Winners Cup in Gothenburg in 1983. Kevin Gilchrist opened the scoring in the opening minutes when he latched onto a long clearance to drive the ball beyond Scotland under-21 cap, David Wylie. It took Morton until the 81st minute to equalise, a penalty kick dispatched at the pavilion end to bring the senior club level.

Earlier in the same year, Kevin Gilchrist was capped at amateur level against Northern Ireland, the first local player to turn out for his country since B. B. Blackwood achieved the same honour prior to the First World War. Kevin later joined team-mate Duncan

McAulay in an all-conquering Scottish Amateur League Select, winning the national inter-league cup, the Baxter Trophy. Of the fifteen goals scored by the SAFL in lifting the trophy, Kevin claimed thirteen and Duncan weighed in with a single, meaning all but one was manufactured in Campbeltown. Other Pupils players followed their example and around this period it was difficult to remember a league select without representation from the 'Wee Toon.'

Entry to the new Premier League was by invitation only – at the time, the only way of enforcing its strict criteria based on standards and facilities. Feathers were ruffled, but in the end it forced clubs to look closely at the way they ran their affairs. After renovating Kintyre Park, Campbeltown Pupils AFC was up to speed and the Kintyre club became Argyll's first representative in the revolutionary new system. Twenty teams contested the initial steering year, with the two leagues divided into sections of ten. The top five clubs from each group formed the first-ever Premier Division, with the remainder competing in Premier Division One. As one of the runners-up, the Pupils made the cut to compete in the top division.

In the years that followed, other leagues adopted a similar blueprint and across the nation we now have an abundance of grass parks instead of the dreaded red blaise or ash surfaces. Although the SAFL was a leader in the grass initiative, once more the credit must go to Douglas Smith of Drumchapel Amateurs. He was the driving force behind the formation of the Caledonian League, the catalyst for change. He stood firm when doubt stalked the corridors of power, believing the choice to be simple – move with the times or become outdated. Given the vast number of amateur clubs in the Glasgow area, it was understandable that doubt was cast upon the ability of the Council to provide adequate grass facilities. Nevertheless, to their everlasting credit, the SAFL management grabbed the baton with both hands and launched forward.

A couple of years later, the creation of Premier Division Two allowed other Argyll sides to join the revolution and Campbeltown Boys and Oban Saints joined the happy throng in 1993/94. At this point, there was a feeling of achievement and harmony and the league's statement of intent encouraged local authorities to address their woeful lack of amenities. There is still much to be done, but a marked improvement of facilities is there for all to see. However, the doors of the Premier League were firmly bolted after the inclusion of the additional Argyll and Bute representatives and this became a bone of contention when Rothesay Brandane failed to gain admission. Although disappointed for our near neighbours, at this point the teams from the far west fully understood the wider politics and needs of the league. The SAFL was in the position of courting well-run clubs and it considered additional travel to be a hindrance to its over-riding ambition – that of being the best league in the country.

Natural wastage means there are only six Argyll clubs left in membership – three premier and three non-premier – where once there were as many as ten. This is a workable total, and the new administration has gone out of its way to re-establish the harmony of past times. A forward-looking initiative has also given clubs outside the premier section an incentive to improve and progress. A 'play-off' has been introduced and the management committee should be commended for initiating promotion and relegation as a link between the two sections of the SAFL. Although invitation still exists as a mechanism for entry to the Premier League, members of section two now have the opportunity to progress simply through ability and the possession of proper facilities.

For Campbeltown Pupils AFC, the journey through the SAFL has been interesting and eventful and it hard to imagine the club has just embarked on its 36th season of top amateur league football, one short of Oban Saints, who joined in 1976. In the words of their secretary David Buchanan, whose club recently hosted the Joe Paterson Memorial Cup match in June 2012: 'If the league is prepared to look after the interests of Argyll football, they certainly can depend on our County clubs to faithfully look after the interests of the league.' The very fact our teams undertake thousands of miles of travel each year speaks volumes for enthusiasm and organisation. In this, actions are indeed louder than words!

And So It Continues

Football is the most popular team sport on the face of the planet, a simple game that has given so much to human society, especially people of the under developed Third World. Anyone watching the African Cup of Nations has to admire the exuberant celebrations and expression of sheer happiness on the terraces. Given this unrestrained enthusiasm, what will it be like if a country from the 'Dark Continent' wins the World Cup? Come to think of it, we may not have to wait too much longer to discover the answer, given the number of African nationals playing with top European sides. Conversely, much has been made of the decline of Scottish football and it does appear that fewer people are playing the game in this country than in the past. The cause of the problem, surprisingly, still remains a mystery. A similar decline is also evident in once-great football nations like Hungary, so a fall from grace is not peculiar to our nation alone.

Home-based entertainment, satellite television, a more affluent society, greater access to other sports, all have been given as a reason for deterioration, yet a country with modern commodities in abundance is now at the forefront of world football – the United States of America. Soccer, as it is known 'across the pond', is not even a major sport in that country, yet its standing on the world stage has improved dramatically. Is it simply their turn to thrive, or are there lessons to be learned from a nation that continually excels in sport?

Education is a buzz-word in the development of sport on the other side of the Atlantic, and many young men from this country have been offered soccer scholarships in the US. Would something similar work here, a competitive, collegiate system similar to Grid Iron, but this time for the round ball game? Denmark had the largest number of coaches at the 1986 World Cup, a government-sponsored initiative which immediately improved the fortunes of one of Europe's smallest football nations. Should the Scottish

Government invest more in the game to help the SFA achieve its goal? Whatever the answer, we continue to search for a solution at a time when our position in world football has slumped to its lowest-ever level.

Although the number of participants continues to fall, according to football historian and author David Ross, our interest in the game as spectators is greater than at any time since the Second World War. In his book *The Roar of the Crowd*, he makes some interesting observations on the aforementioned. He has discovered that, 'expressed as a percentage of population, attendances at League games in Scotland stands at the 80% mark over a season'. (i.e. over 4 million paying customers attend football matches during a Scottish football season). Amazingly, 'this is a far higher proportion than Germany which has the highest attendances, and is a third higher than England which has the highest TV audience'. Therefore, it is safe to say the decline in our game is not due to lack of interest.

So, where do we go from here? Interestingly, our new SFA Performance Director, Mark Wotte, has been instrumental in setting up a number of new performance schools across the country. These are centres of excellence which will hopefully provide a new generation of talent. Our top youth coaches will operate in schools known for achievement in each of the main centres of population, a simple but important step in a new youth initiative. Schools football has always been the hub of our national sport, but in days gone by it was the PE department or a willing teacher who wore the mantle of responsibility. Worryingly, pressure of work has seen depreciation in staff participation, an absence which has contributed to the decline or even disappearance of football in some schools. We now face a 'Catch 22' situation, as our failure to reach major finals means less cash for the SFA and its development programmes, which, in turn, creates difficulty for future qualification. Local authorities and the SFA have been working together for some time, so the introduction of coaches into schools could be the answer to our problem, but only time will tell.

Everything seemed simpler in the past, an era when playing on the streets was part and parcel of a football education. While it was a habit of the times, more than likely the result of growing up in a less affluent era, nevertheless, this informal training ground produced a wealth of talent for the senior game. My earliest memory of playing organised football was with friends on the Meadows Housing Scheme. Our family had moved from the quiet surroundings of

Shore Street to the more populated 'Steel Hooses' in 1953, a time of huge excitement settling into a modern home with extra rooms and for the very first time the luxury of indoor toilet facilities. Friends were easily found and this resulted in my introduction to football tribalism, albeit on a very small scale. We formed a team from the Meadows Avenue area, a bunch of boys to include my long-term friend Alastair Cochrane and his brother Archie. The opposition was predominantly from Ralston Road: Leonard, Malcolm and Alex Gilchrist, all brothers, ably abetted by David Livingstone, Jack McGeachy etc. It was my first taste of competitive football, a round of marathon matches at High Kintyre Park where the winner was the first team to score ten. Every match was played with the intensity of an international, although the absence of a referee was the signal for chaos. Arbitration came in the form of exhaustion, the white flag gladly raised after hours of physical effort and refusal to accept the winning goal. Gluttons for punishment, it started all over again the very next day. Without fear of contradiction, this scene was replicated right across the country in the 1950s.

Football is an obsessive interest, and no-one is telling the truth if he or she is glad to be giving up the game. Nevertheless, be it player or manager, common sense dictates when it is time to stand aside. So it proved when two dyed-in-the-wool enthusiasts were dragged kicking and screaming from the Kintyre Park dressing room at the end of their spell in management. For Bill Hunter and me, the final whistle had blown and it was time to let a new generation take the club forward. Into the breach stepped Campbell Robertson and Duncan McAulay – in the ways of football management at any level, differing styles working together towards a common goal.

Finding ourselves on football's version of the dole, we had the opportunity to reflect on days gone by, happy memories of successful times and a lot else besides. We had many a laugh remembering the antics of the dressing-room, the weird and wonderful rituals performed by players in pursuit of a thing called luck. Don't get me wrong, most of us are fully paid-up members of the 'rabbit's foot club,' it's just that some people are known to take things to the extreme. The football dressing-room is the nerve-centre of eccentric behaviour and as long as there are trophies to be won, it will continue to be so. Superstition in its simplest form is a compulsion to wear the same jersey each and every week and many an argument has developed when an individual was denied his favourite number. It made perfect sense after all – the result depended on it! Then there is the devotee of precision, a player who puts on his team kit in exactly the same order before each match. Never mind kick-off time, it was everything off and start again if he got the sequence wrong.

Then there was the amulet brigade, the wearers of chains, rings and bracelets. Most of the boys preferred to give these items a body-swerve, just as well, as a new SFA directive outlawed the wearing of jewellery to avoid the chance of injury. It was normal practice for the referee to ask players to remove the offending items before each match or, in the case of tight-fitting rings, to cover them with tape, a straightforward request and easy to follow. No chance! Even after instruction, many a game has been stopped to remove the offending baubles; such is the reluctance to give up personal adornment. However, although the rule is well-meaning, the only damage we ever encountered was that of injured pride. Forced to surrender his prized assets in the middle of a match, embarrassment followed as everybody waited impatiently for the game to recommence. One of the mysteries of the dressing room, is it vanity or bloody-mindedness that drives an individual to non-compliance?

Anything, it seems, is worth trying if it brings a greater chance of victory. Take exponents of the 'knock on wood' theory, whether it is Kintyre Park or Liverpool's Anfield Stadium. On Merseyside, the pre-match ritual is there for all to see, a 'touching scene' as players prepare to enter the field of play. The club's 'Liver Bird' emblem is tenderly caressed by the home players in the hope of summoning luck. It is a habit replicated throughout the football world, more often than not in less glamorous surroundings as individuals attempt to gain support from their club totem or badge. Players even have their very own on-field lucky hotspot: touching goal posts, crossbars, corner flags, or, more ambitiously, the match ball securely in the possession of the referee. All of this mumbo-jumbo is aimed at securing fortune in the goal-scoring stakes, but the reverse psychology applies to goalkeepers. A football driven into the empty net before kick-off is supposed to guarantee a 'clean sheet', a ritual more effective if the said item is the preciously guarded match ball. It is of course complete nonsense, but try telling that to a six-foot-plus custodian bent on placating the gods of defence. Naturally, you wouldn't expect any one to admit to these idiosyncrasies, but irrational behaviour is part and parcel of football wherever the game is played.

More surprisingly, top sports psychologists subscribe to the theory that superstition aids athletic performance. Belief in a pre-match ritual, they maintain, breeds the confidence which in turn improves the chance of success, for example, take the great World Cup-winning Brazilian side of 1958. They were first to employ sports psychology in the form a sponge man who carried alternative medicines, natural products from the Amazon Rain Forest with extraordinary healing powers. True or not, simple suggestion was enough to overcome fatigue and injury, something the medical profession call the 'placebo effect'.

Apart from the subject of luck, players also have a compulsive attraction to the first-aid box, in particular the aerosol containing liniment. Used sparingly, it causes little discomfort, but most apply the menthol-based substance like an air-freshener and in the confined space of the dressing room chaos follows. Coughing and spluttering becomes the order of the day as every one struggles for oxygen, the very reason we cannot rule out brain damage as the cause of football's pre-match eccentricities! However, a second opinion is definitely needed on the subject, as after years of exposure, my views cannot be trusted.

Whatever your opinion on the subject of luck, it cannot be denied that man's infatuation with football defies logic. Take the view of one enthusiastic individual, the great Bill Shankly, one-time manager of Liverpool FC. Asked by a journalist if he considered football a matter of life or death, with a hint of mischief he answered, 'No, son, it's much more important than that!' His comment may have been tongue-in-cheek, but there is an element of truth in his statement considering the level of fanaticism attached to the sport. The recent financial trouble at Glasgow Rangers is a case in point. Relegated to the fourth tier of Scottish football, instead of shrinking crowds the club has witnessed its highest attendances in years. It is a statement of intent – mismanaged at board level or not, to their credit, ordinary fans have no intention of walking away from what to them is a life-long obsession.

Having scoured the pages of football literature and spoken to members of different age-groups, my awareness of the importance of football in the lives of ordinary people has grown. Non-enthusiasts will insist that it's only a game, a statement accurate in its perception, but completely at odds with understanding the passion of the ordinary fan. A game it may be, but football's mystique remains undiminished; a sport as popular today as it was in the era of our fathers and grandfathers. It is the focus of millions of people worldwide, a game that satisfies our deep-seated need as human beings to belong. You can call it tribalism or whatever, but there is something very special about playing or supporting one's 'very own' football team. Being part of a partisan crowd is an uplifting experience, and the same can be said of wearing the jersey of your local community team.

This was the case when a group of players pulled on 'the white' of Campbeltown Pupils AFC, a pause before winning back to back league championships in the top two divisions of the SAFL. Asked by the local press if they had seen it coming – the answer was an emphatic, 'No!' After years of hard work and countless miles of travel, the players hoped it would end this way, but never in their wildest dreams thought it would actually happen. In season 1998/99, the Kintyre club was undefeated in away fixtures, an amazing statistic at any level of the game. The culmination of a fine season was a sublime chip from Paul McWhirter, a goal to beat Cowglen and bring the Premier Division One title 'doon the road'. Paul was rewarded by becoming the third club player to be capped at amateur international level, Northern Ireland providing the opposition. He was also selected to play for the 'league team', an accolade simultaneously awarded to his Pupils team mates: Alan Sinclair, Andy Robertson and the evergreen Duncan McAulay. Their team was back in the Premier Division, and the management team of Campbell Robertson and Duncan McAulay could look back with pride on a fantastic season. Happy days indeed!

Campbeltown Pupils v. Cowglen, May 1999: Neil McKay, James Robertson, John Galbraith, Craig Colville, Duncan McAulay, Alan Sinclair, Stanley Irwin, Steve Losh, Norrie Thomson, Calum McMillan, Andy Robertson, Gary McMillan, Paul McWhirter, Ronnie Brown and David Sinclair. Missing from the team that day were Darren McGillivray, Iain Galbraith, Charles Robertson, Neil Brown and Iain Johnstone, from Tarbert.

The new millennium season was christened in style with a friendly match against Irish senior league club, Coleraine. Communication with our neighbours across the North Channel was possible because of the Argyll and Antrim Ferries, a service sadly no longer in operation. Kenny Shiels, now manager of Kilmarnock, brought his side to Kintyre in preparation for the opening match of the Irish Premier League season, a game the following Saturday against reigning champions, Glentoran. The Irish professional outfit was taken aback by the standard of the local amateurs and a hat-trick by Andy Robertson gave the Pupils a creditable 3-3 draw. It was a feat which earned him a trial the following week-end in the Coleraine line-up. The Irish club's weekly match programme commented that, 'This short trip will live long in the memories of all those who made the journey ... Campbeltown Pupils had several very good players who would do well in Irish League Senior football.'[59]

For the Kintyre side, there was a distinct lack of knowledge of what lay in store on its return to the SAFL Premier Division, but at the end of a fantastic season the level of achievement was simply unbelievable. Clear favourites for the championship were St. Patricks FP from Dumbarton, a team fresh from winning the Scottish Amateur Cup in May 1999. Also 'in the mix' were the previous year's champions, Gourock Athletic and our old friends and rivals, Greenock High School FP. It couldn't have been any harder!

The Campbeltown side started where it had finished the previous season, being successful on the road. A creditable away draw to Gourock Athletic kept the local favourites in contention at the top, although the heads dropped slightly after a 3-2 reverse to St. Patricks FP at home. Thankfully, in such a competitive environment, points were dropped by all the leading contenders and, with five games left to play, the championship was still anyone's for the taking. Key to success were two difficult away fixtures, a sojourn to the 'Tail of the Bank' to play Greenock, followed by a mid-week trip to Dumbarton and a final meeting with Scottish Cup holders, St. Patricks FP.

These games were arguably the biggest in the club's history and the Pupils put themselves in pole position with two outstanding victories. Both games were fought as if the players' lives depended on it, a 2-1 victory at the Battery Park, Greenock, followed by an outstanding 1-0 win the following Wednesday at Dumbarton.[60] After two seasons undefeated away from home, the Kintyre team were just three points from the biggest prize of all, the SAFL Premier League Championship. However, this scenario was ignored at the heart of the club. It would take a combination of results for this to happen and everyone was firmly focused on the games ahead.

Failure to win the next fixture, combined with positive results for the two main challengers, would bring the prospect of a week-day league decider against Oban Saints. This was never on the cards, as the Pupils swept to a convincing 4-0 over Busby and, on the same day, Oban and Greenock lost their complementary fixtures. Winning the top title was a sweet moment for everyone at the club, as Pupils were cruelly denied when the first division title went to Knightswood on the last day of the 1988 season on goal difference. As you can imagine, lifting the SAFL Premier title was celebrated in style. Given the week-end that followed, it was a miracle the team could raise a gallop in its final fixture the following Monday night. Nevertheless, accompanied by a rather vociferous support, a joyous squad made its way north to Oban. It was a noisy affair. Well, it was the home of the Kintyre club's great rivals and a 2-0 victory put icing on the championship cake. At the end of the day, the local favourites completed their season five points ahead of their nearest rivals, St. Patricks FP. It certainly was a moment to savour!

The winning of the Premier League was a triumph for a young Pupils squad, as it was for the management team of Campbell Robertson and Duncan McAulay, but it was also the culmination of years of effort by a host of people who contributed to the club's ongoing success: past players, committee members, sponsors and, last but not least, the faithful supporters who had turned out in all weathers down through the years. To all of these people the club owes a huge vote of thanks. The only regret is that time denied others the opportunity to be part of this unique experience, so to absent friends this success is dedicated.

But what is the future of Campbeltown football? As always, the state of our game is closely tied to the economy of the area, so historically it is easy to understand the 'highs and lows' of local football. The early years of the new millennium have not been kind to the 'Wee Toon,' and naturally this is reflected on the playing fields of the community. However, we are embracing a new era and interested parties have forged plans for the development of the game in our remote corner of Scotland.

After ten long years of campaigning, the community is now in receipt of a wonderful, all-weather playing facility, a park which has its UEFA and FIFA Grade Two Licence. To complement this, football has come together under the banner of Campbeltown Community Football Club, a group which will attempt to provide qualified coaching and competition at all levels of the local game. The aim is to develop football at schools and youth level and to steer a course all the way through to the adult game. In an area which has long been steeped in football, it will provide the opportunity to maximise its potential.

In recent years, Campbeltown Pupils and Campbeltown Boys have amalgamated into a single force, a sensible decision given the difficulties of the times. Under the name of the former, the 'new' club has dropped back to Premier Division Two, but continues to develop with its youngest-ever squad. Early signs are extremely encouraging for the future of our local game at amateur level. In 2009, Campbeltown Pupils AFC celebrated its 90th anniversary with a game against the amateur international side, a narrow 2-1 victory for Scotland in a splendid match at Kintyre Park.

Over the past few years, there have been a number of success stories involving people with a Campbeltown connection. Robert Keith Stockdale – Robbie, whose grandmother Lottie McIntyre hails from the 'Wee Toon' – was capped five times for Scotland at full international level. Robbie played football with Premier League Middlesbrough, and also represented Sheffield Wednesday, West Ham United, Rotherham United, Tranmere Rovers and Grimsby Town. He is now youth coach at Sunderland. Joshua McEachran – Josh – made his competitive debut for Chelsea against MSK Zilina of Slovakia in the Champions League in 2010. His grandfather Joe is a Campbeltown man and once played football with Argyll Colliery. Josh, capped 8 times for England at under-21 level, is currently on loan with Middlesbrough. Finally, there is Lawrence Tynes, placekicker for the New York Giants in the NFL. Born in Greenock, he later moved with his parents to RAF Machrihanish, where his father Larry was stationed as part of the American Navy Seals detachment. Along with his two brothers, he was educated at St Kieran's School and played football with Longrow Boys Club, where he was in the charge of Willie Paterson. Lawrence is a major personality in the United States, having twice won the Super Bowl with his club. He also led the New York Tartan Day Parade in 2008.

And so it continues, the story of the people's game, a sport so popular it seems material will always be available to add another page. As an enthusiast, it has been enlightening to research the careers of not only our local sons who made good on the national and international stage, but also those who played the game in the humbler surroundings of our own 'Wee Toon'. Naturally, any record of Campbeltown football is doomed to remain incomplete, as it is impossible to recount every single experience. However, if our young people are prepared to avoid the distractions of modern living and commit to the 'beautiful game', I am certain there is room for another chapter detailing future success. In anticipation of the opening of the Campbeltown All Weather Facility, school children were asked to give their impression of a momentous day. A drawing with a caption summed up the occasion perfectly – 'build it and they will come'. Three thousand people used the park in the first few weeks, proof that interest in our game is alive and well. The stepping stones are in now in place: time will tell if the path to future success has been followed.

Appendix

Here is a selection of Campbeltown adult affiliated football clubs. The list is not exhaustive and is included only as a matter of interest. Some of the sides were disbanded, only to be reformed at a later date – sometimes on a number of occasions. Other started life as casual organisations and thereafter gained a status, such as junior or amateur. The list is only a starting point and hopefully can be amended or added to in the future.

Abbreviations: yth = youth, am = amateur, jnr = junior, juv = juvenile and c= circa.

Team	Founded	Colours	Disbanded	Reformed
1. Campbeltown Jnr	1878	Blue	1923	No
2. Inland Revenue	1879		1880	No
3. Kintyre Jnr	1880		1937	(1958-1964 - yth)
4. Albion	1882	Blue	1887	(1978-1980 - am)
5. St Kiaran	1883		1906	No
6. Athletic	1885		1908	(1949-1952 – juv)
7. Kilbrannan	1885		1920	(1950-52 & 1980-83 - am)

Team	Founded	Colours	Disbanded	Reformed
8. Rangers Jnr	1885	Light Blue	1950	(1973-1978 - am)
9. Victoria	1890		1906	No
10. Thistle	1890	Navy or White	1901	No
11. Hearts Jnr	1899	Red	1956	(1960-1962)
12. Drumlemble Jnr	1900	White	1960	No
13. Heartfield	1900		1901	No
14. Campbeltown Am	1900		1902	No
15. United Jnr	1905	Blue	1960	(1973-1975 - am)
16. Academicals Jnr	1906		1935	(1959-1963 - am)
17. Glenside Jnr	1908	Gold & Black	1955	(1964-65 - am 1969-88 - yth)
18. CGSFP Jnr	1919	White or Red	1939	(1959 - still active - am)
19. Corinthians	1920		1925	No
20. Auchencorvie	1920	Sky - White	1925	No
21. Peninver	1920	Blue	1925	(1950-1962)
22. Carradale	1920	Red	1925	(1950 - various - still active)
23. Southend	1920	Blue	1925	(1950 - c 1990)
24. Laggan	1920		1925	(1950-1952)
25. Strollers	1923		1929	No
26. Argyll & Sutherland Highlanders	1925	Claret & Amber	1929	No
27. Argyll Colliery Jnr	1926	Black & White		(1951-59 - jun) (1958-60 - am)
28. Argyll Thistle	1950	Red	1951	No
29. Dalintober Hearts	1950		1953	(1961-62)
30. NCB Strollers	1951		1952	No

Team	Founded	Colours	Disbanded	Reformed
31. NCB Rovers	1951		1952	No
32. YMCA	1955	White	1957	No
33. Mayfair Thistle	1956	Red and Yellow	1958	No
34. Beagles	1958	Green	1959	No
35. Miners (a)	1958	Black and White	1960	No
36. ATC	1958	Yellow	1959	No
37. Drumlemble (a)	1958	Black/ White Sleeves	1960	No
38. Lochend Church	1961	Yellow or Blue/White	1964	No
39. Grammar School	1962	Red	1964	(1970- 71)
40. Kinloch Thistle	1965	White	1967	No
41. Dalriada Thistle	1965	White	1968	No
42. RAF	1965	Green	1993	No
43. Caledonia	1967	Blue or White	1970	No
44. Youth Club	1967	Red and White	1971	No
45. Largieside	1955	Yellow	c 1985	No
46. A D Rovers	1970	Black and White	1972	No
47. Phoenix	1970	Red	1971	No
48. Shipyard	1978		1979	No
49. Argyll Creameries	c 1985		c 1987	No
50. Kintyre Rovers	c 1983		c 1985	No
51. Fishermen	1978	White or Yellow	c 1985	No
52. Campbeltown Boys	1980	White or Red	2010	No amalgamated with Campbeltown Pupils (CGSFP)

Bibliography

Barnard, Alfred, *The Whisky Distilleries of the United Kingdom,* Harper's Gazette, 1887)

Barrett, Norman S, *Encyclopaedia of Association Football*, Purnell.

Devine, T. M,*The Scottish Nation 1700–2000*, Penguin.

Galbraith, Russell, *The Hampden Story*, Mainstream.

Gillies, Freddy, *In Campbeltown Once More*, Ardminish Press

Johnstone, Frank, *The Football Who's Who*, Associated Sporting Press.

Kintyre Civic Society, *The Campbeltown Book*.

Martin, Angus, *Kintyre –The Hidden Past*, John Donald.

Oliver, Neil, *A History of Scotland*, Weidenfeld & Nicolson.

Ross, David, *The Roar of the Crowd*, Argyll Publishing.

Stirk, David, 'The Distillers of Campbeltown', in *The Angels' Share*, Neil Wilson.

Notes and References

1. *Argyllshire Herald.*
2. *Argyllshire Herald.*
3. *Argyllshire Herald,* 28/12/1878.
4. *Argyllshire Herald,* 4/1/1879.
5. *Campbeltown Courier,* 12/4/1879.
6. *Argyllshire Herald.*
7. *Campbeltown Courier,* 22/4/1882.
8. *Campbeltown Courier,* 4/6/1887.
9. *Campbeltown Courier,* 7/1/1888.
10. *Campbeltown Courier,* 6/6/1968.
11. *Campbeltown Courier,* 6/3/1969.
12. *Campbeltown Courier,* 24/11/1900.
13. *Campbeltown Courier,* 6/4/1901.
14. *Campbeltown Courier,* 21/4/1906.
15. *Argyllshire Herald,* 3/2/1912.
16. *Campbeltown Courier,* 22/2/1913.
17. *Campbeltown Courier,* 15/3/1913.
18. *Campbeltown Courier,* 15/3/1913.
19. *Campbeltown Courier,* 5/4/1913.
20. *Campbeltown Courier* 12/4/1913.
21. *Campbeltown Courier,* 15/3/1913.
22. *Glasgow News.*
23. *Daily Record and Mail.*
24. *Staffordshire Evening Sentinel,* 19/1/1958.
25. *Kilmarnock Standard.*
26. *Campbeltown Courier,* 15/3/1913.
27. *Campbeltown Courier,* 2/11/1979.
28. *Campbeltown Courier,* 27/5/1922.
29. *Campbeltown Courier,* 6/11/1948.
30. *Campbeltown Courier,* 5/1/1935.
31. *Campbeltown Courier,* 22/2/1935.
32. *Peoples Journal,* 18/1/1936.
33. *Peoples Journal,* 22/1/1938.
34. *Campbeltown Courier,* 30/3/1946.
35. *Campbeltown Courier,* 21/2/1948.
36. *Campbeltown Courier,* 5/1/1950.
37. *Campbeltown Courier,* 12/1/1950.
38. *Evening Times,* 31/7/1950.
39. *Campbeltown Courier,* 17/1/1952.
40. *Campbeltown Courier,* 22/6/1979.

41. *Campbeltown Courier, 5/1/1956.*
42. *Campbeltown Courier, 26/1/1956.*
43. *Campbeltown Courier, 10/1/1957.*
44. *Campbeltown Courier, 25/9/1958.*
45. *Campbeltown Courier, 19/10/1961.*
46. *Campbeltown Courier, 18/8/1966.*
47. *Campbeltown Courier, 6/1/1966.*
48. *Campbeltown Courier, 8/9/1966.*
49. *Campbeltown Courier, 15/6/1967.*
50. *Campbeltown Courier, 8/6/1967.*
51. *Campbeltown Courier, 17/7/1969.*
52. *Campbeltown Courier, 25/9/1969.*
53. *Campbeltown Courier, 5/6/1981.*
54. *Campbeltown Courier, 21/5/1982.*
55. *Campbeltown Courier, 27/5/1983.*
56. *Campbeltown Courier, 21/12/1979.*
57. *Campbeltown Courier, 17/5/1983.*
58. *Campbeltown Courier, 26/4/1985.*
59. *The Bannsider, 14/8/1999.*
60. *Campbeltown Courier, 26/5/2000.*
61. *Campbeltown & District Junior Association – Minutes, 1948-1958.*
62. *Kintyre Amateur Football League – Minutes, 1953-1984.*
63. *Personal Scrapbook of Robert Pursell – Toronto University.*
64. *Personal Scrapbook of Sandy Glendinning.*
65. *Personal Scrapbook of Stuart McSporran.*
66. *Personal Scrapbook of Hector McMurchy.*
67. *Second Main Dissertation, Karen Hooker – Exeter University.*
68. *John Burgoyne Papers.*
69. *Kenny McMillan Papers.*
70. *Jimmy Lay Papers.*
71. *'A Walk Round Campbeltown' - John Lees Moffat.*
72. *'The West Highland Football Magazine,'- 1948 - Neil Hamilton Dewar.*
73. *Manuscripts of Willie Mitchell courtesy of Agnes Stewart.*
74. *'Drumchapel Amateur Football Club, 50th Anniversary Booklet.'*
75. *'The Scottish Amateur Football League, 100th Anniversary Booklet.'*
76. *CD Insert Booklet: 'Sons of Somerled' by Steve McDonald, archive material therein, courtesy of Clan Donald Visitor Centre, Isle of Skye, Scotland.*
77. *Web Sites: Manchester United, Liverpool, Everton, Port Vale, Lincoln City, Swansea, Portsmouth, London Hearts, AS Barga, the Scottish Football Association and the Scottish Football Historical Archive.*

Index

All football clubs, regardless of status – amateur, junior, professional, etc – are denoted by 'FC'. Some overlap will be encountered in the cases of club names which have been reused, e.g. 'Glenside' covers junior, amateur and youth teams which all used that name. Individuals mentioned only fleetingly have not been indexed, nor have captions, team-lists and appendices.